# LEGAL and ETHICAL RESPONSIBILITIES

## of School Personnel

WARREN E. GAUERKE

*Associate Professor*
*Division of Teacher Education*
*Emory University*

# LEGAL and ETHICAL RESPONSIBILITIES

## of SCHOOL PERSONNEL

*Englewood Cliffs, N. J.*
PRENTICE-HALL, INC.

PRENTICE-HALL EDUCATION SERIES

*Dan Cooper, Editor*

Library of Congress Catalog Card No.: 59-11037

First printing .......... April, 1959
Second printing ....... March, 1960

Printed in the United States of America
52721-C

To my wife and my son——

Ruth Cora (Fisher) Gauerke
Douglas Warren Gauerke

# Foreword

School personnel work within a complex pattern of social relationships which are governed by both legal regulation and ethical principle. The law establishes the standards they must meet to enter the profession, prescribes the conditions under which they may work as public employees, and defines their duties, obligations, and rights. The quality of their performance is determined in no small measure by their knowledge of the law governing their relationships with others. Nor should this knowledge be confined to school personnel alone; it should be entertained by all with whom they are associated in their work. It is no less important to understand that every obligation and right, legal or otherwise, has an ethical basis. Law and ethics are, in fact, inseparable. The common law is nothing more than an attempt to apply principles of fair dealing, equity, and good conscience to specific social situations. Professor Gauerke's book is a unique attempt to analyze and relate the legal and ethical principles that govern the work of school personnel. All those who read his book will, I believe, agree with me that it is exceptionally well done. It is always a pleasure to commend to the reading public a book that merits high appraisal; such is especially the case when, as in this instance, the author happens to be one of my former students.

NEWTON EDWARDS

AN EDUCATOR SAYS:

Our work demands professional status; we have a substantial basis in scholarship and research; we have the altruistic motive; what we lack is a powerful organization established by ourselves to set standards, to protect the public from incompetence, to enforce codes of ethics, and to stimulate further growth by research.

—William F. Russell, former President, Columbia University Teachers College

THE WRITER SAYS:

Not until educators understand what comprises a powerful organization, standards, and competence, will the goal suggested by Dr. Russell be realized.

# Preface

In his introduction to *The Teacher's Treasure Chest*,* Benjamin Fine, former education editor of the New York *Times,* states that never before in our history "have our teachers been as important as they are today." He notes that we are engaged in a struggle for our very existence. In this struggle the teacher is a key person, for it is he who helps children to understand the difficult thing we call American civilization. "Although a strong army, navy, and air force are essential," continues Fine, "a strong and inspiring devotion to our democratic ideals is even more important. Teachers can help develop that tradition and help strengthen our ideals."

One of our American traditions is that we are a law-abiding nation. If we can truthfully say this of ourselves, what in fact are we saying? Professor Urban defines law as the "ethical minimum." The law must be content to describe the level of behavior which is the minimum we can accept from each other and still be a community. It is little enough, then, to say of us that we are law-abiding. This is only the minimum.

If teachers are to help students understand not only the "legal minimum" but also the deeper moral principles involved in their relationships with their fellows, the teachers themselves must first master the legal and ethical aspects of their roles as teachers. *Legal and Ethical Responsibilities of School Personnel,* is designed to help school personnel, and others too, become acquainted with some minimum legal obligations and rights. It is hoped that the materials will lead also to deeper understanding of ethical choices.

There are nine chapters in all. Chapters 1 and 2 are devoted to introductory materials. Chapter 1 deals with the legal system and the nature of professional ethics. Chapter 2 provides background

* Leo Deuel, *The Teacher's Treasure Chest* (Englewood Cliffs, N. J.: Prentice-Hall, Inc., 1956), p. ix.

materials in order to illuminate the status of educators yesterday and today.

The remaining seven chapters focus on relationships of various kinds among school personnel and between them and the school board, parents, and students. Each of these chapters is preceded by a section devoted to cases involving school personnel. It is hoped that these "problem situations" will serve as a basis for discussion at appropriate times and places. After the chapter proper, there is a list of questions to provoke additional study. Finally, there is a list of appropriate readings.

I owe a special debt to Dr. Fred E. Brooks, principal of Hawthorne School, University City, Missouri. His inspiration and ideas are present in the volume. He and I talked on many occasions about the legal and ethical problems of teachers and their associates. I have gained stimulation and borrowed ideas of a breadth and depth far beyond my own from other persons, too numerous to mention. One such person is Dr. Newton Edwards, my major professor at the University of Chicago, now at the University of South Carolina, Columbia. Others include Dr. Edward Bolmeier of Duke University; Dr. Lee O. Garber of the University of Pennsylvania; Dr. Robert R. Hamilton of the University of Wyoming; Dr. Madaline Kinter Remmlein of George Washington University and formerly of the National Education Association Research Staff; and Dr. E. Edmund Reutter, Jr., of Teachers College, Columbia University, New York. Each has provided me with many hours of happy association and provocative ideas.

WARREN E. GAUERKE

# Table of Contents

Problems in Raising Teachers' Status. The Problem of Teacher
"Loyalty." Economic and Social Ingredients in Teachers'
Status. *Qualifications of Today's Teachers.* State Certification.
Emergency Licenses. *A "Profession" Defined.* Bases for Con-
sidering Teaching a Profession. Characteristics of a Profes-
sional Teacher. The Need Further to Professionalize Teaching.

ASPECTS. Undesirable Behavior Patterns. Some Variations in Supervision. Problems of "Scientific" Supervision. The Realities of "Super-Vision." Employee Orientation. Teacher Evaluation.

Problem Situations. The Teacher in the Large School. LEGAL ASPECTS. Slander as a Civil Action. Libel as a Legal Action. Protection of Personal Property. ETHICAL ASPECTS. Causes of Friction Between Teachers. Attitudes Toward New Staff Members. Supporting One's Associates. Relationships in Staff Meetings and Committees.

Problem Situations. Nonteachers and Noncertified Personnel. *Legal Aspects in General.* Mutual Employees of the State. Importance of Job Classification. *Ethical Aspects in General.* Concern for the Common Goal. Emotional Stresses and Courtesy. CUSTODIAN-PERSONNEL RELATIONSHIPS. *Legal Aspects.* Function of the School Custodian. Custodian's Responsibility to the Principal. *Ethical Aspects.* Recognition of Custodian's Heavy Duties. Teachers' Requests for Extra Services. Custodian's Influence in the Community. Necessity for Avoiding Gossip. Cooperation with the Custodian. SERVICE-PERSONNEL RELATIONSHIPS. *Legal Aspects.* Relation of Food Service to Instruction. Restriction of Pupils at Lunch Hour. *Ethical Aspects.* Teachers' Attitudes Toward Workers and Service. Responsibility for Supervising Children. OFFICE EMPLOYEE-PERSONNEL RELATIONSHIPS. *Legal Aspects.* Scope of Clerical Workers' Authority. *Ethical Aspects.* How the Principal Sees the School Office. Function of the Secretary. Teacher's Concept of the Clerical Staff. HEALTH PERSONNEL RELATIONSHIPS. *Legal Aspects.* Authority of Medical Personnel. *Ethical Aspects.* Cooperation Between Teacher and Health Personnel. Teacher and Therapist.

Problem Situations. The Parent's Attitude Toward School and Teachers. Teachers' Overtures to Parents. LEGAL ASPECTS.

The Teacher's Authority and Control. Detention and the Police
Power. Discipline and Corporal Punishment. Parent's Authority
to Choose Course of Instruction. Sectarian Instruction. Enforcement of Health Rules. ETHICAL ASPECTS. Parent's Respect for the Teacher. Judging the Teacher by the Pupil. How
the Teacher Helps the Parent Understand. Bases for Teacher-
Parent Cooperation. *Records and Reporting.* Reports Must Be
Soundly Based. Should Children Be Compared? The Parent's
Responsibility: Be Constructive. *Home Visits.* Need for Care
in Conversation. Teacher's Respect for the Parent. Keeping
the Interview Balanced. *Parent-Teacher Conferences.* Focus
on the Child. Confidential Information. Truthfulness and the
Constructive Approach.

Problem Situations. LEGAL ASPECTS. *Pupil Control.* Corporal Punishment. *Teacher Liability.* School Trips. What Is
Negligence? The Limits of School "Immunity." Insurance Pro-
tection. *The Curriculum.* Pressure Groups and Public Opinion.
Religious Teaching in the School. *Other Regulations.* Activities
for Personal Gain. Compulsory School Attendance. The "Right"
to Be Taught. Liability of Parents. Secret Societies. Withhold-
ing the Diploma. ETHICAL ASPECTS. Psychological Factors.
The Teacher's Professional Role and Insights. Effect of the
Teacher's Personality. Putting the Child's Needs First. *Social
Factors.* The Teacher's Fairness and Friendliness. How the
Teacher's Behavior Teaches. Working Principles for the
Teacher.

# *Introduction*

## ——— *1*

SCHOOL PERSONNEL are paid a salary by an arm of the state government, the local board of education. They receive their salary checks in return for their helping, or aiding others to help, pupils to learn desirable ways of behaving in our society. The main purpose of teachers and of the school is to serve the needs of boys and girls in planned learning situations.

This purpose has direct relevance to the relationships between school personnel and all others with whom they come into contact. In performing their gigantic task, school personnel need the support of all who directly and indirectly have a part in accomplishing the purposes of the school. They need help in getting answers to the hundred and one problems that arise as they associate with pupils and with parents and patrons. The legal and ethical problems of school personnel are part and parcel of the job.

### Why School Personnel Must Know the Law

School litigation is increasing in state and federal courts as one result of the expanding services of the school to pupils and employees. School personnel need access to readable sources of information pertaining to school law. School employees should examine carefully the facts and implications of situations that produce school law cases. An impressive mass of evidence has accumulated from court decisions regarding what can and cannot be done legally in the dozens of predicaments that daily confront school personnel and parents. The courts have laid down fairly definite lines of authority governing some of the common situations facing school

1

employees. These can be used as guides to conduct when an insistent parent or principal presses an issue or when some other person believes he has a just complaint and demands "immediate action" of someone.

The ideas contained herein are organized to be of help to school personnel when faced with behavior that could be "outside the law." School employees can decidedly profit from an earnest but not necessarily burdensome study of some aspects of school law. The situations are not few in which a member of the school team can act unwisely through ignorance, neglect, or carelessness.

Much of the difficulty stems from the very nature of school work. Definition of school jobs has been attempted by means of statute and contract-phrasing, and by means of the development of professional standards of conduct. The failure to define the work of the teacher, principal, and board members in such a way that the general public may understand its scope has led to court litigation, violations of ethical standards, and endless frustration and heartache. Such failure has actually prevented the achievement of high standards of professional excellence.

### Purposes of This Book

The purpose of this text is to present the common legal and ethical "relationship" problems of school personnel as they engage in their work. The text stresses the legal interests and ethical obligations of school personnel to themselves, children, parents, and to the body politic.

It is impossible in this study to disentangle personnel from the schools in which they work. It can be said neither that personnel were devised in their entirety for the school nor that the school was devised for them. Both have evolved at one and the same time. Certain powerful forces outside both have had much to do with shaping their destiny. It can be emphasized, however, should one be tempted to forget, that the school was not created, and is not now supported, in order that there may be teachers or a profession of teaching.

The main purpose of the text includes two distinct but necessarily related objectives. Objective one is that of re-emphasizing the types of relationships that exist, or *should* exist, between the pupil and school personnel, the parent and school personnel, the teacher and school personnel, the nonteaching employees and school personnel. Objective two is that of presenting the legal principles implicit in these relationships.

School personnel must maintain a complex set of relationships to various parties involved in the educational process. One such relationship, in matter of fact rather than proximity, is to the state and the nation. The position of the school will be derived from the theory of the function of government, as well as from current political and economic conditions. Thus, for example, the theory of democracy as opposed to authoritarianism in the American concept of the state has led to mass education instead of an education to select and train an elite.

Besides relationships to the state, others vitally affect the status and acts of school personnel—relationships, for example, to the various pressure groups of the community and nation, to the nonofficial voluntary associations that work for certain political and social policies. Perhaps of more direct concern to school personnel in their everyday work is their relationship to the parent, both as an individual and as a unit of organized parent-teacher associations. And of course school employees have a relationship to the child. The child associates with other teachers, with the school principal, and with other school personnel. These various relationships frequently make contradictory and conflicting demands upon school people.

This text will not, of course, qualify the reader to be his own lawyer. But he will gain some insight into the very real dangers he can and does face every day—dangers that could be expensive in time, energy, and dollars. Or if a legal problem already exists, the reader may gain some peace of mind and security by comprehending it. It must be borne in mind that no arbitrary answer can be given to most questions of law, for the facts and factors in one given instance can differ materially from those in almost every other case. The text will present some of the more general statements of the courts which can guide school personnel in helping them to decide where to get help when differences arise. School personnel with even this limited understanding of legal precedent would, it is hoped, consult counsel *before* rather than after serious trouble develops.

In other words, the key question for the thinking of school people throughout the volume might be: What would you do if faced with a similar predicament?

Most of the illustrations have been selected from the realm of everyday school activity and school business rather than from the facts of any specific reported cases. By observing the hypothetical employee in terms of the elements in a situation that precipitates legal involvement, all school personnel may form a clear picture of legal principles and of their possible application to their own conduct.

In formulating the "legal rules" governing actions, an attempt has been made to avoid unnecessarily technical phraseology. Enough of court language is used, nevertheless, to acquaint school people with the terminology and method used in reporting decisions of the courts.

## THE AMERICAN LEGAL SYSTEM

### The Need for Laws

With rare exceptions, people do not live unto themselves. The students of sociology and psychology agree that people could not live alone even if they tried and desired to do so. A child is born into society and never escapes from it. Besides the persons involved and their physical equipment for living, society is based upon group habits—approved ways of doing things. The life of one person very naturally touches the lives of others. Contacts among humans have evolved as a series of relationships—one individual with another or with a group.

From babyhood to old age, the actions of one person produce the possibilities of social restraint, of legal involvement with others. For instance, the *status* of the teacher—a subject which bears directly upon his work and responsibility—is expressed to a large measure in the legal codes that have developed.

From the very beginnings of "civilization" there has been accumulating a vast body of rules, regulations, or laws which have as their purpose the regulation of human conduct. The process is a continuous one. By tomorrow, at this time, this body of law will have been expanded appreciably. New rules are enacted each day, and the courts "create" law by their interpretations of new events and reinterpretations of the old. Judicial procedure holds, at least in part, that there is somewhere a known rule of law that will cover the facts of the dispute under litigation. The problem for the court is to discover and apply the rule by means of precedent and "rationalization."

In short, the need for law is that of helping to create a society that is organized sufficiently along accepted rules so that the needs of the vast majority of its members will be best served. It is the task of the legal profession, the courts, and the press to uphold orderly processes of law in order to preserve the greatest amount of freedom for the individual. Ours is a government of laws—laws to protect citizens—including school personnel—and to guarantee their freedom within those laws.

## Three Kinds of Legal Action

In order that man's various relationships to man could be regulated, society developed a system of rules which became known as the "legal system." Within this system there grew up two basic divisions: criminal law and civil law. If the violation of a rule was deemed to be against the state or society as a whole, the act became known as a crime. If the infringement of a right concerned the relation of one person to another, it became known as a violation of a civil right and came under the rules of the civil law.

The enforcement of civil laws (of personal rights) under civil action soon developed a third concept, which was based upon the idea of what was fair, right, or equitable in a particular situation rather than upon what the code or law said. In the English court system, a separate set of courts was established for the purpose of determining disputes involving "what is right?" These were called courts of chancery.

The custom of this separate set of courts was brought to America. Soon after its adoption, however, the idea of special courts for equitable judgments was abandoned. The principle of "equity" was carried on by the civil courts. The two types of cases were distinguished mainly by methods of court procedure and the nature of the legal relief sought. In America, trial courts may hear criminal cases, civil actions, and cases in equity. Equity cases usually do not require a jury. Courts of equity most often act on the person of the defendant rather than against his property. It should be remembered that all three kinds of actions—criminal, civil, and equitable—are included in the term "legal action."

### The Written Basis of Law

Law has been defined as a body of rules for human conduct prescribed and enforced by the representatives of organized society. The term "law," as thus used, involves two groups of documents. The first group comprises the federal Constitution and Congressional enactments which form the body of federal written law, and the constitutions of the several states and legislative enactments which form the great body of state written law. The laws passed by legislatures (or general assemblies) are frequently referred to as state statutes or the "codes of the state." This total body of law, both federal and state, makes up the *written* law of the United States.

The second group of documents comprises the large body of rules which has resulted from the enforcement, by the courts, of long-established social customs. This group, larger by far in volume than the first group, is known as the "common law." To help distinguish it from the constitutional and statutory law, it is referred to as the "unwritten law." This common law, found in the federal and state court decisions, is "unwritten" only in the sense that it is not passed formally by legislators. If laws and codes were not carried by written word, they would be distorted so rapidly, and to such a degree, that the administration of justice in a civilized society would be impossible.

The decisions of the higher courts, along with the reasons for decisions, are published in bound volumes called "reports." From the opinions in the reports we derive our knowledge of the unwritten or common law. It must be remembered here that the unwritten or common law, about which we are now speaking, must give way in favor of any state statute. The judge-made law, too, may be altered at any time by the legislature of a state.

If one were to visit a law library, he would see that the unwritten law has been preserved in the form of court reports by a carefully devised plan, the American Reporter System, generally referred to as the "Digest System." The student of law has no difficulty under the carefully indexed system of court reports in finding the decisions in cases that have been tried in any of our appellate courts. These regularly published reports include all the cases decided by the supreme courts and many of the courts of appeal. Records are also kept of all decisions in the lower trial courts but usually not in law libraries. To get these records, one would ordinarily have to go to the county where the trial was held.

Thus, a vast number of laws have been accumulated which pertain to schools and to school personnel and which govern the relationships of such personnel among themselves and with other persons. School law includes that body of legal rules which relates to the conduct of the educational enterprise. When school personnel have some knowledge of the fundamental laws that govern the conduct of education, they can work with greater purpose and security.

## Court Procedure

Every legal controversy is in reality a fight between two or more parties, each of whom is attempting to persuade the umpire of the rightness of his position. It is not possible to state precisely what the court procedure will be in the event of legal trouble; however, the following descriptive list of steps involved summarizes a typical case.

1. A lawsuit usually results from a disagreement as to legal rights.
2. The first step in a court procedure is the issuance and delivery of a summons.
3. The statement of the case by the plaintiff (the party who initiates the court action) and the answer by the defendant are known as court pleadings.
4. In a defendant's demurrer he temporarily admits the declaration of the plaintiff but alleges that no law makes him liable. This issue is determined by the trial judge.
5. The trial is a legal process by which the evidence in the case is brought before a jury of twelve persons for their verdict.
6. Prospective jurors may be rejected by the attorneys if their knowledge or occupation would tend to make them partial to either party.

7. Witnesses, after having testified, are usually subjected to cross-examination to attempt to expose weaknesses in their statements.
8. The verdict entered in the court records by the judge becomes a judgment.
9. The carrying out of the verdict according to court instructions is called the execution.
10. If errors have been committed in the original trial, the defendant may appeal to a court of higher jurisdiction. Then it is the plaintiff who becomes the defendant if and when the case on appeal is accepted by a higher court.

School personnel can acquire information about the law in several different ways. They may accumulate it by costly experience while on the job. On the other hand, they may familiarize themselves with the legal principles that relate to their professional affiliations. Then when problems arise, they will have the insight to know whether and when to consult legal counsel.

## How the Courts Affect the Law

### Court Hierarchy and "Review"

In the event of conflict between the sources of law, a priority system prevails. Here is the legal hierarchy: (1) the federal Constitution, (2) acts of Congress, (3) state constitutions, and (4) acts of state legislatures and of the bodies created to act legally for the state.

What the Supreme Court of the United States decides in any field, including education, is the *"vox ultima"* insofar as official acts of the state legislatures, departments of the state, and local boards of education are concerned. This Court stands at the very summit of the hierarchy. The decisions on the cases in which it deigns to speak are final. They stand until changed by the Supreme Court itself, by amendment to the Constitution, or by "corrective" legislation—by act of Congress. The decisions rendered by the Court take precedence over those of all other courts. Decisions of "last resort" state courts, on the other hand, usually are final only within the bounds of the respective states.

Only about 1,500 cases out of approximately 50,000 cases per year which come to federal district courts are appealed to the Supreme Court. Out of these 1,500 cases thus appealed, only some 200 are actually handled by that Court, about 1,300 being refused on one ground or another. Of the 200 that receive the judicial attention of the Court, there are but 75 to 100 on which the Court actually issues written opinions.

The Supreme Court has interpreted the language of the Constitution broadly to allow increased legislation by Congress in many fields, especially with regard to all manner of social and economic enactments by governmental bodies.

For further evidence of the weight of the Supreme Court in daily affairs, one will remember that the political complexion of the executive and legislative branches of the federal government changed noticeably when President Eisenhower was inaugurated as chief executive on January 20, 1953. However, the outgoing Democratic President had appointed four of the nine Supreme Court justices. His predecessor had appointed the remaining five. With this Court, the new President had to be content. The stability of the judicial system depends upon this continuity.

The federal Constitution and the United States Supreme Court have had, and continue to have, a profound influence upon the development of school law in the United States. Justices of the federal courts have used the Constitution to challenge public school policies and practices, especially within the past two decades. Under the interpretations of the basic law, certain state school legislation has been declared an "invalid exercise of the police power" of the state.

One of the consequences of review of legislative acts by the judicial branch of government is that of placing the courts in a position to make their views of the Constitution prevail. Educational matters have taken up a great deal of court time, and many pages are needed to cover the topic of "Schools and School Districts" in legal digests and encyclopedias. The courts are thus enabled to influence future readings of the Constitution by other branches of government as well as by themselves. One of the broad generalizations that seems to stand is that the laws of the land are precisely what the courts say they are.

There are those who say that the courts make new laws as effectively as the legislatures which, under the separation-of-powers concept, are charged with that responsibility. This is a matter of practical necessity, because it is utterly impossible for a legislature to provide guides for every conceivable situation that might arise. In theory, under the system of checks and balances, the courts do not create laws. They determine the issues brought before them by what appears to them to be right in the light of constitutions, adherence to the purpose and intent of the laws, and the measure of abuse of discretion exercised.

## Law and Freedom

It has been claimed, on occasion, that the purpose of the legal structure is to repress individuals or to control the activities of free individuals. A careful review of the development of law reveals that this attitude is not sound. Rather than being formulated, adopted, and enforced to restrict personal liberty, laws make it possible for society to enjoy increased freedom.

As a rule there is fairly close agreement among court decisions on closely similar matters. However, opinions vary owing to differences in statutory laws, differences in the circumstances and origins of cases on which decisions have been rendered, and differences in experiences or biases of judges.

Much of the work of the Supreme Court of the United States involves the constitutionality—the legal right to be operative—of federal and state laws. The federal Constitution is the sole criterion for judging such legality when there is conflict between federal and state law. If a majority of the nine justices of the Court find that a law is contrary to the federal Constitution, that law is invalid, or has no legal effect as of the date of the decision. This procedure is known as "judicial review" of the legislative acts. Stated formally, the principle of judicial review is the power of the courts, and ultimately of the Supreme Court, to pass on the validity of laws and other acts of public authority in relation to the federal Constitution.

## State Control of Education

It has been the Tenth and Fourteenth Amendments that have most influenced on the federal level the direction of education.

The Fourteenth, or "citizenship and equal rights," Amendment includes three significant clauses that the Court has often employed to alter legal precedent. These are that (1) no state shall make a law abridging privileges or immunities of citizens of the United States; (2) no state shall deprive any person of life, liberty, or property without due process of law; and (3) no state shall deny equal protection of the law.

The Tenth Amendment reserves to the states all matters not delegated to the federal government. Education was not mentioned specifically in the first ten articles. Under the Tenth Amendment, then, education is a matter for the concern of the states. Also, it must be remembered that the Bill of Rights guaranteed freedom to the individual citizen. It was the Fourteenth Amendment that made these ten restrictions apply to the states. Hence, no state may violate any of them, even in the area of education.

## Precedent, Judicial Power, and Jurisdiction

When a decision, pertaining to whole laws or smaller portions thereof, has established a principle of law, it is considered to be a precedent for subsequent decisions until overruled. However, the precedent applies only within the same jurisdiction or area of authority. Elsewhere, the courts are free not to follow the decision. However, courts are often influenced by the weight of prevailing views in other state courts. It will be remembered that appellate courts record their decisions with written opinions. These records are the foundation of case law which lawyers and judges follow in subsequent cases involving similar circumstances.

It will be helpful here to point out what lawyers consider to be a fundamental distinction between "jurisdiction" and "judicial power." A lower federal court has no jurisdiction except such as Congress has specifically given it. Once a court has jurisdiction of a case, it is thereby put in possession of the power—the judicial power—to decide the case in accordance with the law.

The district courts of the United States have only *original jurisdiction.* This means that they can hear only cases that have not been decided by other federal courts. The United States Circuit Courts have only *appellate jurisdiction.* This means that they can hear only those cases which have been appealed from a decision of a lower federal court. The United States Supreme Court has both original and appellate jurisdiction, depending upon the type of case. To help clarify this, the next section deals briefly with the court structure.

## Court Structure

Despite the keen interest of many persons in the Supreme Court, in its justices and their decisions, knowledge of the American legal system among the public generally, including school personnel, is fragmentary at best. Without doubt, there is need for a fuller, more animate, and more documented knowledge about the functioning of the judicial branch of the government. Even the informed American, familiar with other aspects of government, faces a baffling task when he seeks to form a clear picture of legal institutions.[1]

The Constitution which the thirteen states had adopted proclaimed that "this constitution, and the laws of the United States which shall be made in pursuance thereof; and all treaties made, or which shall be made, under the authority of the United States, shall be the supreme law of the land; and the judges in every state shall be bound thereby, anything in the constitutions or laws of any state to the contrary notwithstanding." So, on April 30, 1789, each state ceased to be a sovereignty. Each state subjected itself to the superior power of the national Constitution and of the national government.

## The Judiciary Act of 1789

Within the first six months of its existence, the First Congress enacted the celebrated Judiciary Act of 1789. This Act created not only the "one Supreme Court" commanded by the Constitution, but also a system of inferior federal courts—a system which has remained for almost one hundred and seventy-five years as one of the distinctive features of American governmental structure. In the Judiciary Act, the First Congress conferred upon the inferior

---

[1] Lewis Mayer, *The American Legal System* (New York: Harper and Brothers, Publishers, 1955), p. vii. This text offers much specific information in readable form.

federal courts original jurisdiction over most, but not all, of the classes of cases enumerated in the Constitution as falling within "the judicial power of the United States."

The Constitution thus created a vast "judicial power of the United States" to be exercised concurrently with that of the states. A notion, unfortunately encouraged by some textbooks on government, is that the three branches of the federal government are coordinate and parallel. The fact is that the three departments are not parallel and coordinate. An understanding of this fact is central to a grasp of the extent of federal judicial power. The legislative and the executive are brought into existence by the Constitution itself. The judiciary is not. Under the American scheme, it can have no real value until Congress and the President have acted.

The dual nature of the court structure is significant for several reasons. Except for the very few federally controlled areas of the nation, the court structure is everywhere dual. It is exclusively federal in the District of Columbia, the territory of Hawaii, and the insular possessions of the United States. In each of the forty-nine states, however, there also functions a system of state courts, side by side with one or more federal courts. Through a system of intermediate appellate courts, they respond to the Supreme Court of the United States. State court systems are similar to the federal pattern.

### Organization of the Federal Courts

The basic plan of the federal courts, established in 1789, has persisted to the present time, despite numerous and important changes. There are district courts, circuit courts, various specialized courts, and, at the apex, the Supreme Court. There are eighty-six federal district courts, covering all states and territories. The state of Georgia, for example, has three federal district courts. For the purpose of hearing appeals, the country is divided into ten regions known as "circuits." In each sits a United States Court of Appeals. The territory of Hawaii and insular possessions are included within the ten regions, but not the District of Columbia. For the District there is a separate Court of Appeals because of the heavy schedule of work there. Except for a few hundred federal cases annually, which are finally passed upon by the Supreme Court, all appeal cases are disposed of by these regional appellate courts created by Congress in 1893. The Fifth Circuit, for example, embraces the states of Florida, Georgia, Alabama, Mississippi, Louisiana, and Texas. The Court sits in New Orleans.

The "legal system" is concerned with every variety of proceeding in which a tribunal of some description adjudicates the rights of the individual. The tribunal is armed with the power of the state and, hence, is part of government.[2] The system includes agencies of several kinds. They are federal, state, and local. Each engages in adjudication on a vast scale. There are voluntary arbitration tribunals and military tribunals which administer a system of criminal justice and occasionally of civil justice.[3] Dominating the system are the courts.

## Jurisdiction

The Supreme Court came into being not by the Constitution, but by the creation of Congress. Alone, among the federal courts, the Supreme Court has its original jurisdiction fixed by the Constitution itself.[4] However, it is the more significant *appellate* jurisdiction that influences education. Unique among the courts of the nation, the Supreme Court unifies the "several" laws.

The Supreme Court has jurisdiction in all cases that involve the constitutions of the several states, the Constitution of the United

---

[2] Mayer, *The American Legal System,* p. 1.

[3] The courts have a dual function—one self-contained, the other supervisory. In their self-contained operations, the courts grant redress to private parties and afford assistance to officers charged with law enforcement, by enjoining and punishing violations of law or compelling compliance therewith. In their supervisory function, they exercise a control more or less extensive over all administrative agencies, and over the special tribunals, arbitral and military, for which the laws provide. The highest courts of the state and the nation exercise a control over the legislative branches of government, as indicated previously. See Mayer, *ibid.,* p. 3.

[4] The Supreme Court is not only the supreme appellate court of the federal court system. To it, for final disposition, come appeals from the state courts in a limited number of cases. The cases must involve a "federal" question. The Court has been reserved by Congress for the right to review on appeal the federal questions involved in the judgment of a state court. In a state court, where there is drawn in question the validity of a statute of any state on the ground of its being repugnant to the Constitution, and the decision is in favor of the validity of the statute, a review of the case by the Supreme Court is a matter of right.

States, and agreements between sovereign powers. It has jurisdiction in all cases that draw in the question of the constitutionality of any state law or any law of the federal government. In addition, the Supreme Court has jurisdiction in certain kinds of cases specifically named. It governs the issuance of "writs of certiorari" to the Court of Appeals. In other cases, the Court of Appeals has jurisdiction.

In most state court cases, other than those reviewed by the Court "on appeal," review by the United States Supreme Court may be had only by permission of the Court. To obtain such permission, there is filed in the Court a "petition for a writ of certiorari," in which are set forth reasons why the case is thought by the petitioner to merit review by the Court. If as many as four justices desire to review a case, the petition for a writ is granted. The Court issues to the state court its "writ" commanding it to certify to the Supreme Court a record of the case.

The First Congress refused to place within the jurisdiction of the newly created inferior federal courts all possible cases falling within the "judicial power of the United States." This reservation illustrates the fact that the federal courts have only such jurisdiction as Congress chooses to give them. All crimes created by statutes of the federal government are prosecuted exclusively in the federal courts. Incidentally, there can be no crime against the United States, except those created by statute. Congress did and still can confer jurisdiction in certain types of cases on the federal courts concurrently with the courts of the several states.

The "judicial power of the United States" has been entrusted to the state courts in considerable measure from the very beginning. Congress still has not deemed it advisable, with certain exceptions, to provide for the removal of cases from the state courts merely because the defendant's pleading raises a federal question.

In most instances, Congress has provided that cases, when instigated in state courts, shall remain there. The cases proceed through the highest court of the state in which a determination can be had. Then, only, may federal review of the federal question be sought. The Supreme Court has also laid down the rule that a federal court should refrain from exercising its statutory power to enjoin (to forbid or prohibit) state officers from following certain action where the state courts are capable of giving relief.

As a result of these limitations imposed by Congress and the federal courts themselves, it is not generally possible to obtain an injunction against a state body in the federal courts. Certain controversies are within the jurisdiction of federal courts only if the amounts of money involved are large enough. Any diversity-of-citizenship case, however, is exclusively within the jurisdiction of the state courts when it is incapable of being characterized as having any given "amount in controversy." A suit against a state by a private party is expressly excluded from the federal judicial power by the Eleventh Amendment.

The process of the courts affects everyone, whether he be involved directly or indirectly. Only the President of the United States as head of the government is regarded as being immune from the courts. Broadly considered, the very survival of constitutional government depends upon its adaptation to changing situations without abandoning the spirit of the system. The courts are an integral part of that system. Statesmenlike judges in the courts play a positive role in their position as "censors on the legislatures" by their interpretations of governmental powers and limitations. With others, Chief Justice John Marshall helped to expound constitutional law as he saw it.

## THE PROBLEM OF PROFESSIONAL ETHICS

Social customs between persons and among peoples have developed gradually over the centuries. They have become the guardians as well as the limiters of personal and group conduct. As humans engage in more and more group-centered activities, their relationships necessarily become more complex. Neither the criminal law, the civil law, nor the "equitable rights" of men can solve adequately some of the problems that arise from new types of relationships.

People realize that "even a man who lives alone, say on a lonely island, has need to establish right relationships." [5] They understand that he is subject to "natural laws" and will suffer if he

[5] William Yeager, *Administration and the Teacher* (New York: Harper and Brothers, Publishers, 1954), p. 504. See also Leo M. Chamberlain and Leslie W. Kindred, *The Teacher and School Organization*, 3rd ed. (Englewood Cliffs, N.J.: Prentice-Hall, Inc., 1958), chap. 23, "Maintaining a Code of Ethics."

does not obey them. As soon as another man comes upon the scene, however, the need for some pattern of mutually acceptable conduct becomes evident.

Guides to conduct are needed especially by professionally employed persons. Here persons come into direct contact with other persons, using predominately mental and intellectual skills, rather than physical or manual ones. The problem of defining professional "right conduct" rests with the professional groups. Some have already found effective means to invoke "codes of ethics" while others as yet have not. The concept of ethics appeared in the medical profession—doctor-and-patient relationship—within the present century. The idea has developed into what today is termed the "canons of the profession."

## What Do We Mean by "Ethics"?

Perhaps an attempt at some definitions is in order here. The set of nonlegal rules—those outside of the legal system—has come to be known as ethics. This set attempts to regulate man's relationship to man. A "concise" definition appears in Webster's dictionary:

> The science which treats of the nature and laws of the actions of intelligent human beings, these actions being considered in relation to their moral qualities; the science which treats of the nature and grounds of moral obligation; the science of human duty; a particular system of principles and rules concerning duty whether true or false; rules of practice in respect to a single class of human actions.

What is generally called the "ethics" of a profession is actually but consensus of expert opinion as to the human duty involved in a vocation, calling, occupation, or employment that involves labor, skill, education, special knowledge, and compensation (but not profit!). Conceptions of what is "ethical" add little. References suggest that the term relates to moral action, motive, or character; that it pertains to what is professionally right or befitting, conforming to professional standards of conduct.

When "moral" is sought out, it pertains to character, conduct, intention, and social relations. *Black's Law Dictionary* reveals the term as pertaining or relating to the conscience or moral sense or to the "general principles of right conduct." What is moral is cognizable or enforceable only by "the conscience or by the principles of right conduct, as distinguished from positive law." It would seem that "moral law" would then be the law of conscience—the aggregate of those rules and principles of ethics which relate to right and wrong conduct and prescribe the standards to which the actions of teachers (and others) should conform in their dealings with each other.[6] Thus, ethics is opinion plus conscience.

Sometimes the phrase "moral turpitude" describes conduct lacking in ethical principles. It denotes an act of baseness violating the private and social duties which a man owes to his fellow men, or to society in general, contrary to the accepted and customary rule of right and duty between man and man. What might a teacher do, for instance, to have his conduct deemed contrary to justice, honesty, modesty, or good morals?

### A Concept of Ethics for Teachers

Here follows a paraphrased definition of a concept of ethics for teachers. It is based on a description of what constitutes legal ethics. See whether it is appropriate:

> Usages and customs among members of the teaching profession, involving their moral and professional duties toward one another, toward pupils, colleagues, and parents, and toward school officials; that branch of moral science which treats of the duties which a member of the teaching profession owes to the public, to school officials, to his professional brethren, and to his pupils.

Law and the ministry had emerged to places of importance as professions even before medicine. Attention was given within the groups to attempts to regulate relationships among members and outsiders. Problems soon arose relating to the manner in which the "code of ethics" was to be interpreted and to the manner of enforcement of provisions.

### The NEA Code of Ethics

It was little different with teaching. Teachers found that if a code of ethics is to be an effective and workable document, it must be more than words on paper. Like a constitution, it can come

---

[6] Henry Campbell Black, *Black's Law Dictionary* (4th ed.; St. Paul, Minn.: West Publishing Company, 1951), p. 1160.

fully alive only when interpreted and construed as specific questions arise. Since the NEA Code of Ethics was adopted in 1929, there have been amendments.[7] Opinions have had to be issued regarding the precise meaning of "using proper channels" and "accepting the obligation imposed by contract for rendering a professional level of service."

The basic principles of the NEA Code allegedly apply to all persons engaged in the professional aspects of education. Interpretations serve to inform the profession as to accepted ethical practices in fulfilling a primary obligation to guide children; in sharing with parents the task of shaping children's purposes and acts; in occupying a position of public trust; in fulfilling inescapable obligations with respect to employment practices; and in acting so as to distinguish teaching from many other occupations by the "uniqueness and quality of the professional relations" among all teachers.

By taking only the fourth principle above (obligations with respect to employment practices) and elaborating it, a teacher can see the problems encountered by those who must render formal opinions. The teacher is "professional" when

(*a*) using proper channels.

(*b*) discussing confidential information only with authorized persons.

(*c*) applying for a position on the basis of qualifications.

(*d*) applying for a specific position in selected school systems.

(*e*) refusing to jump into a position left vacant by somebody's unprofessional conduct.

(*f*) adhering to contract terms unless relieved of them.

(*g*) giving due notice when a change of positions is deemed necessary.

(*h*) giving fair recommendations.

(*i*) accepting no compensation for supporting the adoption of teaching aids and materials.

(*j*) engaging in no gainful employment that adversely affects one's professional status.

[7] These amendments occurred in 1941, 1944, and 1948. The origin of a National Code of Ethics for the teaching profession actually goes back to the appointment of a committee to study the problems in 1924. The NEA Committee on Professional Ethics presented a revised Code which was adopted by the 1952 Representative Assembly at the Detroit meeting.

(*k*) cooperating in the development of school policies.

(*l*) accepting the obligation imposed by contract of rendering a professional level of service.

## Specific Application of Ethical Precepts

Exactly what are the applications of the "canons of professional ethics"? What do the phrases above—all agreed upon as the minima —mean when applied to specific relations within the school? When, for example, should a teacher withdraw from employment? The moral right of a teacher to withdraw from employment, once assumed, arises only from "good cause." What should be considered a justifiable reason? The desire or consent of superiors is not always sufficient. The teacher should not throw up an unfinished task to the detriment of pupils except for reasons of honor and self-respect. What do these terms mean? If, for example, the principal insists upon an unjust or immoral course in the conduct of a situation, or if he persists over the teacher's remonstrances in presenting frivolous defenses, or if he deliberately disregards an agreement or obligation as to duties or responsibilities, the teacher may then be warranted in withdrawing on due notice to the school board, allowing the board time to employ another teacher.

Should, and can, a teacher restrain a colleague from committing improprieties? A teacher should use his best efforts to restrain and to prevent a colleague from doing those things which the teacher himself ought not do to, particularly with reference to his conduct toward children, teachers, parents, and school authorities. If a teacher persists in wrongdoing, a colleague should report the matter to his superior.

What course is open upon the discovery of an imposition or a deception? When a teacher discovers that some fraud or deception has been practiced, which has unjustly been imposed upon a party, he should endeavor to rectify it. He may at first advise the perpetrator, and if that person refuses to take action to keep the other party from foregoing the advantage unjustly gained, the teacher should promptly inform the injured person, so that he may take needed steps. Do you agree? Of course, it is improper for a teacher to make himself a tale-bearer by volunteering statements in a case where they have not been solicited or where they are not absolutely known to be relevant to the situation.

In a problem situation it is improper for a teacher to assert his personal belief in the innocence of one party or in the justice of one cause over another. It is not misconduct, however, for the teacher to express his individual belief in the guilt of an accused if such belief is based squarely on sound evidence and the school authorities are not led to believe that there is other information, known to the teacher but not divulged, justifying that belief.

When a teacher discovers that a pupil has no case against a teacher and the pupil is determined to continue it, or when the teacher finds himself incapable of handling the problem effectively, he should seek professional counsel. Sundry instances may arise in which withdrawal is to be justified. Upon withdrawing from a problem case after certain understandings have been reached and reports of happenings left behind, the teacher should see that all records pertinent to the case are turned over to the principal for study and use by a successor. Such transfer is a minimum obligation.

It is the plain duty of all school personnel to preserve the confidences of pupils. This duty outlasts employment in the school system, and extends as well to other employees of the system as to teachers. Neither should school personnel accept employment that involves (or, they have reason to suspect may later involve) the disclosure or use of these confidences, either for private advantage or to the disadvantage of a pupil. This is so even though there are other available sources of such information. A teacher, for example, should not continue his employment when he discovers that this obligation of silence prevents the performance of his full duty to the former or new employer.

If a teacher is accused of some act by a pupil or by another teacher, he is not precluded from disclosing the truth in respect to the accusation.

The announced intention of a pupil or an employee to commit a crime is not included within the confidences that the teacher is privileged to respect. He may properly make such disclosure as may be necessary to prevent the act or protect those against whom it is threatened.

## Can Ethics Be Taught by Formal Instruction?

There is honest debate about the worth of instruction in ethical principles and practices given on the preservice or the inservice level. There are wide differences in people's conceptions of ethics. Some claim that a remedy may be instruction on a mandatory basis for all those finally selected to teach. Others allege that formal instruction cannot help a person develop moral perceptions.

Rather than attempting to "instill ethical practices," it may be wiser to help all personnel gain understanding through participation in the real tasks of schools. The relationships of the teacher to the board of education, the supervisor, the principal, colleagues, nonteachers, to parents, and to pupils provide opportunities to help the teacher see the operation of ethical principles. There are conferences, group meetings, and seminars to serve as vehicles for study and discussion. Teachers can present issues that involve ethical choices.

The favor that teaching wins from the public, the advantage or benefit that is acquired by the profession, both depend upon a clearer notion of what constitutes the ethics of school personnel relationships.

# Education Yesterday
## and Today

───────────────── *2*

THE LEGAL and ethical problems of school personnel today may seem to have little, if any, connection with the status and organization of education in the past. However, today in the United States school personnel enjoy the legal status they have and the professional favor of the general public at least in part because of the efforts of the pioneers in education who met and solved problems confronting them. These forerunners worked under conditions and with personnel quite different from those existing today.

In America, early interest in education and teaching comprehended training for moral instruction as well as limited intellectual pursuits. Because "education" included more than the improvement and cultivation of the mind, problems arose concerning the place of the school in cultivating religious sentiments and in developing the physical faculties of children. For instance, it is known that the school in America some two hundred years ago played a subordinate role in society. Only in very rare instances did schools achieve a distinct place of their own. Religion and education were so closely related in daily living that there was little distinction between religious and "school" instruction.

Teaching in America is what it is today because of influences which have been molding it since the founding of the first school on the eastern coast. Practices begun by the early settlers, pertaining to education, were the basis for precedents for personnel practices which now are a part of firmly established educational philosophy. Today, classroom teachers "give" moral, intellectual, and physical instruction based upon conceptions of law and ethics that have evolved gradually over the past three centuries.

## Early Interest in Education and Teaching

The attitude of the early people toward education can be deduced from such sources as colonial laws, minutes of town meetings, and documents telling about local customs. Many writers have painted word pictures of teaching in bygone days despite the limited amount of reliable sources of information.

### A New Philosophy of Education

The early history of America does furnish evidence that, as a new philosophy of government came into existence, a new philosophy of education came with it. This philosophy was expressed in the creation of the free public school, which became as essential to the preservation of the "American ideal" as the organic documents in which the framework of the Republic was outlined and by which the freedoms of the people were guaranteed.

Few matters gave the founders of the American government more concern than a plan of education for children. It was the belief of many that the success or failure of the new government depended upon the extent to which the citizenry would be enlightened. This concern was being expressed even before the Declaration of Independence was signed and the federal Constitution adopted.

It is a matter of record that the Scotch Presbyterians had an interest in education even before settlement of the American continent by Europeans. As early as 1560, the General Assembly of the Church in Scotland recommended to the Parliament that there should be a Latin school under a competent schoolmaster in every parish where there was a town of any size, and that in the rural parishes the reader or minister should teach the youth. When the descendants of these folk left their homes to fight and subdue the Pennsylvania wilderness, similar attitudes persisted.

The first action to provide public education in America was brought about by the Puritan influence. In 1642 the Commonwealth of Massachusetts passed an edict which made it mandatory that all children be taught to read. Five years later the legislature of the colony passed a law requiring:

1. That every town having fifty householders should at once appoint a teacher of reading and writing, and provide for his wages in such manner as the town might determine; and
2. That every town having one hundred householders must provide a [Latin] grammar school to fit youths for the university, under a penalty of £5 for failure to do so.[1]

One of the beliefs upon which America was founded was that man has an inherent right to worship God after the dictates of his own conscience. Ethics was thought of as individual morality. There were strong advocates in early days for the education of the youth so that they could read and understand Biblical precepts. As one result, many religious or church schools had sprung up even before the organization of the public schools. As public schools began to develop, certain problems arose when attempts were made to make them serve as instruments of education for various church or sectarian groups anxious to press certain dogma. The selection of a teacher and the content of the curriculum became problem issues of importance in the communities where the religious question arose. What later became the "American ideal"— that of the separation of the church and state—was challenged early.

As noted earlier, the idea of education for youth was not a new idea. However, the idea that education of youth was essential to the success of government was new. The child was to be educated, not to advance his personal interests, but because the law required it. The state would suffer if he were not educated. This concept was expressed by Prussian rulers in the eighteenth century and later by Jefferson, when he said, "If a nation expects to be ignorant and free in a state of civilization, it expects what never was and never will be."

### Federal and State Responsibility

In the political history of early America, certain "vocal" citizens were committed to the principle of requiring free public education by law. A striking contrast existed between this attitude and that

[1] Ellwood P. Cubberley, *Public Education in the United States* (Boston: Houghton Mifflin Company, 1919), p. 18.

of official governments, both federal and state. The federal government was not committed to educating anyone, at any time or anywhere. The Constitution did not include education as one of its responsibilities. No reference was made to it. The power with which the federal government was to influence education was found in the "general welfare" clause. This point should be kept in mind as the legal aspects of school personnel relationships are explored.

A further point concerning the relation of the federal government to education is that the Constitution sets out the powers which the federal government shall have. It specifies that all powers which the Constitution does not specifically delegate to the federal government nor prohibit to the states are powers of the several states. One by one, the states have assumed the responsibility for education left to them by the Constitution. All states now have statements in their supreme law making it mandatory for their legislatures to provide schools for the education of the youth.[2] School laws spell out the details.

One important feature of education as it has developed in the United States is the legal control of public schools by the several states through their constitutions and statutes. The courts have held education to be a state function.[3] In legal theory, public education is considered not only *one* important function of state government, but to be "of government" itself. Where the issue of control over education has arisen, the courts have stated that authority over school personnel and school affairs is "a central power residing in the Legislature of the State."[4]

There is sufficient evidence in the common law for holding that the maintenance of a system of public schools within a state is

[2] Until South Carolina, Mississippi, Louisiana, and Georgia altered their constitutions, as one means of getting around the decision of the United States Supreme Court on segregation in public schools, the then forty-eight states were pledged to maintain free public schools.

[3] Newton Edwards, *The Courts and the Public Schools* (Chicago: University of Chicago Press, 1955), chap. I.

[4] State v. Haworth, 122 Ind. 462, 23 N.E. 946, 7 L.R.A. 240 (1890). This citation means that the case is found in volume 122 of the Indiana official Supreme Court Reports, on page 462. The second reference is to volume and page of the *Northeastern Reporter,* which is a private compilation of cases. The third refers to the *Lawyers' Reports Annotated,* also a series that selects certain cases and gives much background material.

closely associated with the exercise by the state of its police power. In fact, it has been held by the courts that "free schooling furnished by the state is not so much a right granted to individuals as a duty imposed upon them for the public good." Numerous writers have emphasized the same point in declaring that the state establishes schools so that it can better "exercise the state's inherent right to enforce a type of education, looking specifically to the preservation and improvement of the state."

Along the line of state responsibility for education, it is well to ponder one of America's unique contributions to the political ideal of "equality before the law." This was the extension of equal opportunity to each individual to make the most of his talents through education. This ideal was expressed by George Washington when he referred to knowledge as the "surest basis of happiness," and by Jefferson's statement, that among the aims of public instruction are "public prosperity and individual happiness."

So one is reminded that the founders of the American system of government were far from ignoring the value of education for the individual himself. They were familiar with Anglo-Saxon political development and especially with the growth of the idea of equality of every person before English law. This concept of the worth and dignity of a human being had been a long-established tradition of the English people. Their "Petition of Rights" asserted the inviolability of the rights of the most humble subject. It was these same rights that were declared in the Declaration of Independence not to be alienable. The first ten Amendments to the Constitution of the United States guarantee to the individual citizen important freedoms. This "American Bill of Rights" has been a source of protection for "saint and sinner" alike.

One impetus to the beginning of the free public school system in America was the plan of Thomas Jefferson. He proposed a system for Virginia, with its most distinctive feature a system of small local units called "wards." He would have modeled them after the towns of New England. Even though the plan was not approved, it was from such early patterns that present-day school districts have evolved. In accord with early laws of some states, any neighborhood that wanted to organize a school could do so by levying upon itself a tax to defray the costs of building, maintaining, and operating a school within certain prescribed regulations.

## Operation of Early Schools

The operation of early schools provides some marked contrasts to present-day patterns. Administration rested almost solely within the community with little or no regulation from state law. As school district boundaries expanded because of population pressure, the state made provision for the selection of trustees and of school boards to help carry out the business of operating the school. Even though the school was initially administered locally, it should be kept in mind that education had always been a function of the state because it was the state that ultimately controlled education through its constitution.

The preparation of teachers was aided greatly by so-called "Founding Fathers" during the decades immediately preceding the Civil War. Not until after 1865, however, did education really make great strides forward. Court injunctions had held up progress previously in some localities. When the way was finally cleared, it became possible for the affected communities again to make local levies for common school revenue purposes. The public school enjoyed its greatest advance, as far as physical expansion goes, beginning at this time. Townships became the unit of educational administration in the Middle West. The length of the school term for pupils rose from four months to five, and then to six months.

As far as the buildings were concerned, it was not uncommon to have the schoolhouse, in some localities at least, named after the family that had given the plot of ground.[5] This practice was one characteristic of the times and testified to the influence of the family in the school district. The schoolhouse itself, of one room, more than likely had no floor, save the bare earth. In the center, a fire burned under a chimney built of split wooden sticks, laid in log fashion and covered with clay. The school was supported, in all probability, about three feet above the floor by means of four posts set in a square, six feet apart.

The nineteenth century provided for the evolution of the school, from the most primitive type—the isolated one-room log building with earthen floor and benches—to the modern type, with com-

[5] See Millard F. Kennedy, *Schoolmaster of Yesterday* (New York: McGraw-Hill Book Company, Inc., 1940), *passim*.

paratively good equipment. As the twentieth century progressed, some school districts provided for transportation to well-equipped school plants.

At midpoint in the 1800's there were substantial frame and brick schools erected, located so that pupils did not have to walk more than several miles. In some areas, adverse decisions of the courts halted redistricting plans. As a consequence, some school buildings remained unused for several years.

With better buildings came the disappearance of log seats. These backless benches, just the split halves of 10- or 12-inch logs, served as seats with the more or less flat side up. The logs were supported by heavy legs. The upper side was smoothed to remove the splinters. Often the boys' breeches and girls' dresses indicated that the job had not been well done. It was upon these benches that discipline and obedience were inculcated. Before too long a time log seats gave way to seats of plank with back rests. Not all of the pupils in the room had desks. Sometimes the smallest pupil had to do without. The pupils seldom had more than one book to keep track of anyway. Desk seats came into use more and more after 1865. They were usually built for two pupils, boys sitting with boys and girls with girls.

## Status of Early Teachers and of Teaching

### Economic and Social Support

The status of early teachers and of teaching depended upon the interest of patrons as expressed by school laws, general political climate, and funds made available. This early dependence on patrons was not unique. To move away from the United States for a moment, it is known that public elementary education in some countries had its roots in charitable institutions set up as relief measures by the rich. Here teachers were apt to be either women, cripples, or men unable to do hard physical work. Opinions about teachers under such circumstances were bound to reflect seriously upon their status. However, in Western Europe, it was traditionally the priest and later the Protestant minister who explored new ideas, helped to perpetuate formal learning, and instructed the young.

The intervention of the state in education in some European countries and the gradual building up of national systems of education required large numbers of teachers for mass instruction in the three R's. In Prussia, for example, the invalids of the Army became teachers. In Russia, the elementary teacher became synonymous with drunkard or ignoramus.[6]

In the United States, some of the early schools were operated on a pay-you-must basis. In many places there were no public funds, and parents had to pay for each pupil who attended school. This meant that there were children who would not attend or could attend only part of the short term. It was common for some children in one family to go to school while others remained with the mother at home. No compulsory school laws then—even to be disregarded.

If teachers rounded up as many as twenty pupils, they might amass twenty, thirty-five, or fifty dollars in the course of a three-month term, provided everybody paid up. They received some of their pay in food as they boarded with school patrons. More than nine-tenths of annual teachers' salaries came in commodities or in labor performed.[7]

Unmarried rural teachers "boarded around" with patrons, eating whatever mixtures were placed before them on the table. They enjoyed sleeping accommodations that would seem most unconventional today but which were commonplace then. They might spend nights in a one-room cabin, with the whole family, old and young, male and female. Sometimes they might spend the night in the loft of the more affluent patrons, either upon the floor or in a great boxlike bed of hay or dry leaves, wedged in among several active boys. Rural teachers could see the moonlight creep through the chinks and hear a screech owl quaver on the ridgepole

[6] Robert K. Hall, *et al.* (eds.), *The Yearbook of Education 1953* (Yonkers, N.Y.: World Book Company, 1954), p. 6.

[7] In the year 1887, a Mr. Hill brought an action against Balkcom upon a contract. Hill had agreed to teach Balkcom's children, together with other children, for nine months for $45. The lower court had held that, inasmuch as he had showed that he had not taught but eight and a half months, he could not recover on his contract. To this ruling, Hill had taken exception. The Supreme Court upheld the court below since the action was upon a contract itself. Hill had not performed his part of the contract. He, of course, could not recover. **79 Ga. 444.**

above them. On some winter nights, snow might blow in under the ill-fitting roof to melt on the face.[8]

There are records saying that it was not uncommon for teachers in Indiana, in the first decades of the 1800's, to "breathe alcohol" onto a pupil's face when bending over to help him with a lesson. Records indicate that teachers would sometimes face their pupils unsteady on their feet.

## Attempts to Prepare Teachers for Teaching

The status of early teachers was influenced by forces more substantial and long-lasting than unpleasant breath. Status depended upon opportunities for preparation for teaching careers. One of the early objectives of educational leaders was to engender a degree of professional enthusiasm in teachers, to provide them with a better knowledge of the content areas of instruction in which they were teaching, and to provide for possible improvement in methods and modes of discipline. In 1905, Mr. J. L. Hughes brought out a book entitled *Mistakes in Teaching*. This volume was allegedly the work of one who observed the work of teachers and "recorded the errors," as he saw them—errors in methods, management, discipline, and moral training. His avowed purpose was to inform other teachers, who could then profit from his advice and guidance if they so chose.

There were also legal devices to secure better-prepared teachers. States provided for normal schools—but circumstances operated against their early success. The leaders of education in America after the Civil War looked for immediate ways to help improve the staffing of the schools. The reasoning was this: if teachers could not be prepared in advance, something could be done to improve them while on the job. The answer was the teachers' institutes. These agencies were almost universally used during the period between the Civil War and the turn of the nineteenth century. Legislation providing for meetings of teachers to improve their work and prescribing the duties of school officers with reference to the institutes can be found in almost all of the states.

[8] Kennedy, *Schoolmaster of Yesterday*, p. 21.

## Classroom Discipline

The attitude and actions of pupils reflected, in part, the position that teachers "enjoyed" in eighteenth and nineteenth century America. The pupils in Indiana pioneer days carried goose-quill pens. These the teachers mended or recut for the pupils, often while they were reciting lessons. It seemed to be popular to carry the pen over the ear in the schoolroom for the "scholarly air" it gave. Sometimes, though, these same pupils would feel the agonizing whack of the long, flat ferule upon their tender palms.[9] To make the blow all the more painful, teachers might use their free hand to bend the pupil's fingers backward, arching the palm. Some pupils would be whipped with the cat-o'-nine-tails, a bunch of leather thongs on a handle made of wood. It was possible on occasion to see the backs of boys' shirts stained with blood from the stripes.

One thing did set apart the country school of the Midwestern and Southern areas of the early nineteenth century: its rules of courtesy. Whether boy or girl, each pupil was to pause in the door to make a bow in the general direction of the teacher upon entering the school. There were other amenities too. In the yard surrounding the schoolhouse the young teacher often joined the boys' games. After school hours the teacher might go on "coon" and 'possum hunts with pupils, such fun usually centering at the schoolhouse.

Early teachers had their own kinds of trial and tribulation. The health conditions prevalent in earlier days would astound us now. It is reported that itch and lice were still afflicting country schools immediately after the Civil War. There were outbreaks of itch every winter when the pupils came together, for some families were generally afflicted and distributed it among others as soon as school opened.

Regard for schoolhouses, too, reflected the general status of teachers and of teaching. In many communities, it was reported that schools were seldom locked—because rarely was there anything left inside that was worth stealing. There was gradual improvement. After 1865, some schoolhouses became centers of com-

[9] Kennedy, *Schoolmaster of Yesterday*, p. 17.

munity pride. Regulations in some areas indicated that school-houses had to be finished "in a manner calculated to render comfortable the teacher and pupils." Equipment began to be worth safeguarding.

## Qualifications of Early Teachers

As time wore on, the citizenry became increasingly dedicated to the ideal of the "free public school." State statutes and local regulations created the organization. A necessary step was a supply of teachers to instruct the children.

### Fundamental Skills

Home was the first school, with parents the first teachers. So, schools began actually as an extension of the home. Much that a child needed to know about certain skills was adequately taught in the home. Such skills as reading and the writing of numbers could not be so well taught by the parents. Hence, the first teachers were persons in the community who could teach those skills. There were few people trained in reading in early days, other than members of the clergy. It was natural, then, that in many cases the local minister became the schoolteacher in the neighborhood. With no state requirements, the qualification for teaching was ability to read, write, spell, and "do sums."

Material on the masters and dames who constituted the teaching personnel of earlier days is scarce and fragmentary, allowing us to construct only a partial, and therefore inaccurate, picture of the early teaching corps. Many excellent volumes have treated the subject of the early interest in public education and the general lack of preparation of early teachers. In general, the younger the children "to be taught" and the more rural the community, the lower were legal obstacles for becoming a teacher. There were no examiners, no examinations to be taken. If one believed he could teach the young, or was not strong enough to work the soil, he just "got hold of a place," if he could.

The academic qualifications of teachers during the Colonial period ranged from bare ability to read and write the language to the scholarly attainments of a graduate from college. Again, it must be emphasized that no reliable generalizations can be made about the competence of him who was called a teacher in the thirteen colonies. It is known that wide differences existed in academic preparation and cultural backgrounds. To what extent early teachers came from the agricultural and trade classes is not known.

Considerable evidence does point to the fact that there were then some poorly educated teachers in every community. Commenting upon the ignorance of teachers, one writer has said: "It is a general plague and complaint of the whole land that for one discreet and able teacher, you shall find twenty ignorant and careless." [10] Hall, in the first work on pedagogy written in the United States, entitled *Lectures on School Keeping*, commented in much the same vein on the teacher. He stated that school keeping was a casual, makeshift, part-time job, the last resort of the business and professional incompetent. He said that teaching was not a well-defined trade with standards of preparation and fitness, let alone a profession.

### Method of Selecting Teachers

Until relatively recently the appointment of teachers, in most communities, was a simple affair. It consisted of locating interested parties either through hearsay or by advertisement in some journal. The persons sought were to be both "qualified and willing" to teach and be content with the salary that had been voted for the purpose. The supply of well-qualified teachers was never so large as to necessitate any involved machinery for eliminating the weak applicants. It is not surprising that the requirements for teachers in many localities were practically nonexistent. One need consider only the loosely knit machinery of existing government and the scarcity of individuals who wanted to teach school to understand why legal minima were unnecessary.

One observer stated that all the qualifications needed in a community in Massachusetts as late as 1800 were "the knack to continue in the schoolroom the discipline of the kitchen, and being

[10] Charles Beard and William Carr, "Colonial School Days," *National Education Journal*, XXIV (February, 1935), p. 43, as quoted by Willard S. Elsbree, *The American Teacher* (New York: American Book Company, 1939), p. 33.

a good mender of quill pens." Twenty years later a teacher in Kentucky stated that "of course not one of us had had a day of professional training" for teaching. The teacher and his grandfather had been invited into the teaching ranks by school patrons who regarded both of them as "eminently qualified." A person went into teaching usually of his own accord and had little trouble finding places to work. There was not even the semblance of examinations to test ability or aptitude.

As the nation grew and settlements were established beyond the chain of the Appalachians, the status of teachers changed very little at first. Teachers of the early 1800's in the pioneer Midwest were a part of a motley group. It seems likely that none had earned a diploma of any sort. Perhaps a majority of the teachers in rural areas had done no previous work to prepare them for the jobs they occupied. Those who taught still included all types. As one writer put it, they were "drifting westward, vaguely looking for something to turn up in a business way." Meanwhile, those who taught temporarily were following paths of least resistance. There were those who did not hesitate to make known their feeling that teaching school was the special province of those who were too lazy to do real work.

There being almost no state educational machinery, it was the local school community that could accept or reject persons who applied for teaching positions. It had almost unlimited power in operating the school. In the beginnings of publicly supported education, all of the electorate—the men, in other words—met at the schoolhouse, where they decided many important matters. One of the most important, usually, was the selection of the teacher. There was one qualification usually thought of as important. "Scholarship attainments" were to be considered, but the chief qualification was ability to keep order in the schoolroom.

Teachers had few planning problems, so far as lessons were concerned. When finished in one spot, they could go on to another community and conduct a school term there. They could use the same materials, the same methods. Demands upon teachers were light.

Persons thus "hired" needed no license to practice their trade. They needed little understanding of their place in the larger setting of education. They needed no understanding of contracts. They were usually referred to as the "Master" or the "Schoolmaster," and the esteem in which they were held by the community varied with each individual and each group.

As the nineteenth century progressed, there was agitation in favor of graded schools. Supporters of the movement pointed out from the very first that the plan had one strong advantage. The "graded room" arrangement would make it possible to employ "females" for the younger and less advanced children. In Massachusetts, a prominent citizen recommended that all primary schools be taught by women. He stated that the "moral advantage" was the most important reason. However, he was quick to add that the "cheapness of such a policy" would entitle it to public acceptance. In Boston, the superintendent stated in 1848 that the ideal school was to be a large one with six hundred pupils being taught in separate rooms by teachers with low salaries, the salary of a woman teacher being then about one-sixth that of a master. One writer stated it this way:

> With women teachers possessing such manifest moral and professional superiority over men and being employable at a fraction of the cost of men, it is little wonder that they should be preferred in the new graded systems which were developing rapidly between 1830 and 1870.[11]

To look to the brighter side for a bit, many individual communities insisted on higher academic qualifications for their teachers. This tendency developed despite absence of certification laws. For example, in Dorchester, Massachusetts, the teacher was almost always a college graduate. As early as 1648 Henry Butler, the teacher there, was a graduate of Cambridge University, England, holding the Master's degree. Of forty-five colonial masters of the Dorchester school more than forty were graduates of Harvard College. In Pennsylvania, likewise, the Quakers boasted of high qualifications for teachers. They laid great stress on the competence of the candidate to teach the subjects included in the school program.

### Beginnings of Teacher Certification

It was in the Midwest where teacher certification was made a matter of statute. The state of Indiana passed a law in 1837 which

---

[11] Edward H. Reisner, *The Evolution of the Common School* (New York: The Macmillan Company, 1930), p. 388.

authorized the circuit court of the state to appoint examiners to look into the qualifications of teachers and to certify as to their fitness. When enforced, this law might have eliminated many incumbents had it not been for one fact: The teachers to be examined often knew more than the persons doing the examining. Not until 1850 were licenses to teach school issued in Indiana. Such permits certified that holders could teach arithmetic "to the single rule-of-three," which meant that teachers could solve such problems as "2 is to 4 as 7 is to what?"

From this point, it was not far to the appointment or election of county examiners. Such officials usually devoted full time to their job. They examined candidates and were supposed to pay visits to schools. It was their duty to give advice as to school management, to promote institutes, and to make periodic reports to state school officials.

## Normal Schools

After 1865, as pressure mounted to place education on a more nearly professional plane, the normal school was adopted by the states to a considerable degree. It came to be *the* teacher-preparing institution of the latter part of the century. The United States Commissioner of Education in 1871 reported that there were 51 normal schools supported by 23 states. Sixteen cities had also inaugurated the normal school for the improvement of the local supply of teachers.[12]

An entry in a journal of one of the officials of an early normal school reads:

> This day learned authentically that one of the pupils of the normal course is under matrimonial engagement. The school will not suffer a great loss. Her promise in the profession of teaching is not very encouraging.[13]

Besides the normal schools supported by public funds, there were in 1871 more than 40 private schools for the preparation of teachers.

[12] To understand better the conditions that existed in the early normal schools, read A. O. Norton's *The First Normal School in America;* the Journals of Cyrus Pierce and Mary Swift (Cambridge, Mass.: Harvard University Press, 1926).

[13] Reisner, *The Evolution of the Common School*, p. 398.

By 1890 there were 135 normal schools in 39 states supported either wholly or partially out of tax funds. The number of private normal schools remained at 40.

The American normal school was really little more than an American academy adapted to the objective of preparing teachers for the common schools. The normal schools had large numbers of students who had no other schools to attend. Even where students were prospective teachers and in need of professional preparation, their lack of academic equipment made it necessary for the normal school staff to include instruction in common learnings. This was especially true for those students who came from rural schools.

One qualification of mid-nineteenth century teachers should not be overlooked. In some respects teachers were closer to the young people than was the minister. Teachers who were sympathetic were often drawn into giving advice and aid in personal affairs. More than the minister, teachers were the promoters of many homes, the "repositories of many secrets."

Quite naturally, the persons who became competent teachers under the limiting conditions were influenced by the characteristics of the period and the place in which they lived. The really great teachers have been of many different and often contradictory types. However, despite variations, great teachers have shared a number of basic ideas and ideals. Especially have they recognized the need for having better-prepared teachers. The improvement in the competencies of teachers was recognized early and continues today. The policies and practices inaugurated by pioneers in selecting, compensating, and supervising teachers established patterns for many of the personnel policies now in vogue.

## Curriculum Requirements Before 1900

In the "pioneer days" there seem to have been very few legal requirements regarding the curriculum to be taught. In some areas of the school program, the whole school recited en masse. Sometimes each pupil worked individually with the teacher. Each teacher must have literally created his own curriculum, which varied from term to term and from place to place as the circumstances dictated.

Webster's speller was the "basic text" and about the earliest of all textbooks to appear in the pioneer West. Sometimes it was the only one that could be found in an entire neighborhood. The subject of spelling was considered of prime importance in the 1820's and '30's in the West. In pioneer opinion, poor spelling was one of the surest marks of ignorance. It had been so common among those who had had no opportunity for education that their shame placed added emphasis upon its teaching. The emphasis persisted until new ideas invaded notions about teaching beginning about 1900.[14]

For advanced reading, the New Testament was used until something more nearly practical could be afforded. It is reported that arithmetic was hardest of all to teach, for there were few textbooks to be found, few slates, and no blackboards. State machinery for education was barely thought of.

The McGuffey Readers were the most important series of school-books in early history. Some feel that no other text has ever exercised so profound an influence on teaching and learning in any country of the world. It is known that the Readers were very widely distributed, especially so in the rural areas.

The curriculum of the grammar school did not expand rapidly. However, required subjects increased from the three R's until there were seven. The four additional were spelling, grammar, geography, and American history. Physiology at last became number eight. This subject made headway slowly in rural schools. As someone stated, "No one ever saw any bold manifestations of sex at our country schools." At a celebration in 1885 a patron is reported to have exclaimed:

> I tell you that the seeds of vice and wickedness is [*sic*] often sowed at school in the minds of the young by teachers who are paid a large salary to do far different. What do you think of a man who would open a school with prayer and then converse freely about the alimentary canal? Such a man would lead a life of the deepest infamy if he had the least encouragement. Last winter we paid thirty-four dollars per month to a man who opened school with prayer and then made a picture of the digestive organs on the blackboard. And yet we wonder that politics is corrupt.[15]

[14] Again, it is hard to generalize. Yet, Mann, Sheldon, Parker, Peabody, and Harris had all contributed reforms before 1900, and the Herbartians were in full swing by then.

[15] Kennedy, *Schoolmaster of Yesterday*, pp. 224-25.

Even with the heavy demands of physiology in some schools, the school day was often too long. It is reported that by two o'clock in the afternoon on some days, the pupils had recited everything they knew. To save fuel, teachers would send pupils home to walk through wind and snow. One of the accounts of early learning states:

> As a small boy, I remember my father, with books under his arm, striding with yard-long steps on a nippy winter morning toward District School No. 3. This school stood only a few rods from our rural Indiana home. During the day, if the wind blew toward our house, it carried with it the distinct hum of children reciting their lessons in chorus. And we knew it was recess time when their hum changed to shouts of joy.[16]

## Status of the Modern Teacher

When teachers instructed only the elite in religious dogma or in the classics, they were indeed "masters," men who had it within their power to pass on esoteric knowledge. With the development of the common school, designed to impart to all young people certain rudiments of knowledge considered indispensable to the structure of society, the status of teachers changed very rapidly—legally and ethically.

Many have written about the major competencies and traits of modern teachers. They speak about the tremendous contribution that the teaching corps makes to the development of the nation. On the other side of the ledger, teachers can find this kind of comment being made about them:

> . . . the hard-working, dedicated mediocrity who teaches from a more or less standardized syllabus in one of the less progressive secondary modern schools of England or high schools of the United States . . . an adequate but unimpressive member of the undifferentiated horde that walks briskly from subway to office. . . .[17]

Surely, mass education of the young today has shattered the simple archetype of the educated elite, the "complete man" who was able to master the major essentials from an encyclopedia of human knowledge. Today, no such person can exist.

[16] *Ibid.*, p. 45.
[17] Hall, *et al.*, *The Yearbook of Education 1953*, pp. 2-3.

Education today is a process that must be carried on within an institution. Rarely is it carried on in the intimate and personal way between a master and a pupil that once could give teachers high status. Today teachers take on, in major part, the attitudes and manner of the institution in which they work.

Conceptions of the teachers have been influenced by the stereotype of the schoolmaster, surviving perhaps only in files of old magazines and newspapers. The status of teachers today is a very puzzling paradox: they are at once admired leaders and neglected public servants. They may enjoy a prestige approaching that of other professionals and yet be burdened financially and go unnoticed by the parents of the very children entrusted to their care.[18]

One difficulty in evaluating the status and social position of teachers is in deciding upon what the term "teacher" means. One is prone to lump together the scholar and the instructor, the research worker and "the professor," the man of theory and the coach in motor skills, and refer to all as teachers. When one notes how difficult it is to say precisely what is meant by a "teacher," one begins to be plagued with doubt. As one group of writers asked, "Is there point in attempting to group together into a single profession a philosopher and an officer instructing a novice in swordsmanship, or a lecturer explaining how best to prepare salads for school lunches and a physicist working with a cyclotron?"

There is some agreement that the responsibilities laid upon teachers cannot be properly discharged unless the teaching profession as a whole is everywhere regarded with more respect—that is, such respect would be accorded teachers if standards were raised.[19] It is doubtful that the establishment of normal schools and of colleges for the preparation of elementary teachers and the issuing of state teachers' certificates made much difference in raising the status of

[18] *Ibid.*, p. 2. Perhaps some evidence of "neglect" as far as teachers are concerned is revealed by the resolutions adopted by the delegates to the NEA Convention in Chicago, July, 1955. Two top items were: increased salaries and "some free time" for teachers during the school day. It was felt that industry was far ahead of the teaching profession on both these counts.

[19] In some recent studies, it was reported that in those areas where high standards for teaching plus high salaries have been maintained, there were no teacher shortages. However, in those areas where standards were lowered, and salaries were low, acute shortages of teachers existed. See Chamberlain and Kindred, *The Teacher and School Organization,* chap. 1, "Scope of Education," and chap. 5, "Preparation for Teaching."

teachers. These efforts were generally limited to elementary teachers. Because of different backgrounds of preparation for personnel, and different opportunities for advancement, the social status of elementary teachers and of secondary teachers varies greatly.

## Problems in Raising Teachers' Status

Within the profession itself there continue to be practices that militate against securing a high status for teachers. It need not be labored, for example, that the acceptance by teachers of arbitrary personal restrictions is one factor in lowering their own professional status. Often, restrictions are enforced by imperceptive administrative personnel. It should be noted that perhaps members of no other profession could be forbidden to smoke in lounges. Yet, the "undignified spectacle of teachers hurrying out of school to smoke" is not unknown. It is one thing for teachers to accept willingly restrictions which are based upon judgments arrived at through deliberation. It is altogether in error for them and others to put up with petty tyranny.

It is a truism that power always earns respect. Those who wield it in any form will be accorded higher status than those who do not. It is for this reason, among others, that university teachers everywhere enjoy relatively high respect and prestige. Rightly or wrongly, they are accorded deference not extended to their junior colleagues.

Of course, it is difficult to ascertain specifically the position of the "man of ideas" in the social class structure. The research that has accumulated is helpful in revealing the general status of various occupations. Here, all signs seem to point to the esteem in which the professional man is held in America.[20] Russell Lynes has suggested, more or less seriously, that the familiar class system, based on family lineage or wealth, is gradually being replaced by a status order predicated on intellectual ability. Some observers interpret signs of stepped-up "anti-intellectualism" in the ideological and political realms as one indication of the increasing importance of the "man of ideas" rather than the other way around.

Be that as it may, an essential element in determining the status of teachers today is the prevalent public attitude toward the value

[20] American Association of University Professors, *Bulletin*, Winter, 1954-55, p. 523.

and credibility of the material taught in the schools. One need look only at the wave of criticism of the public schools, or sample some of the articles critical of teachers and other school personnel.

One of the certain tests of an educational system, despite pros and cons, is its contribution to the culture in which it exists. Today, for example, the culture, termed technological and dynamic, could not possibly survive without an adequate system of education. To the extent that the cogency of this concept is grasped by adult, thinking members of society, both intellectually and emotionally, to that extent do teachers employed take on the prestige of their profession, and thereby acquire high status.

## The Problem of Teacher "Loyalty"

To a certain degree, the status of teachers must be affected by their choice of loyalties. Teachers have their own loyalty to the profession, to a political party, to a religious sect, to ethnic minorities, and to economic classes. They have strong loyalties to ideas and social ideals, to concepts of universal education, and to moral codes and ethics.

By virtue of becoming teachers, individuals do not cease to be citizens. In theory at least, teachers retain their right to run for political offices, to campaign for candidates of their choice, to make contributions to organizations they feel are worth their support, and to express their views on politics. As we know too well, teachers may have their political freedoms and academic freedoms restricted very substantially.

The Feinburg Law was passed in New York to rid the schools of subversive teachers.[21] Reports on each school employee were required by the provisions of the law. Its constitutionality was attacked on the basis that the law violated the right of free speech of teachers.

[21] Adler v. Board of Education of City of New York, 342 U.S. 485, 72 S. Ct. 380, 96 L. Ed. 517, 27 A.L.R. 2d 487 (1951). This notation is interpreted as follows: The Adler case can be found in the official reports of the United States Supreme Court Reports in Volume 342 on page 485. In the National Reporter series, the same case is reported in Volume 72 on page 380. The Lawyers' Edition of the Supreme Court Reports is an unofficial edition with much editorial comment. The same case is found there in Volume 96 on page 517. The case is also found in the American Law Reports, second series, in Volume 27, beginning on page 487. This series annotates some opinions of appellate courts in all jurisdictions.

According to the decision on the law by the United States Supreme Court, it was established that school authorities legally may inquire into the past conduct and past loyalty of school employees. Justice Douglas attacked the majority opinion. He found it impossible to accept the doctrine that one who enters the public service can be forced to sacrifice his civil rights. According to him, the law is destructive of one of the most cherished and indispensable privileges held by teachers, that of academic freedom.

The status of teachers is affected adversely when enactments of the legislature make it "dangerous" for them to think or say anything except what a "transient majority happens to approve at the moment." Teachers lose when the legislature injects itself into the internal affairs of the administration of schools. It would be much better for teachers and community if control of subversives were thought of as a problem for planned action on the local level. Then jobs of others can be saved and their prestige maintained.

When teachers accept positions, they are removed, at least legally speaking, from the local community. Professional employees of the board of education are employees of the state. Under few circumstances can they be considered to be in the employ of the local school district. In some situations, this has value for teachers. On the other hand, the immunity from liability (freedom from suit in court) enjoyed by the school district, by virtue of its being a part of the state government, does not extend to teachers. They are liable for their negligent acts just as if they were not engaged in school work.

### Economic and Social Ingredients in Teachers' Status

The status of teachers also depends upon a host of lesser concerns. For example, leaves with pay from the job are by no means universal. They are granted on the basis of state statute and local regulation. If the legislature so chooses, it can change or discontinue retirement allowances for teachers. Only in those cases where such allowances are part of teachers' contracts are they protected. Such limitations do not enhance the value of teaching in the eyes of the public.

Fortunately, marriage is no longer a legal ground for dismissal in many localities. The status of teachers is raised to the extent that the specific grounds named in the statutes of the state serve as the sole grounds for the discharge of teachers.

Teachers fare not so well as businessmen when it comes to allowances that are deductible for federal income tax purposes. If their attendance at school is necessary to continue in present positions, teachers can be allowed a tax deduction. Also, if schooling is for the purpose of maintaining qualifications for present positions, they can deduct that expense. However, if the purpose of attendance is to qualify for a better position, permanent tenure, or other improvement in status, the answer from the Internal Revenue Service authorities is still "no." [22]

Another index of the status of teachers in the community is the extent of their social life. A rich and varied social life enables teachers to do their work well. However, salaries that are low in comparison to those of manual laborers make it difficult to maintain social status. Competent persons to staff schools who are a credit to the profession at "going rates" are difficult to find.

The National Education Association indicated that many teachers have little or no income other than their school salaries. Generally speaking, teachers with higher salary incomes received larger proportions of their over all income from outside the schools than teachers with lower incomes. Earnings in other occupations and contributions from relatives comprised most of the nonschool income of the rural teacher. Investments were relatively important sources of the supplementary income received by city teachers, especially at higher income levels. It seemed likely, from the report, that outside earnings were more prevalent during the period of World War II, but there are no figures to indicate this.[23]

There are data to indicate that salaries of teachers generally compare unfavorably with average incomes in most of the other professions and in some nonprofessional salaried occupations. In some larger cities the salary of female teachers compares favorably with the income of business and professional women outside of

[22] Interpretations of 1958 modifications of tax laws for teachers do not change restrictions markedly.

[23] NEA, Research Division, "Professional Salaries for America's Teachers," *Education Digest*, Vol. XX (September, 1954), pp. 42-44.

See Donald H. Ross, "Employment Practices and Working Conditions in the Elementary and Secondary Schools," chap. IV of *Teacher Personnel*, in *Review of Educational Research*, Vol. XXV (June, 1955), pp. 231-32.

teaching. In the period of inflation beginning in 1940, teachers lagged far behind other groups in sharing in the increased national income of the period. It would seem clear that salaries of teachers must be made to compare more favorably with those of other occupations requiring comparable ability and academic preparation if teachers are to be respected. This adjustment is also needed if an adequate supply of persons is to be attracted to the teaching field, persons who will serve to raise and not lower the status of teachers in the eyes of their contemporaries.

Studies have attempted to show variations in the cost of living of teachers and in the purchasing power of their salaries from one year to the next. Results generally show that teachers often have little or nothing left for savings, and that the total current expenditures of teachers actually exceed current income. The social life of teachers under these circumstances must necessarily be circumscribed.

Other studies indicate that even after thirty or forty years of teaching, the assets accumulated by teachers are, on the average, insufficient to provide an adequate retirement program. Teachers have generally had to spend their current incomes which leaves little cash for retirement years.

There is a wide acceptance of the idea that teachers should be better financed. The wave of popular interest in education that arose in response to reports on the emergency in education created by war and postwar shortages of funds and of personnel would seem to suggest that there is a "reservoir of good will" and approval for education and teaching.

There has been no current comprehensive study of the prestige value of teaching. However, several clues to attitudes toward the teacher are to be found in the nation-wide opinion polls. One such poll conducted several years ago by *Fortune* magazine surveyed women aged twenty to thirty-five. Each was asked: "If you had your choice, what kind of work would you do?" Those who preferred teaching number 6.8 per cent. Two other polls contacted male teachers. Only 1 per cent of those contacted stated that they seldom enjoyed teaching. There were 7.2 per cent who said that their work was dull and boring. Perhaps some inference can be drawn from such data concerning the community attitudes on teachers and their services.

## Qualifications of Today's Teachers

Everyone seriously interested in teachers and the teaching profession must be concerned about the qualifications of the persons admitted into the ranks of the profession. The day has long since passed when the task of the teacher could be said to be merely that of supplementing in a minor fashion the education that is provided by the home. At an earlier period in our history, when life was much less complex than now, the home could provide for most future adult needs. Today, however, society is so interdependent and family life has been beset with so many outside attractions that the school has had to assume increasing loads of responsibility. As a result, the nature of the school program and the quality of school personnel have undergone startling changes as compared with earlier days.

### State Certification

It is teachers primarily, confronted with these changes, who must measure up to increased demands and pressures, academic and personal. Fortunately, practices prevalent today bring these demands into sharp focus. Almost every state has established qualifications for those wishing to be teachers. The services of teachers have been placed under contract. More and more, examinations conducted for applicants for certificates to teach actually test candidates' qualifications for school positions. There are "objective" standards, the results of which can be interpreted with some accuracy by independent individuals.

In all of the forty-nine states the statutes generally require licenses of teachers. Licenses to teach are *prima facie* evidence of a teacher's qualifications. Professional employees must hold proper licenses or certificates to be eligible to receive salary from state tax funds.

Many state departments have become so alarmed by the shortage of qualified teachers that they have been stampeded into approving and adopting short-term programs of preparation. Shortage problems have been met by programs of substandard preparation, flooding the market with teachers who possess something less than minimum preparation. Of course, many are conscientious persons. However, the danger is that many may thus come into the teaching ranks who could not do so were qualifications kept high.


## Emergency Licenses

The granting of "emergency" certificates during periods of economic crisis can be explained on so-called "practical" grounds. From the standpoint of maintaining professional status, such a practice is open to serious question. In times of stress, there are shortages of dentists and engineers too. There has been little serious thought regarding the suggestion that "emergency" licenses be granted to people who did not meet the professional standards for dentists and engineers.

Today, less emphasis is placed upon teachers' command of specialized disciplines and more on personality and command of teaching methods, at least at the elementary school level of instruction. Boards have the responsibility of employing persons who can teach children. Teachers do not carry out this board function but carry out their own function for which they are licensed to practice as teachers. They are licensed by the state and not the locality.

A fundamental feature of the work of teaching is the attitude of teachers. Persons who spend much time in discoursing upon the "difficulties" of their work and lamenting the "sad lot of teachers" are hardly in a frame of mind to ferret out the emotional problems of others. They, in fact, may add to the store of problems.

A last thought on the topic of qualifications is this: In some localities it is not enough that teachers possess the academic qualifications and that they be "good." It is further required of them that they be "considered good"—on the assumption that even suspicion and rumor of violation of ethical standards would destroy their moral influence over the pupils and render them unfit to be their teacher.

## A "Profession" Defined

The teacher during the year and during the summertime remarks occasionally that "I get awfully tired of hearing that I must be professional." He is understandably confused. He knows, of course, that professional status, in the abstract, is both necessary and desirable.[24]

One reason for the confusion that abounds is the meaning of the term "profession." Teachers are accustomed to hearing that lawyers are "professional men." But the morning news commentator speaks about the "professional tennis player." At the Kiwanis Club luncheon, the speaker states that "a professional man is one who conducts his own business and works for fees rather than being employed on a salaried basis."

We have been committed to getting along with a teaching "profession," almost as loosely defined. In addition, the ranks of this profession have been such that great numbers have been able, not only to move into the profession, but also to move out with great ease. There have been some doubts expressed as to the propriety of calling "teaching" a profession at all.

It is true that teaching, like law, medicine, and the ministry, is usually referred to as a profession, to help set it apart from business and the "ordinary run of callings." But the professional activities, which should carry special prestige, privilege, and ethical responsibilities, have not always been so easily discernible.

### Bases for Considering Teaching a Profession

From the days of Ichabod Crane, one of the itinerant teachers who "boarded around," on through the period of the Westward movement with the Hoosier Schoolmaster and up to present-day career teachers, there have evolved certain practices, customs, and laws which continue to make for less and less confusion regarding

[24] See Myron Lieberman, *Education As A Profession* (Englewood Cliffs, N.J.: Prentice-Hall, Inc., 1956). In the preface, the author states that "the experience of the established professions clearly indicates that occupational groups do not achieve professional status until the members of the groups concerned participate en masse in the movement to achieve professional status."

the status of teaching as one of the professions. There are some distinguishing elements in teaching, some historical bases, and some present conditions that justify considering teaching as one of the professions. The conception of teaching as a profession is useful to us today in examining specific questions regarding individual conduct and group practices.

One of the indices of the existence and strength of a well-established profession is the control of admissions and of the preparation courses by the profession itself. Thinking people recognize that the welfare of a profession, and the quality of its services to the public, depend largely upon the level of professional standards that are required. Adequate standards, developed and applied to all within the profession, are a *sine qua non*. Unfortunately, teaching lags behind in this important matter.

The history of the stable professions in the United States indicates that both the character of service provided and the prestige and security of those engaged in any profession rest largely upon the extent to which the professional organization or group determines and controls the standards of preparation and admission. There have been studies to show that certification requirements are an important factor in the building of a profession. Within the past decade, there were some half-dozen states where the candidates for county superintendent of schools did not have to have any schooling beyond high school, nor any teaching or administrative experience to be part of the "professional" group.

There seems to be general agreement that those who seek to be teachers should possess "adequate" scholarship. Teachers need special knowledge and skills based upon general education and professional preparation. They first need a liberal education befitting any competent citizen. They should be students of world cultures and students of the sciences.

The one main device that professions have used with success to help establish preparation for their respective fields on a professional level is the instrument of accreditation. To develop standards that are valid, to apply these impartially, and to limit official approval for entrance to those institutions which meet these professional standards—all these are important tasks and not easily achieved. Accreditation is closely related to influence of a group upon the formation of policies affecting the group. The teaching corps is professionalized to the extent to which teachers help establish important policies affecting their work. In some areas teachers take an active interest in shaping policies on teacher selection and preparation, the organization and development of the curriculum, the quality and direction of supervision, and academic freedom. In general, no large professional teaching group exists in the sense that the influences of the group cause members to perceive the education-task in light of these advances in professional thinking.

To the degree that a profession helps protect the welfare of its members, it has achieved maturity. If teaching were clearly a profession in every sense, teachers would maintain, through their own organizations, active committees to handle the matters of certification, group insurance, leaves, retirement, loads, rating, and tenure. To have high professional status, the existence of well-organized professional associations is essential. They must be able and willing to defend the economic interests of their members as well as to support scholarly activities.[25]

For teaching to become a full-fledged profession, teachers must be accorded a greater level of responsibility. They must have freedom to go in and out of the school when not teaching; they must have freedom to join professional unions or political parties. They ought to be granted periods of paid leave, easy interchange between schools and between schools of foreign countries. Teachers should be a part of a democratic or nonauthoritarian team of principal, supervisor, and superintendent. All of these are indices of professional status. Teachers must have complete security of tenure, public advertising of vacancies, appointment to position by a committee, freedom to choose the school in which they work, freedom from having to submit to any kind of religious or political test.

Opinions differ as to whether the teaching profession should have a single, universally accepted code of ethics. The medical and legal associations are noted for their strict codes. Both groups are characterized by the formulation of and adherence to their codes, setting forth guiding principles for conduct as they apply to the performance of their professional work. Some regard all such codes with cynicism. In contrast, there are those who believe that codes have

[25] The organization of teachers must be strong enough to exert pressure against such practices as dismissing a state supervisor because that supervisor had a private luncheon meeting with a member of another race.

contributed materially to the high regard in which the public holds these groups. They believe that codes are worth while in maintaining standards.

There seems to be little doubt that teachers hold teaching to be a profession. They hold that one of the most important characteristics of a profession is the duty of public service. Though compensation is attached to the work as a livelihood, duty is a primary and inseparable part of the work. Existing codes serve as a guide to conduct and merit serious attention by all teachers. They should adhere as strictly to codes as possible. Codes stem from insight into teaching problems and cannot be legislated as such.

### Characteristics of a Professional Teacher

Teachers may well ask, "What makes me a professional person?" Within very rough limits, the following general statements hold. "Professional" teachers do not require close or constant supervision. They do not regard themselves as employees, working for a boss. They do not perform their work "by the hour," basing salary on hourly rates. They take full responsibility for the results of their efforts and actions.

Also, professional teachers continually seek out ways in which to improve themselves. They contribute to the skills and insights of their profession. They respect the confidences of others by never consciously violating them. They demonstrate loyalty to colleagues by refraining from gossiping with or about them. They avoid repeating rumors and hearsay. They refrain from passing information received through the "grapevine."

Professional teachers adjust their grievances through proper channels. They refrain from complaining habitually and from grumbling to others. They meet their obligations, legal and moral. They are sensitive to the problems of fellow workers. They never attempt to advance themselves at the cost of others. Professional teachers are proud of their profession and are desirous of rendering the highest quality of service they can perform.

The challenge to teachers to be professional persons is one of great magnitude. There is no mechanical formula for determining whether a group like the teaching corps can be regarded as a profession. What is significant is that the general public has come to identify certain characteristic features, which can serve as criteria. Some features that help identify professions are:

1. The work (of the teacher) calls for specialized preparation over a considerable period of time and must be based on a good background of general education and culture.
2. The members of the group strive through the use of selective admission procedures to maintain a high level of performance of duties.
3. The work consists of the practice of an art, based upon the application of scientific principles.
4. The members of the group formulate and abide by a code of ethics.
5. There are varied specialized services within the occupation.
6. The members of the group intend to make the occupation their life work.
7. The members of the occupational group involved are characterized, in spite of their specialized differences, by a high degree of unity of purpose, spirit, ideals, and organization.
8. The members of the group carry on continuing inservice study.[26]

The profession of teaching, as the legal profession, must ignore commercial standards of success. If it is thus set apart as a profession, it must have traditions and precepts of its own which are to be mastered and lived up to. This living spirit is embodied in the ethics of the profession.

There is evidence that teachers who are professional workers do put emphasis upon nonmonetary values. They exhibit an eagerness to acquire educational degrees which may heighten competence. They have the desire to continue to read. They are interested in contributing to their professional literature.

### The Need Further to Professionalize Teaching

The standards just described that relate to making teaching a profession are far from being realized. Measured by these standards, and by those of other professions that are well recognized, teaching falls short.

How to select, prepare, and reward an adequate supply of competent teachers remains one of the puzzling issues at the middle of the twentieth century. To the extent that care is not exercised by

[26] M. H. Willing, *et al.*, *Schools and Our Democratic Society* (New York: Harper and Brothers, Publishers, 1951), p. 347.

members in admitting candidates for entrance into teaching, teaching remains less than a profession. Teaching has seldom come out well on this criterion. Without the support of local, state, and regional groups, the "up and down" and the "in and out" features of supply and demand will remain.

Besides being stabilized as a profession, teaching must be made a full-time job. It, alone among the professions, denies to its members the right and the responsibility of practicing every month of the year. Only a small part of the teaching corps holds its positions on a year-round basis. The actual number of months that teachers are "teachers" varies from state to state and from district to district. The period ranges from seven to twelve months. The average is approximately nine months, or 175 days. This means that for three months of every year teachers must sever their connections with the profession because of contractual demands. The existence of teachers depends upon their ability to transfer membership from the group representing teachers to another representing nonprofessional interests. One hundred per cent loyalty to professional standards and ethical precepts can hardly be expected from a profession that offers only partial security, and that offers status for three-fourths of the year.

The extent to which members of an occupational group stay in that line of work over a period of time has much to do with the professional status and recognition accorded that occupation. If many teachers leave the profession, it is evident that conditions are unsatisfactory and the status low. Oversupply of teachers is a concept that is talked about in periods of economic depression. The notion militates against the selective-admission criterion of a professional group. A return to prosperity causes shortages because the "haven-in-a-storm" teachers move to what they claim to be "better" jobs. It is unrealistic to expect to build teaching into a genuine profession by relying upon the law of supply and demand. Such a dependence works against a decreased interference by boards of education with the work of the school, with the personal lives of the personnel, with the increased efficiency of services performed, and with the raising of professional standards and sights.

Lastly, the codes of ethics in the field of education are not real codes since they make no provision for legal or moral enforcement. There is no established machinery for enforcement of the National

Education Association code. Perhaps the development of adherence to it depends upon continued education of all teachers. It is important to have teachers adhere because they see its values, not because of fear of sanctions that may injure their reputations.

Probably the single greatest need for strengthening the preparation program for teachers is the development and application of discriminating professional standards for the institutions that prepare teachers. Teachers themselves can do much to advance their professional insights. They can study the meaning of professional conduct, think through issues that require ethical formulation, join informally with others to discuss ethical problems, promote consideration of ethics at local and regional meetings, write about ethical problems in journals, talk with lay groups to help inform them, and take an active interest in committees concerned with ethical problems.

Without the support of many elements in the community, the profession of teaching cannot hope to obtain full-time job status for teachers. Nevertheless, the teaching group is the logical one to initiate action through intelligent and persistent propaganda in every community of the land. The building of standards is a long-range task. Progress already achieved is but the beginning of a long uphill pull. Teaching is far from being a profession in most parts of the land. There is no state and territory where it may be said that teaching has reached adequate professional status. The main tasks lie ahead. The machinery for advancing standards is being extended rapidly through cooperation between local and national teacher groups and accrediting associations.

# School Board-School Personnel Relationships

———————————————— *3*

The "problem situations" given here and at the beginning of each of the subsequent chapters in this book are typical of those that arise among school personnel. What would you do in each instance? Analyze each entanglement for answers to the following questions:

1. What are the crucial issues in the case for a teacher, for the board of education, or for others involved?
2. Which issue do you feel needs prompt attention so that the effectiveness of the school program will not continue to be endangered? What is the reason for your choice?
3. What facts are known about the issue? (Be careful to distinguish between a fact and a conclusion or value judgment based on facts.)
4. What are several alternative courses of action to be taken in order to help resolve the conflict?
5. What is your decision regarding the most desirable attack? (Here concentrate on the over-all strategy or plan of action. The tactics may depend on many variables.) Support your decision with reasons. In giving reasons you will, of course, be calling on your personal judgment.

CASE A

The law of the state of ————————— provides that failure to give a teacher notice of his re-employment or lack of it by April 20 of the current contract year shall constitute re-employment on the same terms as those provided in the contract of the current year. It was admitted

56

by the ————————— Board of Education that the required notice had not been given to the teacher. Another teacher was employed instead. Two teachers therefore reported at the school on opening day.

Board members were also present. "The scene of utter confusion which resulted can readily be imagined! The first teacher arrived early and entered upon the performance of his duties. A member of the Board urged the pupils to pay no attention to the first teacher; told them that the first teacher was not their teacher, but that the second was. Upon refusal of the first teacher to surrender the school to the second teacher, the Board sought an injunction against his acting as teacher of the school. The lower court granted it, but the ————————— Court of Appeals reversed the decision of the lower court and held that the injunction should not have been granted and that the first teacher was entitled to retain his position."

The court stated that the efforts of the Board members to get out of the "mess" were solely the result of their own failure to proceed in accordance with the statute.[1]

CASE B

There are four schools in Centerville, U.S.A. It has become necessary because of reorganization to effect the transfer of certain teachers who have taught in the Central School. The contracts of the teachers do not specify any particular assignments to schools, but simply state that teachers are employed to teach in the county school system. One of the teachers scheduled to be transferred has raised the question of fairness concerning her transfer to another school in the Centerville District. She has had correspondence with the principal of her "old school" and with the County School Superintendent to whom she registered her protests. The Superintendent called her attention to the wording of the contract, but the teacher states, "The Board can't do this thing to me."

CASE C

Packages are occasionally delivered to the wrong person by mistake. If a teacher knowingly takes advantage of this kind of situation and makes use of the items delivered, must he pay their reasonable value? Although no express contract was ever made, will the courts, from the nature of the situation, imply an agreement? Will liability for payment arise if the teacher upon whom the benefits are conferred is not aware of receiving them until after it is too late to return the items? Does he impliedly promise to pay for them only when he has had the opportunity to return them?

(Here is an answer to some of the questions raised in terms of some of the principles involved. If a teacher knowingly receives valuable services or property from another, with knowledge that no gift was intended, the teacher impliedly promises to pay the reasonable value of such bene-

[1] Robert R. Hamilton, *The Bi-Weekly School Law Letter* (Laramie, Wyo., March 15, 1951).

fits. Like most persons, the teacher usually accepts a definite offer of goods or services by written or verbal assent. However, if he receives something under circumstances which make it appear that no gift was intended, he must pay the value of the goods if he keeps them. If, for example, the teacher regularly takes and reads a literary journal sent to him, without any subscription being sent, the teacher's act constitutes acceptance. He is liable for the subscription price of the periodical.)

CASE D

A superintendent has two vacancies in the school system. He offers a teacher one of them for a stated salary. Thinking of the chairmanship of the social studies department, the teacher accepts the offer of the superintendent. No contract results if the superintendent had in mind the opening in the seventh grade. Because they are not in agreement, there is no contract. A mutual mistake as to the position to be filled and duties to be performed renders an agreement void.

CASE E

A contract entered into on the assumption that need for certain services exists is void if the need does not in fact exist. If a teacher contracts to teach the seventh grade at the Military School and, at the time the agreement is made, the Air Force Base loses men and their families by reorganization, no contract results. Fewer classes would be formed. Similarly, in other cases, if an element or factor which both parties assume to exist is lacking, no contract results from the negotiations.

CASE F

A teacher purchased some photographic equipment from Smith, the Coach, and desires to have the agreement set aside because of fraud. The alleged misrepresentation was a statement by Smith that the camera and enlarger were in "A No. 1" condition. The court refused to set aside the agreement because statements as to value are matters of opinion and not of fact.

CASE G

Mr. Brown writes to a teacher on April 1, 1955: "I have the job open at the figure agreed upon. If I do not receive a letter to the contrary by April 15, I shall consider that you accept the offer." The teacher did not write to Mr. Brown. This situation contained the essentials for an acceptance, according to the teacher. Mr. Brown decided that he did not need a teacher and wrote to the applicant on April 10 withdrawing his offer. However, on April 9, the teacher wrote accepting the offer.

(In the same case, the teacher might not have written but could have come in person on April 11, requesting course outlines and textbooks. The teacher might not have received the letter withdrawing the offer. The teacher might have believed that Mr. Brown was under obligation to accept his services. On April 11, the teacher might have sent a telegram of acceptance which was not received by Brown for three days.)

CASE H

A teacher received a written offer of a position from the Denton School Board, offering him a position in their junior high school, at a salary of $3,400 for nine months. The teacher replied at once by mail accepting the offer. After a short delay, he again wrote the superintendent concerning the offer. He was informed that his acceptance had never reached them and that the position had been accepted by another. The teacher, as a consequence, was compelled to accept a position at a reduced salary in another state. The Denton School Board refused to make good in any way the salary differential, and the teacher brought suit to recover. He was awarded $550 in damages, the court finding that a contract had been made as soon as the acceptance was mailed. However, if the teacher had replied by telegram and it had been lost, no contract would have resulted.

CASE I

A teacher received a letter on June 20 from an insurance company offering to insure his car, covering all liability including fire, for $85. On June 21, the teacher mailed a letter of acceptance, enclosing a money order for the full amount. On June 22, his car was burned at a service station fire. Who must suffer the loss? Why?

(In the above situation, instead of writing, suppose the teacher remitted and accepted the offer by telegram. It was received by the company after the fire. Would the teacher be able to collect damages? Why?)

CASE J

Mr. Jones, a retail supplier, offered a teacher a ditto machine for $75. The teacher said, "I will take the machine at that price if you will throw in a stand and ten reams of paper." Explain the nature of this transaction. Remember that acceptance of an offer must follow the terms of the offer, and any variation is a counteroffer.

The school board occupies a place of importance in the operation of American public schools. The reason is that schools are managed by school boards. It should not be inferred from the discussion that follows that the only or chief school board responsibility lies in the area of its relationships to professional and nonprofessional employees. The focus here, however, will be limited to the legal and ethical concerns of school personnel in their relationships with the board of education that employs them.

## "School Board" Defined

The term "school board" ordinarily refers to any board that controls the public schools. Boards have specific titles and are known by many names. In 1958, the United States Office of Education estimated that there were more than 50,000 administrative units in existence in the country. This means that there were literally thousands of school districts or their legal equivalents.

Each of the school boards is "a creature of the state" and subject to its laws.[2] Under varying state designations, school boards are separate governing bodies. They are responsible directly to the people of the separate school districts. However, the boards are held accountable to provisions of state law. Original authority for the control of the public schools lies in the states—not the nation nor the local communities. The school board is usually vested with authority, responsibility, and function making it independent as a governing body. Under state law, therefore, the school board is a sovereign governing body in the performance of its legal functions.

The basis for the legal status of school boards is the constitution of each state. This formal document places the control of public schools in the legislative body. A second basis for the legal status of the school board is the body of state school laws. A third basis which sets the limits of legal control of the board is the decisions of courts, particularly of courts within the same state (remember the meaning of jurisdiction).

The courts are generally agreed that education is a state rather than a municipal function. They are in agreement that boards serve as agents of the state.[3] The school district has been created for the

[2] Charles E. Reeves, *School Boards* (Englewood Cliffs, N.J.: Prentice-Hall, Inc., 1954), chap. I. See also Robert R. Hamilton and E. Edmund Reutter, Jr., *Legal Aspects of School Board Operation* (New York: Bureau of Publications, Teachers College, Columbia University, 1958), chap. I, "Local School Board in the Legal Structure"; chap. 4, "Authority of School Boards in Relation to Employed Personnel"; chap. 7, "Contractual Authority of School Boards"; and chap. 8, "School Board Membership and Meetings."

[3] In William A. Yeager, *Administration and the Teacher,* p. 174, appears this comment: "No attempt will be made in this chapter to document all references to principles and practices, especially those based on court decisions." Yeager lists appropriate references that explain the relation between the state and public education.

specific purpose of making effective the state's plan for education. The district aids the state to fulfill its obligation to provide public schools for its children.

The school board of necessity employs personnel and must adopt rules and regulations governing policies that apply to the school system in general and to personnel in particular. The board can even set precedents in its actions on specific matters and cases. These actions, when challenged, do precipitate differences of opinion relating to school board and school district authority. Some reach the courts for settlement.

By way of introduction one more aspect of the importance of the board of education in the community should be noted. The actions of a board are very important in determining the quality of public education. The type of school provided is determined by the board that controls and directs it. The board must meet minimum state standards but can go beyond them in deciding many matters. The board can and does affect the community directly by going beyond minima in deciding teacher qualifications, the kind of school buildings to be constructed, the location of the buildings, the transportation of pupils, the number of elementary schools in the district, the breadth of the high school offerings, administration of athletics, bases for the discharge of the superintendent or a principal, the extent of pupil health services, and scores of other matters.

Chapter 3 is divided into two main parts: legal aspects of board-personnel relationships and ethical considerations in such relationships. The discussion elaborates some of the important elements in the legal and ethical relationships between personnel and the board. It must be general in character and cannot be an exhaustive treatise or be authoritative for all states under all conditions.[4] The code of each of the 49 states contains the specific information for the administration of the schools within the state.

[4] See Reeves, *School Boards,* p. 62.

## LEGAL ASPECTS

### The Nature of Teacher Employment

**Certification**

Every one of the forty-nine state governments possesses, within the borders of that state, the legal responsibility for "certifying" that certain individuals have met the qualifications for positions in the schools as set out in state law. The Constitution of the United States reserved the matter of education—and thus the certification power—for the attention of the states.

The requirements for certification for teachers in some states are met when prospective teachers complete planned degree programs for teaching at one of the recognized public or private colleges and are recommended by the director of teacher education of the institution. Thus, graduation from a planned degree program, for all practical purposes, results in "automatic" certification within the state.[5]

More than 1,200 colleges and universities in the forty-nine states are accredited by education officials for the purpose of certification of teacher personnel. There is some general agreement that an adequate plan of cooperation is needed between state authorities who certify and institutions that help prepare persons for positions in schools.

The legislatures of the several states have delegated to state departments of education the important task of seeing that a core of qualified personnel is available for teaching in the state's public schools. These departments in turn work with colleges and universities, which plan the courses of study, and with individuals who may have specific certification problems. For example, a teacher who

---

[5] See Yeager, *Administration and the Teacher,* chap. 6, pp. 103ff. Chamberlain and Kindred, *The Teacher and School Organization,* contains the following relevant chapters: 4, "The Local School District"; 6, "Securing a Position"; 7, "Salary"; 8, "Welfare and Security"; 9, "Retirement"; 10, "Legal Status"; 16, "Keeping Records and Reports"; and 17, "Using Buildings, Equipment, and Supplies."

has taught in state *A* may require clarification of his status in distant state *B*, where he plans to teach and where requirements are different. Even though all state certificates are issued on the basis of college credit earned, a real problem is to decide what should be included in the credentials of a teacher if and when such documents are the sole basis for certifying one for teaching.

When requirements for a degree have been met, with specialization in education, the granting of a certificate to the graduate is a legal duty imposed upon the certifying officer. This kind of duty is termed by the courts to be "ministerial" in character. It is a duty which the officer may not legally refuse to perform under specified circumstances.

As one would expect, there is still much variation in the specific requirements to be met by one desiring to be certified to teach in a state. In 1955 all but three states required the candidate to have credits in student teaching in order to secure the professional certificate to teach in high school. In general, two years beyond high school graduation is the very minimum requirement for certifying an inexperienced person for teaching in the elementary grades. In some states there is a minimum age requirement. Often evidence is required of a prospective teacher's good health. Some states demand "proof" of good moral character.

The legal meaning of the term "certificate to teach" is oftentimes unclear. It is certain, however, that admission to the ranks of the teaching profession within a state is regulated by the school laws (state statutes or code) of that state. A board of education is prohibited from employing a noncertified teacher, except under special conditions. A teacher is "unqualified," in the legal sense at least, unless he has been duly and properly certified. A teacher who expects to be eligible for a teaching certificate before the opening of a school term may enter into a contract to teach. In other words, the board is on safe legal ground since the issuance of a license to teach before the actual beginning of teaching must follow when requirements for certification have been met by the candidate.

Some states and cities go beyond graduation from an approved program in recommending initial certification. They may require applicants to "pass a written examination." A test of this sort is used by the state or city in order for persons to obtain school positions, not to obtain certificates. Courts have supported such requirements saying that, in the "exercise of their discretion," school authorities may establish reasonable qualifications over and above the minima provided by state law.

Most states continue to retain control over school personnel by means of issuing a variety of certificates bearing various labels. Again, states and certain cities exercise such powers. The law may specify exactly what personnel must do in order to renew their certificates—how much and what kind of summer or inservice work will be required. In some instances, the law spells out the manner in which applicants shall be examined and what the evidence shall be which indicates that the applicant is entitled to a "better" or at least a different certificate.

When a teacher receives a certificate—his license to teach—the state issuing the license is granting to him the privilege of public school teaching. However, the state is *not* entering into a contract with the teacher. The certificate which the teacher then holds, of whatever type or grade, indicates merely that the possessor is qualified to practice his profession under the law.[6]

In fact, teachers may not enter into binding agreements to teach unless they possess the certificate required by state law. If a person who holds no certificate places his signature on a piece of paper indicating an agreement to be employed, he has no contract at all. The courts do not recognize such an act under the circumstances as a valid agreement. Also, a court will not permit employees to recover funds if they serve with no valid license. A board of education may not authorize the payment of money (which must come from public or tax funds) to one who teaches but does not hold the legal certificate. In order to receive such money, teachers must have their certificates on file with the appropriate state authorities. If they do not, the courts will consider that they have "volunteered" their services.

Parenthetically, there is the general rule indicating that "payment should be made for services rendered." However, when personnel work without a license and a board accepts such services, this rule cannot apply. The nonapplication in such circumstances is sound.

---

[6] A teacher has no legal "right" to be employed as a teacher in the public schools. The courts have stated that such employment is not an "uninhibited privilege" and that the teacher has no right, upon constitutional grounds, to serve except on such terms as the state prescribes.

If a board were bound to pay for such services, licenses of professionally prepared personnel would be worth no more than scraps of paper. If a board were bound by law to pay, certification laws would be defeated. A board would thus be free to employ anyone not holding a license. The basic purpose of legislation on certification is to protect children from persons who want school employment but who do not possess proper credentials, which are at least legal evidence of competency.

The period during which certificates are legally in force varies greatly among the states. Some certificates must be renewed after three or seven years; others are valid for a "lifetime." The so-called "life" certificates, however, remain in force at the pleasure of state authorities. In all states, certificates are issued to inexperienced teachers but teaching experience is one of the requirements for earning certificates that warrant pay increases.

Most certificates may be revoked for stipulated reasons. The list of causes for revocation includes such items as immorality, negligence, incompetency, violation of contract, intemperance (as used here, it perhaps relates to drink and not food or talk), violation of "the law," and unprofessional conduct. Court cases exist by the hundreds because there seem to be real differences of opinion about the definition of "stipulated reasons." It is difficult to know precisely what behavior of a teacher will be deemed to reflect unfairly, unjustly, or unreasonably upon the school.

As would be expected, requirements for certifying and for revoking licenses have changed from time to time. These changes have sprung from periods of economic depression or war-stimulated economy rather than from greater insights as to the kinds of demands made upon school personnel. Requirements are revised upwards during periods when many persons want to teach because schools look like a "haven in a storm." They are relaxed during periods of war-induced shortages of personnel. During World War II, for instance, there was a decided increase in persons holding emergency certificates. However, even in periods of "abnormalcy" when temporary certificates are plentiful, there is a tendency in some places to raise rather than lower professional standards for school personnel. Where this has been the rule, there has been an ample supply of teachers who are qualified, at least on paper.

## Securing a Position

When vacancies in the staff of a school system are created, the chief administrative employee of the board of education (usually the superintendent) should know or review the provisions of the school code that set out the procedures for employment of professional personnel. These must be followed exactly. The courts will permit no discretion in this area. Personnel who are employed by irresponsible boards may have no jobs at all.

It is common practice for superintendents, as representatives of boards of education, to make offers of employment. The question should immediately arise whether a "mere representative of the board" can legally employ personnel. The reader should be under no illusion that the point involved here is merely a technical matter. Many court cases arise because of this "technicality."

If employees are not clear about this point, they can get themselves into socially and economically embarrassing situations. It happens that the summer months find school officials away from their posts at a time when decisions regarding staff need to be made. Miss A, for good reasons, may have waited until August to secure a position. She may have completed graduate work in an institution within one state and may desire to teach many hundreds of miles away. If she carries on all the negotiations by mail, failing to make a personal visit to the office of superintendent and the board of education, Miss A may believe she has a contract to teach when she does not. All she may possess is a letter inviting her to teach, which was sent her by a person not legally authorized to negotiate any contract at all. For instance, a supervising principal may send out telegrams to several directors of teacher-preparing departments of colleges and universities asking for applicants for two eighth-grade positions. In another office, in the same school system, the superintendent may have given instructions to "look around" for two secondary-school English teachers. If Miss A acts on the basis of one telegram, she may find herself in trouble and with no job. To complicate matters, the board may feel that some local people may be qualified.

Under no circumstances should personnel rely on the promises or vague statements of one not authorized to employ them. They should request and wait for bona fide offers from the secretaries of boards of education written on official letterhead stationery. The superintendent may, of course, be the means of conveying the wishes of the board to the employee. But in almost no instance does the superintendent or principal do the actual employing of personnel. That is the right and duty of the three-, five-, or fifteen-person board of education, acting in its capacity as a legal unit.

Employees will better understand the importance of this matter when they realize that boards of education of school districts receive specific authority, express and implied, from the legislature of the state. The question is this: Can the authority thus received be legally delegated to (shared with) an individual? This question is vital because it is the practice in many districts for boards to "give" to administrative heads of systems the task of employing personnel as they see fit.

The courts have held that boards of education cannot legally delegate their authority to the superintendent in matters regarding the employment of professional personnel. He can only recommend persons. He cannot legally enter into a contract with them. It is boards that are vested with the power to make employment contracts.

When the laws of a state specifically authorize a superintendent to make such contracts (when they expressly confer such authority upon him), then of course the superintendent acts within the law. It would seem that the law in most states regarding contracts with personnel should be amended to conform more nearly with the practical situation. On the other hand, there is the argument that the placing of unqualified authority in the hands of one individual subject to few or no restrictions might prove to be a dangerous practice.[7] The board of education, runs this argument, is an agency of the state, doing the business of the state, with employment of personnel as its most important function.

## The Contract to Teach

Boards of education continue to be involved in legal controversies with employees. The powers of boards of education to contract vary

[7] Where permitted by law, the county superintendent may employ a teacher for the school district on nomination of the school trustees and may not refuse to employ a teacher so named. Even here, the basic authority to employ is vested in the board of education of the school district.

considerably from state to state. This accounts in part for the legal harassment of personnel and of the boards, too. Unfortunately, many cases arise because of loose business practices in the employment of personnel. This fact ought to be of real concern to teachers and other school workers. Employees must take the initiative to protect their own interests. Dependence upon others may lead to trouble. No school person need be a party to one of the many lawsuits that reach the high courts of the land each year.

One of the basic elements in "business" relations with a board of education is the notion of what constitutes a contract. The courts have generally held that a contract is an agreement between two or more parties which is enforceable at law. In all forty-nine states, boards of education are authorized by state law to make such agreements with personnel for their employment.

To be legal and binding, the agreement between an employee and board representing the state must conform to all of the general requirements of a contract. This is to say that the contract (1) must be entered into by parties who are legally competent to enter into an agreement, (2) must be supported by what courts call "adequate consideration," (3) must be sufficiently definite as to its terms of agreement so as to indicate what the parties intend by the contract, and (4) must conform to any special laws that may apply in the particular state.

The requirement of "adequate consideration" is an essential but not obvious element in a binding agreement. It deserves special mention and will be "spelled out." Simply put, the requirement is actually the price that one party pays for the act or the promise of another. Consideration, then, in the legal sense, consists of the act —or the promise—of surrendering some legal right at the request of another party. No promise of a prospective employee can be binding unless the board of education does, or promises to do, something for the interested party. In other words, a mere promise by *A*, not supported by a price agreed upon by *B*, does not obligate one legally. No such "agreement" could be enforceable in court. Consideration demands that "something be done" in return for the promise of another, in order to make the promise enforceable.

Those interested in school employment should keep in mind other factors besides what constitutes a contract if they would avoid legal trouble. They must realize that a contract can be completed only at a meeting of the board that has been legally called. There is no contract at all if one or two board members hastily draw up a "legal-looking" document and pass it around for approval at a board member's place of business. No contract can ensue even though approval is given to such agreement by a "quorum" of the board at the "on-the-spot" meeting.

Thus, independent action by individual board members will not serve as the basis for school employment. Action at the unannounced meeting constitutes illegal procedure. Because a board of education is termed a "quasi-corporation," it must act as a body, at a meeting called in advance. The seeker after a school job will save himself grief if he remembers that board members must meet together at a regularly scheduled time and meeting place in order to transact business that will meet the scrutiny of the law.

Besides the necessity for accomplishing business at a regular meeting in order for that business to have legal force, a board of education is confronted with other requirements regarding employment contracts. It must extend an offer to the applicant. He must then "accept" the same offer if a contract is to follow. Fundamental to the formation of a contract is an agreement consisting of a definite offer and an acceptance of that same offer. His acceptance must be communicated to the board, for communication is another basic requirement to fulfill an agreement.

The "offer and acceptance" aspects of the contractual relationship between employee and board will be elaborated upon here because they must be *thoroughly* understood. It must be clear just what a teacher does to become "legally bound."

This problem has several ramifications. An employee should know whether he can legally accept a job offered to him by remaining silent regarding the offer. To understand this, he should be familiar with the meaning of such phrases as "implied acceptance" of a contract and "counteroffer." In short, the question is, "When is a contract actually completed?"

There is agreement that an offer for a position becomes effective only after such offer has been "communicated" to the one intended to receive the offer. To illustrate, an offer in a letter that is never mailed does not form a legal offer. Even though the person concerned learns in some way of the contents of the letter, there has been no legal offer of a position. Likewise, a telegram that is lost cannot be the basis for a position.

A communication from a school board to a teacher, for example, becomes an offer only when the communication contains terms definite enough for the teacher to accept if he wishes. The following situation illustrates the point. A superintendent may say to a conventioning teacher, "I expect to need an additional music man next year." The teacher might reply, "I'll take the job, Mr. Bills." No contract could possibly result here because the parties have not definitely agreed upon such matters as annual salary, method of payment, or the starting date for services. Because of the very real possibility of misunderstandings regarding such vital items, the courts have held that mere announcements of job openings or casual words about them are not legal job offers.

If one through sheer accident does exactly what a board of education plans should be done, no contract can arise either. Receipt by a teacher of a circular, an advertisement, or a postcard from a teachers' agency usually does not form the basis of a job offer. All of these types of communication are too vague to indicate what the parties intend.

If the teacher happens to return a form to a commercial agency asking that papers be sent to a board and a letter of availability mailed, this makes no demand upon a board. Even though the same board were to make a request for a teacher holding the identical qualifications and the teacher mailed his papers to the board, there could of course be no basis for contending that a contract to teach had been entered into.

To keep away from legal involvements, an applicant for a job should remind himself that an offer for a position, made to one person, cannot be accepted by another as though intended for him. There can be no binding agreement under that circumstance. One who receives an offer of a position that does not interest him must avoid passing the information on to a friend, no matter how well qualified he may be. If he does pass the offer on, he implies that the original offer to him can be a valid one for someone else.

An offer for a position remains open for acceptance until it has been rejected, has been withdrawn, or has been allowed to lapse. In other words, if the board of education stated a definite time during which the position would remain open, the offer would be withdrawn automatically upon expiration of the stated period.

However, an offer may be revoked by the negotiating board at any time *before* the applicant has accepted the terms of the offer. Of course, a rejection terminates the offer. It cannot later be accepted unless the board has reopened negotiations.

A teacher may have occasion to be familiar with the meaning of "counteroffer" and what it denotes. One example will clarify the idea. A teacher may have been corresponding with a superintendent concerning an opening in a particular school. One day the teacher decides he wants that position. He then writes a letter mentioning a desired annual salary of some $300 above that quoted in the offer of the board of education. He drops his letter in a mailbox. That very same day the teacher receives a letter from the superintendent informing him that the board offers him a teaching position at the salary $300 above that originally mentioned. Although the figure corresponds exactly with the wishes of the teacher, no contract exists between the teacher and the board of education. The reason is that the teacher is now the one making an offer, which the board is free either to accept or reject. A contract of employment will be completed only when the teacher accepts the board's new offer and drops his acceptance in a mailbox.

An acceptance of a position is indicated when the job seeker communicates his willingness to be bound by the exact terms stated in the board's offer. The acceptance "takes effect," legally speaking, at the moment it is communicated to the board of education.

Willingness to be bound by the precise terms of an offer may be made known in several different ways. If the offer is made by letter and the acceptance is mailed, a contract is formed as soon as the letter to the board is dropped into the mail chute. Likewise, when an applicant receives an offer from a board by means of a telegram, he has bound himself legally the exact moment his message of acceptance is actually placed in the hands of the telegraph employee. In other words, the contract is completed as soon as the acceptance is in the proper channel of communication. There is one stipulation: the foregoing is true only when the prospective employee accepts a position using *the very same means* of communication that was used in delivering the offer to him.

This point is worthy of deliberation. When one chooses to respond to an offer by means different from that used by the negotiating board, his acceptance is technically effective only when it is actually in the hands of the employing board. In general, a contract will not result if the communication of the acceptance is lost or delayed after the applicant chose a mode of reply different from that used by the offerer.

## Types of Contracts

A contract may be described in terms of whether the agreement is oral or written. In the absence of a statute requiring that contracts of employment be in writing, a formal written contract is not required. An oral agreement will be binding. Even when an agreement of employment must be written, there are instances in which failure to do so did not render the agreement invalid.

Whatever the law, a contract between an employee and a board of education should be in writing to avoid later misunderstandings. Especially should the contract to teach be formally drawn. Difficulties between a teacher and a board are reduced to a minimum when their final understanding is written and the document is signed by both parties. The protection that a written contract affords a teacher and the board is considered important by the courts, even though oral agreements are enforceable where the requirement of a written contract is not mandatory. The courts hold that there can be no recovery of damages for the "reasonable value of services rendered" under the oral agreement when the law plainly requires the contract to be in writing.

If required by law, the execution of a written contract is more than a "ministerial" detail in the process of employment. No valid contract exists until all the requirements of the law have been complied with. If a written contract is one such demand of the law, the employee for his own protection should request a written contract. Any action taken by the board, outside of the law, is subject to revocation by that board if it so desires. There can be no accurate measure of possible embarrassment to an employee under such circumstances.

The written contract offers an additional legal protection. The courts agree that oral evidence may not be introduced to vary the terms of a written contract. The protection thus afforded the employee *and* the board is substantial. Neither party can later introduce oral evidence in a court to vary or to contradict any of the terms of the written document.[8]

A second means of describing a contract is to distinguish between an "express" and an "implied" contract. To be termed an express contract, a document must contain all the essential elements or terms of an agreement in the language of the parties to the agreement. An employee is bound by the express provisions of the contract as is the employer. Legal trouble arises when either employee or board seeks to determine the nature and extent of "implied" obligations in the contract.

If an employee, say a teacher, flags a public bus that is running on an established route in his community and enters the vehicle when it stops for him, an implied contract is formed. If the same teacher goes into the corner grocery and walks out with a loaf of bread after waving it high so the shopkeeper sees the teacher with the bread, an implied contract is formed. Though no word was

[8] Statutes which require that contracts of employment be written sometimes do not apply with respect to the teacher entitled to benefit of a permanent tenure act. Statutes providing for the automatic re-election of a teacher for the ensuing year, in the absence of notice, do not eliminate the requirement of a written contract in some of the states. A provision of a tenure statute specifying that the statute "shall not be construed as requiring written contracts with permanent teachers" does not prohibit the school authorities from requiring written contracts with such permanent teachers. This is in order that authorities may have a record and avoid vexation of disputes arising over the substance of oral agreements.

A statute merely requiring the contract to be in writing does not thereby require it to be in a single document. It does not require that the formal contract shall be in all respects sufficient to charge the school board with liability if it is supplemented by a written record of the action of the board establishing its liability. Neither is it necessary that the contract should be in written form at the meeting of the school board, provided it is reduced to writing later on.

The record of the school board disclosing the employment of a teacher and the oral acceptance by the teacher of the employment is not sufficient to constitute a contract in writing. However, a contract is sufficiently evidenced by the minutes of the board where the only statutory requirement of a written contract is a provision ordering a record of all action of the board to be kept. Even where the law requires a contract in writing and a written contract exists, the minutes of the board are the evidence of the authority for making it. The contract as written must be in conformity with the law, of course. See Gerritt v. Fullerton Union High School District, 24 Cal. App. 2d 482, 75 P. 2d 627 (1938); Costello v. Hazle Township School District, 241 Pa. 179, 88 A. 363 (1913).

spoken, the teacher impliedly promised to pay for the bus trip and for the bread.

To be termed an "implied" contract, the agreement must "infer" certain duties to be performed from the relation of the parties involved. Certain essential features of the implied contract are thus not expressly set forth. They are inferred as a matter of reason and justice. The circumstances surrounding the agreement make it a reasonable and necessary assumption that certain duties are expected to be performed.

A teacher thus may wonder whether the small print in his contract "implies" any obligation or extra duty. The explanatory material in small print can be significant, since courts consider the contract as a whole and give effect to the intention of the parties from viewing the entire instrument. The general rules regulating the construction and operation of contracts ordinarily apply to the teacher's contract of employment. Wherever possible, the courts follow the construction put on the contract by the parties themselves. Courts hold that all of the parts of a contract must be considered in order to determine the meaning of any one particular part. Individual clauses in an agreement and particular words, in small or large print, must be considered in conjunction with the whole document in order to determine the total effect of the instrument.

Also, a contract is distinguished by classifications called "executed" and "executory." So long as the agreement has not been carried out by the contracting parties, the agreement is said to be "executory." Some future act is to be done. When the parties have fully completed all the contract calls for, it is said to be "executed." Nothing remains to be done by either party to the contract.

Another useful classification is that which distinguishes between a "void" and a "voidable" contract. A void contract is one that never had any legal existence from the beginning. It is no contract since it is without life. The existence of a mistake, however unintentional, renders an agreement void or invalid. For example, the contract is void if there is a mutual mistake as to the position to be filled or the "extra" duties to be performed. No contract can be formed unless the minds of the parties meet. A contract is also considered to be void when it does not contain all of the essential elements.

A "voidable" contract is something quite different. It is one that has no force and effect as to the wrongdoer but is not void as to the wronged or injured party, unless he elects so to treat it. In other words, one of the contracting parties, for some reason, may have the legal privilege of withdrawing from the agreement entered into. The contract is considered to be defective. It can be cured (made right) through acceptance by the party who could have avoided the contract. It is "avoidable" if defectively executed. The injured party, then, may choose to avoid the contract by withdrawing from it.

Also, a contract is rendered voidable where proof of fraud exists. The courts define fraud as the "intentional misrepresentation of a material fact which induces another to contract unwisely." It is intentional misrepresentation, then, plus reliance by one of the parties on the "fact," that forms the basis for fraud. Fraud suggests that one party chose to gain unfair advantage of another. The elements of fraud are (1) misstatement of fact, (2) intentional deceit, (3) reliance upon deceit by one party, and (4) certainty of damages suffered.

If an applicant conceals his malformed leg by special supports when interviewed by a board, his behavior misrepresents the "true facts." His action to conceal his physical condition constitutes fraud, if he knows that such defect would eliminate his candidacy. Whenever facts are covered up, the second party to a contract is misinformed and has the right to avoid any agreement that may be formed.[9] It is *intent* that defines fraud. Innocent misrepresentation causes a "legal mistake."

In addition to the right to rescind a contract because of fraud, it is possible to sue the party who misrepresented and to recover the actual loss suffered as the result of the fraud. The guilty party is said to have committed a "tort" against the other party, where the elements of fraud are present. He becomes liable for damages caused by his acts. The rule is firmly established that where one

[9] An exaggerated statement of opinion is not a misstatement of fact and is no basis for the charge of fraud. If a teacher states that he feels he can manage a dramatic club or chorus, he is stating his opinion. Should the teacher fail in either venture he tackled, the board could not rescind his contract. Fraud results when a teacher states positively that he can perform a certain clearly understood function and, on test, fails to perform as represented. His contract could be avoided by the employing board of education.

acts in bad faith and with fraud, he may be held personally liable.

One caution must be stated in connection with using fraud as a basis for avoiding a contract. The mere failure to disclose certain known facts does not, in and of itself, constitute fraud, thereby making a contract voidable. One party to a contract is under no legal duty to *volunteer* information in its possession. It is up to each party to study the problem and to make its own investigation. When it does, and questions are asked, partial or evasive answers may result in fraud if replies are made so as to be misleading. Members of the board, for example, are duty-bound to give direct and complete answers to questions when they are asked by prospective employees. Replies can be refused, of course. The board could be guilty of misrepresentation wherever answers were partial and therefore misleading to applicants.

To summarize, a number of adjectives can and do modify the word "contract." An agreement can be either oral or written. It can be "express" or "implied." A contract with unfulfilled provisions is termed "executory," and one completed is called "executed." A "void" contract is one that was never legal. A "voidable" contract can be rescinded at the option of *one* of the parties to it. In order to help protect himself, the employee under contract should know these differences and the conditions regarding contractual relations.

## Board Powers

School boards are legal bodies, organized to govern the school districts and to enforce the laws relating to public schools. As agencies of the state, boards are established by law for the specific purpose of making effective, within the respective districts, the laws of the state pertaining to public schools.

As a quasi-corporation (a seeming one) of the state, the local board has important duties. The employee should know the specific powers and general duties of the board of education. The board is the employer. The employee should be aware of the legal requirements in his state that pertain to contracts, and he should check his school contract against these. The board has the duty to check its employment contracts against the legal restrictions obtaining within the state and local school district.

Essentially, the board of a school district is a corporate body with legal authority to make and execute contracts in the name of the school district. Members of the board may be personally liable for the acts of the board if the board intentionally exceeds its authority acting in bad faith. The board may be sued by an employee and declared liable for failure to fulfill the provisions of a contract. This is so despite the protection it enjoys from suit because of the common-law doctrine of immunity from suit by government. This immunity applies only to personal injury or damage claims due to negligence (tort). It has no bearing whatever on the business dealings of a board. These are contractual in nature.

Salary received by employees is one of the major problems over which differences may arise. A teacher who does not hold the required legal certificate cannot expect a board of education to pay him. Members of the board may be held personally liable for such misuse of school funds. Once legally employed, a teacher can negotiate with the board to have it make provision for individual differences in salary schedules. The board may use ability and effort as distinguishing criteria among teachers having similar duties, experience, and educational preparation. Provisions for individual differences in salary schedules cannot be challenged successfully on the ground that the standards provided are "subjective" in nature. This is a prerogative of the board.

On the other hand, salary provisions that are clearly discriminatory are open to question. The ground for attack is that such provisions are outside the authority of the school board. They are not reasonably designed to promote any legitimate objective of the school enterprise.

Sometimes the period of service of employees and the period of salary payment do not coincide. To avoid trouble, employees should request that the arrangement concerning payment be "spelled out." It is very easy to do so using simple language. Guesswork is then removed. The employee and board can be sure about the salary part of the contract at least. A teacher will not obligate himself on the basis of nine salary checks when the board has a different basis for payment of money due the employee.

The plight of an employee under contract is serious when the district "runs out of money" before the close of the school term or fiscal year. Is the contract valid for the balance of the school year? The lack of school funds to pay for the operating expenses for the school year has been held a valid reason for breach of contract when the contract provides for its termination "on reasonable grounds." The courts have said that lack of funds is a legal reason for nonperformance of a contract by the board of education.[10]

A board may not arbitrarily cancel a contract without the consent of the employee. There may be a provision in the contract for its termination and the discharge of the obligations of the parties. However, the board may not act willfully and deliberately.

At the termination of the contract, the employee must be notified if the board does not choose to renew it. Notification by the board must be made according to law. This means that the employee must receive word from the board generally by the end of April, or thirty days prior to the close of the school term. No reason for nonrenewal of nontenure employees' contracts need be given by the board. It is good practice for the board to pass a ratifying resolution on contracts so that the record of the action appears in the minutes of the meeting.

### Board Rules and Regulations

Frequently an employee will sign his contract without any specific knowledge of the existence or nature of the rules and regulations of the board. He should know that a board has the authority to adopt reasonable rules and regulations with which the employee is obliged to comply.

A teacher, for instance, should understand that upon signing a contract, he is bound by the laws of the state and rules of the state board of education and the local board. The board has inherent power to make reasonable rules. No statute is needed specifically to confer such power. The only restrictions placed on these rules are that (1) they must be reasonable and (2) they must be within the legal framework of the state. It is beyond the province of the board to pass any rule or regulation that has for its object anything outside of instructional matters. However, there are many

---

[10] Where the statute of a state provides for the suspension of school "on certain contingencies," the suspension of a school on the happening of the statutory contingency is a valid excuse for the nonperformance of contracts with employees.

court decisions that have established a body of law regarding rules that affect the personal freedoms of the teacher.[11]

A teacher should know to what extent current rules and those adopted after employment become a part of his contract. In the absence of state laws, a teacher is bound by regulations of the board of education adopted after the time of contract-signing as well as before. Courts have held that all rules and regulations in effect at the date of the making or renewal of a contract are integral parts of the contract. To put it bluntly, rules and regulations in existence when a teacher signs on the "dotted line" to work as a teacher for so long and for so much are just as much a part of that instrument as though they were printed and attached thereto.

A teacher's contract by implication contains the promise by him to "observe all rules and regulations of the school authority." Knowledge of the *existence* of rules is legally unimportant if and when the teacher "breaks" a rule. Ignorance is not bliss! The rules of the board are literally "read into" the contracts of employees, and they are chargeable with infraction of them.

To justify the position that an employee is bound to observe rules made subsequent to his employment as well as those in existence at the time of employment, the courts have emphasized the educational necessities of the situation. In the light of such obvious necessity, a teacher should encourage the board to provide him with a copy of board rules and regulations at the time of contract signing. This would help to insure that the teacher at least has the opportunity to know what is actually part of the contract he has signed.

From even cursory reading of board rules and regulations, a teacher should realize that the pronouncements of the state board of education, when within the law, are just as much a part of his contract as are the regulations of the local board. He should have little doubt that his contract subjects him to present and future by-laws, rules, and regulations of the contracting board. By reading appropriate documents, then, the teacher can acquaint himself with the "full scope" of the agreement that he and the board have given assent to.

[11] For further information consult Robert R. Hamilton and Paul R. Mort, *The Law and Public Education* (Brooklyn, N.Y.: The Foundation Press, 1941), pp. 336ff.; and Edwards, *The Courts and the Public Schools*, pp. 467-508.

Thus, the full extent of a contract should be comprehended. A teacher also faces some "restrictions" that stem from the contract. He must "keep records," refrain from engaging in certain "disloyal" activities, follow curriculum prescriptions, look after the safety of school property, and abide by a variety of "reasonable limitations" on his personal life.

The assignment of a teacher to a school, after signing a contract, means that the new employee is faced with the duty to comply with specific requirements. Merely to hold his new job and be a functioning member of the system, he must know policies regarding admission of pupils to the school, the legal age for "early school-leavers," nonresident tuition fees, care of school funds, provisions for kindergarten and preschool education, and the health requirements for school attendance. The information on all such items can be procured in the office, it is true. It is better, though, for the teacher to be acquainted, at least in general, with such requirements.

As soon as the schoolbell sounds, a teacher embarks on a "record keeping" chore. One of his important tasks is that of helping the office keep tab on the tardiness and attendance habits of pupils. A teacher has the legal responsibility to keep such records as may be required by statute or local board regulation. This is his legal duty. Obviously, his responsibility as a teacher goes far beyond record keeping, important as this one duty is.[12]

All violations of attendance regulations must be reported to the principal, who, in turn, compiles the data for the superintendent and board. To make this work not impossible, a teacher is asked to report daily or weekly, on prescribed forms, the days and even half-days of absence. He may be called upon to aid the office in compiling data concerning the number and distribution of pre-school and school-age children in the attendance area served by the school.

Besides accounting for pupils, a teacher is asked to report periodically on pupil progress. He is urged to complete information

[12] A teacher may not wrongfully exclude a child from school. It has been established as a principle that a teacher does possess the power of suspension of a pupil when his behavior is such as to render the teaching situation ineffective. The right of the child to attend a public school is not a right without qualification.

required for the cumulative folders, such as indicating scores earned on achievement and other tests, and to include appropriate anecdotes. A teacher is sometimes involved in the making of schedules of classes or courses, in supervising the playground, and in using cafeteria facilities. He is charged with seeing that reports of "school" money collected are made on required forms.

Regulations that pose problems to teacher freedoms are not new. The more recent revolve around the issue of loyalty and are promulgated more by state agencies than by the local boards of education.[13] In the absence of a board rule forbidding it, a teacher may engage in political activity without affording the board grounds for dismissing him. According to legislative action in some states, membership in the Communist Party, or a "subversive" organization, keeps that teacher from exercising his "right to teach" even though he possesses proper credentials.

The "Loyalty Oath" legislation has occupied the attention of administrative boards. One question raised is whether an employee legally may be discharged for "political" activity. It has been established by court decisions that school authorities may inquire into the past loyalty and conduct of employees.[14] Too often the one who takes it upon himself to "volunteer" information to school authorities regarding the loyalty of employees possesses no such authority. The innocent suffer with the guilty. It was not long after World War II that daily newspapers carried such headlines as "Hunt for Reds Holds Trap for Teachers," or "Unwritten Charges Fire Three Teachers."

As a duly certified employee of the state, a teacher in more than two-thirds of the states must take an oath of allegiance to the United States Constitution. Local boards will often insist that the prospective employee make additional pledges by filling out forms and documents to "prove" that he maintains no membership in the disallowed groups. For instance, a local board may require "certificates of endorsement" and proof of residence signed by county ordinaries or judges. The real problem appears to be one of the

[13] See Yeager, *Administration and the Teacher*, chap. 20, for a discussion of academic freedom and loyalty oaths.

[14] Adler v. Board of Education of City of New York, 342 U.S. 485, 72 S. Ct. 380, 27 A.L.R. 2d 472, 96 L. Ed. 517 (1950). This is only one of many such cases.

extent to which a state is willing to go in protecting itself from subversives. This is a problem for all who would take seriously the duties and privileges of citizenship.

Arguments have been cited for and against the written formalization of the employee's rights and obligations. For the teacher, this too often has meant he must be preoccupied with statutes, rules, and regulations without regard to particular provisions relevant for him.[15]

A first step toward clarification might be to define the phrase "rights and obligations." The question of what *are* the rights and obligations of a teacher is a legal one. A concern for what they *should be* is a philosophical matter. Rights exist in varying degrees, ranging from legal and logical expectation to moral commitment. Some rights of teachers are indeterminate. Privileges exist for teachers that, if claimed as rights, might well be lost.

It may be helpful for teachers to define their rights and obligations as "those expectations of and by the faculty member" that are recognized by his school system as reasonable. If the right is clearly recognized in any way as a reasonable expectation, it is important, regardless of the legal enforceability. The "Academic Bill of Rights and Obligations," detailed in Dennison's work, forms an excellent guide for adoption by a board of education in its relationships with teachers.[16] There are sixteen principles "spelled out" with subpoints explaining the significance of each proposition. The first six pertain to appointment and dismissal. They say that a teacher has: (1) the right and the obligation to be governed by clear and mutually binding terms of appointment; (2) the right to an understanding of the conditions governing duration of appointment and chances for promotion; (3) the right to fair and objective processes in matters of reappointment, promotion, and increase in salary; (4) the right to achieve continuous tenure after sufficient time to prove himself; (5) the right to advance notice of nonreappointment or dismissal, and the obligation to give advance notice of voluntary resignation; and (6) the right to some

---

[15] See Charles P. Dennison, *Faculty Rights and Obligations* (New York: Bureau of Publications, Teachers College, Columbia University, 1955), pp. 13-18, for an "Outline of Principles and Related Practices" that apply to the college level but have direct implications for public schools.

[16] *Ibid.*, pp. 14-18.

"due process" to assure fairness in case of nonreappointment or dismissal.

Principles seven and eight pertain to salary policies. They indicate first an employee has (7) the right to be governed by a salary policy that is understood, consistent, and determined in the light of consultation with those affected by it. Second, he has (8) the right to such assistance in matters of personal and family responsibility as the school system is in a position to provide, and the obligation to avail himself of such help as may forestall his ever becoming an economic liability, moral or legal, of the system.

Principles nine through thirteen pertain to rights and obligations relating to personal and professional freedom and growth. They state that a teacher has: (9) the right to encouragement and protection in the activities appropriate to a member of a professional body dedicated to teaching; (10) the right to equal consideration with others, regardless of creed in religious or other matters; (11) the right to assistance from the school system, through sabbatical leave or other means, in furthering his development as a professional person, and the obligations associated with receipt of such assistance; (12) the obligation to exercise his professional freedom within the limits of service to the educational enterprise of which he is a member; and (13) the obligation to observe duly the rights and responsibilities of the pupils.

Principles fourteen through sixteen pertain to the rights and obligations relating to the faculty member's share in directing the education enterprise. Here a teacher has: (14) the right to work in a departmental or divisional unit that is reasonably free from the arbitrary domination of an individual or a limited group; (15) the right and the obligation to play a responsible role in the overall functions appropriate to a public school staff; and (16) the right to a direct means of communication with the board of education. It is well to have "rights and obligations" spelled out as suggested above. Nevertheless, there are matters that cannot be settled by saying, "Take a look at the policies." These provide the bare minima only.

Despite the fact that public education and religion are generally considered to be separate under our laws, the subject is one that plagues teachers and local boards. An employee may not be refused employment, or discharged, because of his religious beliefs. Regulations concerning the ban on the teaching of religion, however, are generally in harmony with state law since the board gets its authority from the legislature.

Regulations of local boards indicate whether Bible reading and the teaching of sectarian songs are violations of the separation principle. The reading of a portion of the Bible "without comment" is the established practice in some school systems, especially in the South. State supreme courts have approved the practice by saying that reading from the King James Version does not constitute "religious" teaching.

Some local boards require that teachers refrain from appearing on school premises attired in certain garments. The local district must follow provisions of the school laws pertaining to regulations of dress. In the absence of statute or regulation forbidding it, boards legally may permit the wearing of religious garb by public school teachers. This does not mean they may engage in sectarian teaching. In some districts, a teacher must not wear religious garb since it may imply the teaching of religion. Contrariwise, boards of education may require, for participation in physical education activities, that teachers be attired in prescribed dress.

The question of who may legally use school facilities under board jurisdiction at times concerns employees. This is especially true if they have the responsibility for working with pupils on school premises after school hours, or if they belong to groups desiring to use school facilities for private purposes. Teachers should be familiar with the policy of the board regarding use of the gymnasium or auditorium by political organizations, farm and labor groups, religious bodies, secret societies, and by agencies outside the community with no local sponsors.

As custodians of board property, teachers should be certain about the authority of the school to require pupils to pay for damages they may inflict on school property during the "special" use of the building facilities. If teachers give thought to the possibilities of legal involvement, they will not encourage a wrong and may avoid embarrassing situations.

To summarize, the rules and regulations of a board of education may not conflict with any constitutional or statutory provision. They must meet the test of "reasonableness." This test is a question of fact in each individual case. "If boards could remember that rules are tools to aid them in the administration of the schools, and are not profound edicts, the integrity of which must be preserved at all costs, many lawsuits would be avoided." [17] The enforcement of rules and regulations must meet the "common sense" test. Some flexibility is needed in their enforcement so that rules will "serve and not enslave" the teacher and the board of education.

### Legal Obligations of Employees

The legal duties of employees have often come under the scrutiny of the courts. The nature and scope of an employee's duties under contract, extra pay for extra work, and salary increases during the contract period are kinds of issues that continue to bring board employees into the courts. Such problems concerning those under contract must be interpreted by the courts in the light of relevant board policies and state statutes, if any. Sometimes the school law is merely a general commitment to an idea; sometimes specific obligations must be complied with.

Many job concerns are involved in fulfilling contractual responsibilities of teachers. They include specific class duties, after-school assignments, agreements as to daily schedule of hours, and the length of the "teaching year." Specific issues that have grown out of these include the legal dates for resignation, suits for damages against a teacher for resigning in a "fit of anger," leaves of absence for "personal" reasons, seniority rights, membership in labor-affiliated groups, "rights" of married women teachers, and policies regarding "substitute" teachers.

It is generally agreed that a teacher must perform his contractual duties personally. He may not name a substitute unless allowed by terms of his contract or approved by the board of education. In the  absence of contract stipulations, a teacher need not perform other than "teaching services." This is to say that a board may not require a teacher to perform janitorial service, police service, or work that is unrelated to his field of "regular preparation and service." Of course, a teacher cannot be forced to teach. However, his failure

[17] Hamilton, *The Bi-Weekly School Law Letter*, Vol. III, No. 17 (October 15, 1953), p. 66.

or refusal, without justification, to perform services in accordance with his contract constitutes a breach of the contract.

Ordinarily, a board may expect "reasonable duties" to be performed by teachers under contract. The courts seem to sustain actions of boards since they hold that "extra duties and work" are normally within the duties covered by teachers' contracts.[18] Courts state that a board may prescribe the duties to be performed by school personnel. They have said that the board has such power in the absence of any specific statute. The courts have added that teachers expect to and do perform a service. They have stated that teachers expect to and do put in extra hours when service requires such additional hours.

In general, teachers may be assigned duties quite foreign to their subject-matter area. They owe wide general duties to the school in which they work. "Any reasonable assignment" would probably be sustained by the courts.[19] It has been stated that the direction and supervision of nonclass activities are usually an important part of the duties of teachers. Such extra duties are not always taken into consideration in the contract of employment. It would help teacher and board if such understandings were made a part of the agreement to teach.

An agreement to pay an additional sum to teachers for the performance of a contract is legally binding if the teacher agrees to do something different from, or over and above, that which is stipulated in the contract. For example, if a board wishes to increase the salary of a teacher during the contract period because he is performing additional duties, the original contract should be terminated. Then, by mutual consent, a new contract can be formed with the increased salary for the new duties accounted for. The point to remember is that additional payments to a teacher under his original contract may be illegal. Payments made by a board under separate and independent agreements are valid. Each would constitute a separate agreement.

[18] Two such cases are Parrish v. Moss, 106 N.Y.S.2d 577 (1951); and McGrath v. Burkhard, 280 P.2d 864 (Cal., 1955).

[19] Robert R. Hamilton, *The National School Law Reporter* (New London, Conn.: Arthur C. Crofts Publications), Vol. V, No. 12 (August 4, 1955), p. 48.

## SOME BASIC PRINCIPLES OF CONTRACTS

1. An acceptance of a teaching position is a communicated promise to fulfill the conditions of an offer.
2. Silence alone is not an acceptance of a job.
3. An offer to one teacher cannot be accepted by another teacher.
4. Any change in the terms of the offer by the teacher is a counter-offer and thus a rejection of the offer.
5. Requesting additional information about an offer is not a counter-offer and a rejection.
6. An acceptance takes effect as soon as it is communicated to the board or its agent.
7. If the method of communicating the acceptance is the same as that by which the offer is made, or is by any special means stated in the offer, it becomes effective at once.
8. An implied promise to pay for benefits knowingly received arises as soon as the benefits are received.

## Employee Welfare

Legal protections of employees by way of "fringe" benefits have had "ups and downs." At one time, an employee was simply "hired" for a single short term and was not accorded the protection usually given a domestic servant. To afford some protection, a number of states have enacted legislation requiring various degrees of security.

### Leaves of Absence

One authority in school law has raised several issues regarding one kind of welfare benefit for teachers—the administration of leaves of absence.[20] Three pertinent questions are posed: (1) May an eligible teacher demand a leave of absence, or does the local board have discretion in granting the leave? (2) May a teacher demand, at the end of a duly granted leave of absence, his reinstatement without loss of salary, tenure, or retirement rights? (3) May a board of education require a teacher to take a leave of absence that the teacher has not requested?

[20] Madaline Kinter Remmlein, *School Law* (New York: McGraw-Hill Book Company, Inc., 1950), p. 137.

Remmlein states that a sick leave may be "demanded as a right" on a teacher's part and that a board may compel such leave if the disability might interfere with the efficiency of the teacher. A teacher should not guess what provisions have been provided for such leave. In the state school code and the local regulations are the provisions governing the granting of sick leaves for employees.

When the statutes of a state specify the bases and conditions of "leaves of absence" as such, those stipulations exclude all other bases for which leaves may be legally granted. A teacher will find the rulings of the state attorney general's office regarding accumulated sick leave a helpful guide when needed. The local board may require proof of illness. Considerable time is spent by employees in discussions of sick leave regulations. Such talk should be based on evidence rather than on imagined obligations or supposed legal principles.

A board may terminate a contract of an employee because of sickness when all available leave has been used and the employee is still unable to fulfill a "substantial part" of his contract. The courts usually decide what constitutes a "substantial part." In almost every instance, a teacher who is absent from his duties may not choose his own substitute or pay such a supply teacher for services rendered.

Professional leave is usually a privilege granted by the board of education. Unless provision is made in the statutes, leave for reasons other than illness is a matter within the discretion of the local board. Generally, boards have become more liberal in defining professional leaves of absence. Travel, with the special purpose of study, is being gradually included within the scope of such leave. For those returning from such study leave, the practice is to have the employee present some evidence to the board of how the time was spent.

All procedures pertaining to leave have legal implications for employees involved. Almost half of the states include in their school laws provisions either permitting or requiring local boards to grant leaves for personal and professional reasons. More and more, local boards are supplementing the basic provisions of the state law.[21]

[21] There are several texts that deal adequately with the general topic of leaves. Two recent ones are: Yeager, *Administration and the Teacher*; and Willard S. Elsbree and E. Edmund Reutter, Jr., *Staff Personnel in the Public Schools* (Englewood Cliffs, N.J.: Prentice-Hall, Inc., 1954).

## Dismissal

A board of education sometimes acts in a hasty and arbitrary manner in discharging teachers. When such action is challenged in the courts, it is seldom sustained. The law is clear on the point that an employee under contract cannot be "fired" before the termination of his contract unless there is cause.

The innocent party may not, under law, enhance his damages when a contract has been breached. On the contrary, the party is obliged to take reasonable action to lessen them. A teacher who has been illegally discharged may not sit and "twiddle his thumbs." He is obliged to exercise reasonable diligence to procure other *similar* employment. In other words, the teacher may not sit idly by and be entitled to damages in the amount of his salary. He must make an effort to get another position to reduce the sum the district would have to pay in the event of the loss of the suit.

When a teacher has been illegally discharged, the rule is that he is obliged to accept only work as a teacher or work of "equal dignity and standing." The courts decide what lines of work are not inferior and whether one teaching position is considered inferior to another. It is clear from decisions that a teacher is not obligated to accept a position in another town or community, however desirable, in order to mitigate his damages. As far as the mitigation-of-damages rule is concerned, the privilege of remaining in the community in which the teacher has chosen to live and work is protected by the courts. The burden is upon the school district to prove that a teacher did not seek similar employment when illegally discharged from his position. It does not rest with the teacher to prove that he did seek it.

Not all cases of "dismissal" involve a teacher who is illegally discharged. Most times, in fact, the board waits until the termination of the teacher's contract. If a board does not choose to renew the contract at its termination date, it must notify the employee prior to that time. The notification by the board must be made generally by the end of April, or thirty days prior to the closing date of school. The board need give no reason for nonrenewal of a nontenure teacher. In all cases, failure by the board to give such "legal notice" does not *entitle* the teacher to re-employment for the next year. He may not receive notice and still have no contract if he lacks the capacity to hold the position or if he waives service of the notice. If the school where he was employed is closed by the board in accordance with the law, the contract will provide that, in such event, the contract "shall be void."

Under the express provisions of some statutes, a teacher is required to give notice of acceptance of employment for the succeeding year. The employee must notify the board to the contrary on or before a specified date. If he does not, the board can presume that the employee has accepted other employment.

The judgment of administrators of schools in the troublesome area of "teacher competency" is tested very frequently in the courts. Teachers have vague notions about who or what decides whether a teacher will remain in the system. This is usually all that is known about the subject. Where does the burden of proof of competency lie? Teachers need information about where such judgment rests.

What competency is, or what competency is not, cannot be determined in the abstract. The courts uphold some reasons and reject others as legal bases for discharge of teachers. The livelihood of teachers depends upon precise meanings of the concept. The broad term, "incompetency," is unfortunately not a definite and clearly definable one. Usually, meaning must be secured from the facts and special circumstances of each case. Because incompetency is a valid ground for dismissal of a teacher at common law and under laws of most states, some discussion of the topic is necessary.

This explanation of the term is as helpful as any: "A relative term without technical meaning. It may be employed as meaning disqualification; inability; incapacity; lack of ability, legal qualifications, or fitness to discharge the required duty." [22] However, the fact that a teacher is the holder of a certificate to teach is prima facie (on the face of it) evidence of his competency, not incompetency. By accepting a teaching position, a teacher thereby represents that he possesses a reasonable degree of understanding of pupils, of one or several content areas, and of the teaching-learning process.

When a teacher accepts a position, he expressly or impliedly

[22] Horosko v. Mt. Pleasant Township School District, 335 Pa. 369, 6 A. 2d 866 (1939).

makes certain agreements with the board concerning his qualifications for carrying out his duties. A properly certified teacher implies that he has ability to manage a classroom and will be diligent in the execution of his work. The presumption of competency is on his side. Therefore, whether a teacher meets standards is a question of fact to be determined by legal means. The burden of proof is upon the board when it asserts that a teacher has fallen short of his obligations.

When the charge of incompetency is raised by a board of education, the presumption of competency must be refuted by positive evidence if the incompetency charge is to be sustained. The burden of proof rests with the school board. If it fails, the teacher may not legally be discharged, regardless of how thoroughly convinced the board may be of that incompetency.[23]

When cases involving incompetency have come to the courts, it is generally agreed that "competency" is both physical and mental. If a teacher, otherwise highly competent, becomes unable to perform his duties because of illness or injury, he may be held to be incompetent in a legal sense. A married woman's pregnancy has been held to make her incompetent to teach. It is well to point out here that physical inability of a teacher to perform duties does not necessarily imply "incompetency."

The law is well settled that a teacher under contract can be removed "for cause" before the termination of his contract. A teacher's certificate and therefore his contract may be revoked in most states for certain stipulated reasons as: immorality, negligence, incompetency, violation of contract, intemperance, violation of the law, and unprofessional conduct. Some states list only general causes for termination of the contract. Where specific causes are actually enumerated for the legal termination of a teacher's contract, the general rule is that the contract cannot be voided for any causes "other than those specified" in the regulations of the board or state statutes.

A board is required by some courts to make a finding of facts setting forth the evidence relied upon in reaching its conclusions

[23] The serious charge of incompetency cannot be sustained merely by showing that the teacher does not possess the highest qualifications. The law only requires average qualifications and ability equal to that of the average teacher. It does not demand abilities equal to those of the most eminent members of the profession.

concerning the discharge of a teacher. This practice seems desirable in that it makes judicial review of the decision less cumbersome and requires the board to "think through" its decision concerning the dismissal of teachers.

Of course, the question of whether a hearing is required is resolved if a statute expressly provides that certain action regarding employees can be taken only after a hearing has been held. The question of whether a hearing is required arises by implication when a statute provides that certain action can be taken only for cause. The inference here seems to be that cause can be established only after a hearing has helped to establish the facts in the case. There seems to be a growing inclination on the part of the courts to hold that a hearing is necessary in order to remove a teacher under contract when a particular cause is stipulated, even though the statute does not expressly require such a hearing.

The practice of withholding increments rather than dismissing a teacher forthwith is one resorted to on occasion. This kind of "inaction" by a board is generally permissible if the teacher's work is not considered satisfactory by the board and it gives adequate reasons to the teacher. In all such cases, however, the state minimum salary must be met. In case of a suit by a teacher when salary or contractual problems arise, no hearing may be scheduled during the summer vacation unless the teacher agrees to it. When the hearing is held, it may be private or public in nature, depending again upon the wishes of the employee involved.

The right to a hearing for the teacher, before legal action is taken against him, does not exist in all school-connected controversies. The important question, then, is this: Is a hearing by school officials required, and under what conditions, before legal action may be taken by them against a teacher? [24] "To be heard" is an important right which the courts carefully protect. In fact, it is basic in the philosophy of American law that a person shall not be condemned before he has been given the privilege of being heard in his own behalf.

[24] A discussion of when a hearing should be a prerequisite to administrative action is contained in Hamilton, *The Bi-Weekly School Law Letter*, Vol. III, No. 10 (July 8, 1953), p. 40.

## Tenure Laws

A teacher with tenure does not have a single contract that extends over a period of years. Rather, there is automatic renewal of his contract. Basically, a teacher can possess tenure under three types of laws.[25] Besides the automatically renewed contract, there are the continuing contract and the implied contract. The school laws in the various states provide that a teacher shall be deemed re-employed or re-elected, or his contract shall be renewed for the succeeding year, unless the employing board of education shall, within the time specified, "give or cause to be given" notice to the teacher that he shall not be re-employed or re-elected or his contract renewed for the succeeding year.

In each state, the laws regarding tenure apply to such school districts and to such teachers as the legislature of the state so designates. Some school laws apply only to the probationary teacher and are not applicable to the teacher who has attained permanent tenure or a continuing service status. Other laws of the states specifically omit the probationary teacher. The laws do not change the legal effect of a teacher's employment contract and do not establish permanent tenure.

It is most important, regarding the meaning of the concept "teacher tenure," to note that tenure is not necessarily anything permanent.[26] Since tenure is usually not in the nature of a contract, the laws supporting it may be amended or even repealed completely by the enactments of future legislatures. A typical example of the wording of a board rule covering the topic of tenure is the following:

> *Rule 4.* It shall be the policy of the Board to recognize and to reward efficiency in service, to offer permanent tenure only to those who have clearly and fully demonstrated competency in training, personality, health, and a will to grow in knowledge and skill, to cooperate with others, and to keep abreast of the community needs and of the profession.[27]

[25] Employees should consult the statutes of their state for the laws regarding tenure.

[26] See Yeager, *Administration and the Teacher*, pp. 456ff., for a discussion of "Teacher Tenure and Termination of Service."

[27] *Administrative Code of the San Francisco Unified School District* (Board of Education, San Francisco, California, 1946), p. 25.

The fact that tenure is not necessarily permanent may be disturbing to some teachers. Teacher groups in many regions are continuing to work out ways to have tenure included as part of the contractual relationship between teacher and board. Teachers feel that tenure cannot be what it purports to be when it merely reflects the particular legislative policies of the day.

Statutes on teacher tenure generally permit discharge only for stated causes established by a hearing. Within or outside of tenure provisions for teachers, the dismissal by a board of education means complications if malice is involved. If a teacher has been arbitrarily and maliciously dismissed from his position, he has a right of action for damages against the board members personally. The teacher's counsel must show that members of the board acted in bad faith. It must be remembered here that mere mistakes or errors in judgment in dismissing a teacher create no personal liability for board members.

The real goal of tenure laws has been the attempt to get greater stability in and improvement of the educational enterprise. However, it is generally conceded that school laws of the states covering dismissal favor teachers. Tenure laws were established by the states for the benefit of education generally. Any benefits conferred on the individual teacher were merely coincidental to this main objective.

## Retirement Laws

One of the most productive sources of school litigation is the area of teacher retirement laws. A substantial amount of it arises from the fact that apparently much retirement legislation has been drawn and enacted hastily, without adequate consideration of its implications or consequences.[28]

Numerous cases have come to the courts in which retirement laws have been the issue. Examination of these shows that the legislation has been attacked on several grounds.[29] Almost without

[28] According to Robert R. Hamilton, Dean of the Law School, The University of Wyoming at Laramie.

[29] Hamilton and Mort, *The Law and Public Education*, pp. 422-27. Retirement laws have been attacked for being class legislation, for granting extra compensation to public employees, for spending money for private purposes, and for taking property without due process of law.

exception, however, the retirement laws have been upheld by the courts. The decisions have materially strengthened the laws by making clear their intent to better education generally.

With little exception, a teacher who has served during good behavior under tenure rules of the board is officially and automatically retired from service at the expiration of the school year in which he reaches the legal compulsory retirement age. Each teacher is then entitled to such annuity as may be legally provided by the district under state laws.

If a retirement allowance is an annuity, it may not be changed subsequently, since such a change would constitute impairment of contract. When a teacher possesses a right based on contract, his right is a vested one. Here, the legal difference between an annuity and a pension must be understood.[30] A pension is said to be a bounty "springing from the graciousness of the sovereign." The state is under no obligation to pay a pension to any person. It may do so legally if it so chooses. An annuity is unlike a pension in that it is in no way a gratuity. It arises out of a contract or legal obligation. The teacher has contributed some of his earnings to a fund from which the annuity is paid.

Retirement systems for teachers in vogue in various states and the Social Security Plan of the federal government have been compared in recent years by teacher groups to discover the possible advantages of one plan over local plans or the possibilities of coverage under both systems. Agitation has increased since teachers in private schools have begun to enjoy the benefits from membership both in a retirement system and the Social Security Plan.

The question of participation by the public school teacher in the Social Security Plan has raised the issue of the constitutionality of any such venture. In some states, the long-established retirement plans must be altered before the teacher can be enrolled in the federal plan. In short, the question of getting wider coverage under local or state plans by strengthening them, and the question of seeking membership under the federal plan, will, of necessity, be widely debated for some time. To date, there appears to be only one state where the retirement system was not re-instated when the Social Security plan was adopted.

[30] Yeager, *Administration and the Teacher*, chap. 18.

## ETHICAL ASPECTS

To supplement the legal controls that affect the relationships between employees and the board of education, there exist the professional codes of ethics (national and local). These codes impose "additional moral control." [31] The discussion that follows is concerned with some aspects of conduct of personnel and the board, not covered by law. The topics considered are: credentials, letters of application, the professional interview, contractual obligations, orientation to a position, and evaluation of job performance.

### Securing a Position

**Credentials**

As one of the most important aspects of their work, teacher placement offices assemble credentials of candidates for teaching positions. Prospective employers take the statements written about a candidate with varying degrees of seriousness. Unfortunately, the information contained in the "confidential papers" is not always compatible with the "true facts." Every teacher knows of instances where very serious trouble occurred between a teacher and a second party. The administrative official, instead of indicating the strengths of the dismissed teacher along with the precise nature of the problem, may camouflage the statement in the credentials. It may be so garbled that no one could get an accurate picture from reading it alone. Since employers place some degree of confidence in credentials of a candidate, it is essential that any comments made about the competency or personal habits of the candidate be as complete as possible as well as informative.

It is the responsibility of the teacher-candidate to see that data he submits to become part of his professional file are truthful, not only in being factually accurate but in giving no misleading impression. The teacher injures himself when he purposefully insinuates that he has had a kind or type of experience that he has not had. The teacher restricts the usefulness of the credentials of all applicants for positions when he acts unethically. A board of edu-

---

[31] Elsbree and Reutter, *Staff Personnel in the Public Schools*, p. 397.

cation must be able to depend upon the statements included in credentials if it is to discriminate validly among candidates and choose those with recommendations that seem best to fit with the school philosophy and policies.

A code of ethics applies only to a particular occupational group such as teachers. It does not apply to all persons within a jurisdiction (city, state, or nation) as does the public law. The ethical code for teachers speaks of the need for representing one's qualifications accurately. What constitutes a misrepresentation of professional qualifications? Deliberate outright lying is fraud. What about inferences?

The exhortation is made that the teacher "will apply for or offer employment on the basis of competence only." [32] What does this actually mean? What criteria of a nonprofessional nature is the administrator able to use in considering the employment of a particular teacher? To these questions, answers had best be supplied by the reader. In fact, there may be no answer.

If a teacher leaves a school system because of low salary, he should contact the institution from which he earned his latest degree, requesting that his credentials be brought up to date. Then another system can write for information prior to employing the teacher at a higher salary.

Boards of education should regularly include within their annual budgets items for the purpose of paying the expenses of those whose job it is to seek out likely prospects for positions that become available in the system. For the benefit of both himself and the system, a teacher needs the sincere cooperation of boards that are actively seeking out potentially desirable persons to fill current and future vacancies. Such a practice, if generally followed, would tend to discourage the employment of the drifter who is waiting for "something special to turn up," and would tend to work a disadvantage to the board that consistently followed the policy of waiting for applicants "to show up."

### Letters of Application

A letter of application for a teaching position is actually a putting to, or placing before, a person a request or petition for a position

[32] Lieberman, *Teaching As a Profession*, pp. 417ff.

in a particular school system. It is a written request to be employed for a specific opening at a certain specified time. A request of this sort is governed in part by ethics.

The teacher who is anxious, for one reason or another, to locate in a particular community, should write his letter to the superintendent (or supervising principal, as the case may be), not to a member of the board of education. By this observance of direct line of authority, the teacher can secure from the professional head of the school system the detailed information required to make an intelligent choice as to whether he wants to make a formal application for a job opening. He avoids dependence upon the making of "connections" to aid him in securing more favorable consideration than another would receive without "pull."

There are several reliable means open to a teacher in his search for the position of his choice. Many school superintendents have established and maintained the practice of announcing vacancies for positions for the ensuing year. Institutions that help prepare teachers customarily maintain appointment bureaus. Teachers also have a wide choice if they wish to enroll with commercial teachers' agencies. Here complications may arise when it must be determined whether a position has been secured on "one's own initiative" or by means of the agency. Another limitation is that an agency usually sends out notices of vacancies to many "prospects" in the hope that one will be suited for the position and help defray the costs connected with maintaining a reputable service.

The teacher should, quite clearly, place himself in the best possible light when mailing out information about himself. He should avoid, though, creating the illusion of broad and rich experience along certain lines when such does not exist.

Contrary to what job aspirants maintain, it would seem unwise to write letters of inquiry about openings in an indiscriminate manner. If one feels that "something good is bound to turn up" in this way, he must invariably meet disappointment. Almost always, such "buckshot" applications fail to accomplish the purpose intended. Many find their way unanswered into nearby wastebaskets. The mimeographed form or scribbled note suggests to the reader that the writer possesses the "any-old-job-is-good-enough" attitude.

All are familiar with the many suggestions that appear in the literature regarding the standards to which acceptable letters of application should conform. Here are three: (1) Letters of application should emphasize the qualifications of the applicant for the particular opening rather than any disparagement of other applicants. (2) The letters should demonstrate that the applicant seeks the position on his own merit, not because of the real or assumed influence of friends or relatives. (3) The letters should include no complaints about the position presently occupied and no promise of skills that the applicant does not in fact possess.

It should be unnecessary to labor the point that notices should be sent promptly to all offices where applications are on file as soon as the applicant has accepted a teaching position. This professional behavior will aid a teacher in getting and then holding the quality positions he would deserve. It enables boards of education that have been previously contacted to drop from their active files persons who are under contract.

## The Interview

The professional interview should be used by the board of education to discharge its responsibility to provide the best possible personnel consistent with desirable employment practices.

Regardless of the locale, the professional interview should be held for the sole purpose of bringing the best-qualified person to a vacancy. An adequate interview is a two-person relationship in which the applicant gives honest impressions of fitness for the position and the employer explains in detail what the position entails and the rewards offered.

It is well known that the strengths and weaknesses of a candidate do not reveal themselves when the pressures of the office interview bear down upon the interviewer and a teacher trying to appear "at his best." Because of the many serious limitations of such perfunctory interviewing, it is a wise procedure for a representative of the school system to visit prospects so that impressions will be made while the worker is "on home territory." If time and money permit, such a visit and conference bear fruit. The board gets a first-hand picture from its contact of how the prospect "looks in action." The person being considered has the security of doing his regular job. He can invite the board representative to "his" office and ask him to his home if that seems appropriate.

It is elementary that information discussed between two persons during an interview is "privileged" information. As such, it is highly confidential. For a teacher to repeat to others what was said to him under "interview" conditions is grossly unprofessional. For a teacher, in the momentary absence of the board representative, to examine papers that may have been part of the discussion, is the action of either a benighted or a vicious person. An interview is precisely what the term implies.

When a teacher is interviewed by several persons, either individually or by a group, there are psychological factors that may make the procedure questionable as far as any real value to the board is concerned. If demands are not made on the candidate that border on the unethical, the multiple interview often places the candidate for a position at an unfair advantage or at a serious disadvantage regarding opportunities for employment by that board of education.

The follow-up after the interview is an important step in the professional chain of relationships between the prospect and an interested board. As in the interview itself, the follow-up makes demands upon both the applicant and the board. Someone representing the board is obligated to notify the candidate immediately regarding the decision the board has reached. There can be no legitimate excuse for failure to let the teacher know "where he stands." The board sometimes delays, saying that the teacher interviewed "is their choice," but it has to wait and see others "for the record." Depending upon the particular time during the year, a teacher cannot be left waiting with the prospect of leaving the present board "in the lurch" if and when an offer finally comes through.

In short, a teacher should learn directly whether the board accepts or rejects the recommendation of the superintendent or whether it wishes to delay action for some specified reason. In all fairness, a board must reveal in writing to the candidate its decision to employ another for the vacancy.

On the other hand, if a teacher decides that the opening is not attractive to him after the interview, he is obliged to notify the board without delay of any sort. He must not "hold off" in the hope that the board will meet some particular stipulation advanced during the conference. When the applicant has accepted a position elsewhere, he should make this fact known to the board that arranged for the interview. These suggestions are valid ones regardless of whether there appears to be an undersupply or oversupply of qualified teachers at the particular time.

The controlling concern of teaching as a profession is one of "efficient service." The interview between prospective employer and applicant should be geared to "placing the cards on the table." The representative of the board of education may well talk with the applicant about the general problems facing teachers as citizens and as professional workers. He may well point out that the code of ethics for teachers attempts to embrace all important ethical problems of teachers. He and the prospective teacher should explore the fact that the code of ethics assumes agreement on basic policy and purpose among members of the profession.

The careful interviewer ought to make it clear that the nonacceptance by the candidate of one role of the school—to provoke critical thinking—is a matter of personal understanding and commitment, not a matter of ethics at all.

In the course of the conversation, however, some agreement should be reached about possible pressures that may make the employee succumb to regulation of his behavior that lies outside the realm of his occupation as teacher. Only confusion can result if a board includes within the code of ethics insistence upon arbitrary standards of behavior by the teacher. Provisions of a code of ethics must relate only to the professional work of the teacher, not to unrelated activities of a purely personal nature, if professional ethics are to make sense.

Surely the teacher ought not be left with a feeling of uncertainty about what would be included in the admonition "not to act improperly." He should realize that a difference exists between prohibiting unethical conduct and prescribing desirable conduct.

## Contractual Obligations

Even though a contract creates, modifies, or destroys a legal relation, there are ethical considerations for personnel implicit in such promissory agreements. Of course, the law will enforce the legal obligations but not those related to ethics. Nevertheless, some yardstick is needed to help the employee and the employer to distinguish scrupulous from unscrupulous professional conduct.

Although not a part of the contract, use of public property by the employee for his private purpose is clearly unethical. Giving lessons after school hours and using school instruments would be such violation. A nonpublic purpose is being served by use of tax-purchased equipment. A related problem is that of the kind of outside employment that "tends to lower the status" of the teaching profession. What are the prohibitions here?

Should the teacher under a teaching contract expect to be shielded and protected from adverse but unjustified judgments by members of the public or the teaching staff? There is no clear distinction between "disloyalty" and "disrespect" in some quarters. Employees and employing board do not understand clearly enough the difference between the rights and obligations of a teacher as a leader in the community and the emphasis by boards upon conformity and loyalty.

Whatever the cause, the code of ethics for teachers is not clear regarding contract obligations. It does not distinguish between the unethical and the undesirable types of conduct of a teacher. Violations ordinarily do not carry penalties. One result is that there is substantial agreement among informed groups that the attitudes of a teacher toward his obligations of contract are generally less professional, less ethical, than those of boards of education.[33]

There are many kinds of problems facing an employee, it is true, that relate to his contractual obligations. Despite difficulties, a teacher avoids breaking his contract if he comprehends the full meaning of being a professional employee. He takes the provisions of his written or verbal agreement seriously. He does not ignore, at least knowingly, any of the terms. Regardless of more generous subsequent offers and the "emergencies" that arise, a teacher with some insight into the meaning of a contract stands by the agreement into which he willingly entered. All know of the teacher who leaves for a job in industry a week before school opens or who "quits" during the term because "things aren't going the way he thinks they should."

[33] One conclusion reached by participants in the Conference on School Law, sponsored by the Ohio State University, Summer, 1953.

A release from a contract can usually be had by giving the board due notice." A teacher should inform the superintendent that his resignation will be withdrawn if the board is unable to secure a qualified person to replace him. When a teacher acts in this professional manner to secure a bona fide release, he helps prevent embarrassment to the school authorities who do not have to "look around" at the last minute for a replacement. Recognition of the importance of his contract by the employee and respect for his welfare by the board enable the schools to maintain high levels of service to the communities they serve.

## Ethics and Orientation

It is perhaps not expecting too much to require that the ethical code serve to orient the novice into his professional obligations, his rights, and his privileges as a member of the group. Too often, though, the new employee is not "initiated into the fraternity" properly. He is compelled rather to resort to time-consuming, and often disheartening, trial and error in meeting the problems with which he has a right to expect professional assistance, at least initially.[34]

If the code employs phrases that are understandable, the code can be a device for helping a new teacher. To be workable, clauses should be clear statements of principles, should contain reasonable provisions, should indicate basic agreement among the members, and should include all big problems to be encountered.

Every position in the school system should be charted and its specifications listed for employees to examine. These should include the nonclass load of teachers, other services to be rendered, and the nature of the community work needed, as well as the direct teaching load of subject or grade combinations. Good practice in orientation is followed by the administration when a teacher is assigned to fill a specific position on the basis of preparation. The nature of that position should have been previously determined very carefully. The system acts in a manner less than professional when, for reasons unknown, it places a teacher with a content major in English in history and purposely places a teacher with a major in history in the area of teaching English.

[34] Yeager, *Administration and the Teacher*, p. 159.

A teacher should bring to the new job understanding of his teaching assignment, including both in-class and out-of-class (extracurricular) activities. He should not hide any large responsibilities he has assumed in outside organizations for fear that "reprisals" may be taken should difficulties in school work develop as the term progresses. On the other hand, the board in assigning an employee should not ignore his outside interests and commitments and burden him unduly with "extra" duties. The board, acting through the local school administrator, should encourage full and complete understanding regarding the all-important orientation process.

Perhaps being a good citizen is taken as a matter of course in most communities and is not something to dwell on during the first year of teaching. It may be questioned whether good citizenship is directly concerned with ethical behavior. At least the code of ethics should help the board of education and its new employees to determine the professional etiquette needed between the teacher and the nonteacher or "outsider." There should be agreement between the board and teacher as to what "reasonable patterns of behavior" are that will be acceptable to the community. Parts of the ethical code should be used by the board employees to help the lay person understand the meaning of "professional conduct" in its broadest and most useful sense.

An effective plan of orientation as a teacher enters his new position may very well make the difference between his success and failure and assure initial confidence in the classroom and with parents. Full and complete orientation is perhaps an ideal never quite fulfilled. An ultimate goal is the realization by the teacher of the full significance of teaching as a profession wherever the teacher may be employed.

### Evaluation of Teaching Performance

Surely the code of ethics in and of itself does not serve to exclude an incompetent teacher from continuing as a member of the teaching profession. But ethical considerations loom large as factors in teacher ratings and possible dismissals. What constitutes a relationship that is "inconsistent with a teacher's professional obligations"? This phrase has been used times without number in citing "just cause" for nonrenewal of contract. There is no one answer that applies for all times and places.

What must a criterion of conduct be like to enable a board to distinguish ethical from unethical conduct as a basis of evaluating teacher effectiveness? Surely exhortations and platitudes are not good enough as guides for either the teacher or the employing board. For instance, is it not unethical (unprofessional, in other words) for the teacher to engage in class in a furtive and concealed type of partisanship so that it cannot be subjected to critical analysis? Can a teacher incur community disapproval and administrative ire but still be a highly effective teacher in the classroom? These are questions that need much thought and reflection before answers are propounded.

Many feel that whatever instruments are used for evaluating teaching success, those instruments employed at the present time permit too wide a margin of error. There are some boards of education that use personality tests and character tests widely and, some think, uncritically. A teacher may believe, with a measure of support, that the results of many evaluation instruments must not be taken too seriously. The tests are not refined enough to warrant the conclusions drawn. Indiscriminate and unintelligent use hurts a teacher, it is felt, rather than helps him. The elaborate statistical procedures to which some have been subjected are not warranted.

At the last official count, there were more than 120 personality and character tests available.[35] Some are simple in construction, while some are elaborate. A teacher has friends if he insists that these tests "simply do not work"[36] One of the teacher's friends is the psychiatrist who views with suspicion the idea of attempting to measure what makes the teacher "tick." When asked if he thought that a test could pick out the potential teacher, one professor stated that there is nothing in our present knowledge that promises such a test in the near future.

It is difficult to evaluate the "evaluation" devices. Their usefulness depends upon the kind of person supervising the whole

[35] Oscar K. Buros, *The Fourth Mental Measurement Yearbook* (Highland Park, N.J.: The Gryphon Press, 1953).
[36] One is psychologist H. G. Gough of the University of California at Berkeley. See Robert Wernick, "Modern-Style Mind Reader," *Life*, Vol. XXXIX (September 12, 1955), p. 98.

program. If the tests are used under the direction of one who is "out to hurt" someone, the results can be construed to fit the prejudices of the evaluator against the best interests of a teacher. If one has a vested interest in "making a device work," he may carefully interpret the results to suit his biases and preconceived notions about the strengths and weaknesses of a teacher.

The general public does not expect the average person to be a teacher. However, members of a board of education may expect the teacher to behave like the average man. When he is unable to, there may be trouble. If expectations are different from performance, a teacher may resort to various compensatory devices, none of which may be very helpful. In times past, teachers have sought defense in such violent reactions against conformity that they went to school or appeared in public with open-toed slippers or walked the streets with a turtle on a string. Nowadays we are more likely to find that instead of flaunting his profession, a teacher does his best to disguise it. He wants to take on the "protective coloration" of the masses so that he will not be pointed out as "a teacher."

Several suggestions appear below that may be helpful in establishing areas of agreement between the teacher and board of education.

1. A teacher should avoid getting into the middle of a "heated" discussion. He should play the role in the community of the interrogator, the prober, and the summarizer.
2. A teacher should look on the members of a board of education as private citizens, no more, no less. He should not initiate talk about school affairs with a board member.
3. A teacher should attend the church of his preference, despite probability of criticism, rather than attend where it "may be good to be seen."
4. A teacher should govern his personal habits (food, drink, dress, and entertainment preferences) by local standards when "on the job."
5. A teacher should, if in a small community, make purchases at local establishments where possible.
6. A teacher should avoid limiting social contacts only to the "Nob Hill" families. The children come from many different neighborhoods.
7. A teacher in a small town should avoid being only a five-day-a-week resident.
8. A teacher should be active in community affairs. He should avoid, however, joining all "worthy" groups. Be "hard to get" when the chairmanships of committees are extended or when

vacancies in the officers' ranks are asked to be filled by a teacher. Be selective!

Sometimes a teacher and a board of education will differ on what appear to be "little" matters. Trouble is likely to be precipitated. Solutions depend, of course, upon many things—such as the moral standards of the teacher and what he personally considers to be honorable. Much depends upon how a teacher, in case of a "flare-up," thinks he will feel when he comes face to face with colleagues. It is important whether a teacher feels he can "trust the board again," or whether he can trust himself.

Mostly, a solution to such problems depends upon the sincerity of the employee and board members and whether both can "forget as well as forgive." There should be no secret hates between employee and board to plague both in the already difficult work of teaching children. Whatever the issues, they should be faced squarely and not allowed to drift. Practical steps should be taken to deal with them.

## QUESTIONS FOR STUDY

1. What is an acceptance of a position?
2. How may an acceptance be made?
3. Is silence a good cause for thinking an offer is accepted?
4. Is it possible for a teacher to accept an offer of a position made to someone else?
5. What is a counteroffer?
6. Is asking for information a counteroffer?
7. When does an acceptance of a job actually take effect in the following circumstances?
   (a) When the offer is sent by mail.
   (b) When the offer is telegraphed.
   (c) When the teacher uses a means of reply other than that used in the offer.
8. What is an implied acceptance?

## SUGGESTED READINGS

*American Jurisprudence*, Vol. 47, "Schools." Paragraphs 29-47 for Administrative Officers and Boards; paragraphs 48-55 for Contracts; and paragraphs 108-145 for Teachers.

*American Law Reports.* See Index for topics under "Schools," "Board of Education," and "School Teachers."

Chamberlain, Leo M., and Leslie W. Kindred, *The Teacher and School Organization,* 3rd ed. (Englewood Cliffs, N.J.: Prentice-Hall, Inc., 1958), chaps. 4, 6, 7, 8, 9, 10, 16, and 17.

*Corpus Juris Secundum,* Vol. 78, "Schools and School Districts." Paragraphs 83-143 for Administration; paragraphs 154-238 for Teachers, Principals, and Superintendents.

Edwards, Newton, *The Courts and the Public Schools* (Chicago: University of Chicago Press, 1955), chap. XVI.

Fisk, McKee, and James C. Snapp, *Applied Business Law* (Cincinnati: South-Western Publishing Company, 1955), chap. I.

Hamilton, Robert R., *Legal Rights and Liabilities of Teachers* (Laramie, Wyoming: School Law Publications, 1956), chap. II.

————, and E. Edmund Reutter, Jr., *Legal Aspects of School Board Operation* (New York: Bureau of Publications, Teachers College, Columbia University, 1958).

Remmlein, Madaline Kinter, *School Law* (New York: McGraw-Hill Book Company, Inc., 1950), chap. 3.

# Principal-Personnel Relationships

# 4

## PROBLEM SITUATIONS

What would you do in each of the following situations? Analyze each in terms of questions raised at the beginning of Chapter 3 (page 56).

CASE A

Mrs. A is a fifth grade teacher who is well liked by the pupils. The principal believes she is a competent teacher. She works easily and with no apparent tension. Mrs. A is working toward a B.S. degree in Education and has almost completed the degree requirements.

The principal received his fifth complaint yesterday from another parent. The general tenor of each is that the teacher lacks judgment and tact in remarks she has made to the parents. Mrs. A is alleged to have repeated information and odd bits of conversation that were presumed confidential.

When called into the principal's office for a conference, Mrs. A said that she felt that she understood and seemed repentant. However, the principal felt that before too long a time another aspect of the problem would cause the office telephone to ring again.

CASE B

All seniors of Country Day High School were cautioned to return from their senior trip by means of transportation provided by the school. Mr. C, the class sponsor, "made a deal" with the top-honors girl, who was to make the graduation address, that she might return with another girl and two boys in a private automobile. Part of the arrangement was that neither the girl's father nor the school principal was to know about the plan.

On the trip back home the car in which the four students were riding collided with a gasoline truck. The girl who made the "deal" was seriously injured. The day following, Mr. *C* was called to the principal's office at 7:45 A.M., following a telephone call the principal had received from the father.

## Case C

Two boys were "discovered" matching coins in a small room adjoining the school lunchroom. Miss *H* reminded the two boys that school board regulations specifically stated that "gambling" in any form was not permitted on any property owned by the school system and that offenders would be sent home, temporarily suspended from school.

One of the two boys involved, with a previous record of rule infraction, left the school premises directly. His father called the school principal to complain within fifteen minutes after getting his son's message at his office. The second boy went to the principal to inform him that neither of his parents was at home, but that his pal went home. The principal asked the clerk to ring Miss *H* directly.

## Case D

Miss *P*, the principal of Parks School, was concerned about a first grade teacher. It seems that she had lost status in the community through an incident involving slapping a child. The teacher denied the incident, but a mother claimed to have "witnessed the act."

The teacher had encouraged the mother to visit the room without having "signed in" at the office. The mother called several other parents to arrange a meeting of protest, to which meeting the principal was invited. No invitation was extended to the teacher in question.

The occasions are many where an employee and principal have opportunities to establish firm relationships. There are, consequently, opportunities for misunderstandings to develop. The principal can give the employee the impression he thinks he is a "clock-watcher" who is not interested in doing a satisfactory job. The employee may get the impression from the administration that "they think" he is not contributing to the life of the community in which he lives and works. The employee may have received two notices from the principal about the need to formulate a plan for his self-improvement. The teacher may blame the principal for having stood in the way of the teacher's making a significant contribution to the teaching profession within the past year. A teacher may feel guilty about not being able to name any tangible accomplishments in improving the quality of his service. He may not be proud to be a teacher and may let his principal know it by word and deed.

## The Principal as Teacher

Why have teachers and principal, in too many instances, grown apart? Why do they have such different conceptions of each other's role in the school system? There are no easy answers. It would help, though, if the employee thought of the principal as a teacher, with all that this implies—regardless of whether the employee thinks the particular person merits the title.

Because of differences in outlook, teachers have tended to set themselves apart from the principal. Legal and ethical problems have thus arisen which would not have been nearly so perplexing had this dichotomy not been fixed in the thinking of teachers. The concept "principal" has meant for one teacher promoted to that position that he be responsible for "discipline cases." For another the term has meant "head teacher," and so he has assumed a full load of classroom work in addition to doing "extra duties" like reporting on attendance, distributing supplies, and checking on the general condition of school facilities from time to time. For a third it has meant his being a full-time supervisor of instruction.

The relationships between employees and principal—whatever title he may happen to hold—are the province of the present chapter. The first half of the chapter is devoted to some of the legal relationships that affect employee and principal. The second half points out some of the employee's relationships to administrators that are essentially ethical in nature. The materials show that what ethical conduct is considered to be is determined by many factors. One such is the tradition of the teaching profession itself. In the school, ethics begin where legal provisions leave off. When the professional worker acts or keeps from acting, not only legal compulsions but also professional obligations govern his choices.

## LEGAL ASPECTS

The legal aspects of the relationship of the employee to the school principal are varied. To serve as a framework for comment, a teacher's relationships will be discussed with reference to assignment to a particular job, the program of instruction, records and record keeping, rules and regulations, and exertion of authority or "chain of command." First, some comments are in order concerning the role of the principal.

## The Principal's Job

There is confusion not equaled elsewhere in the public school system about the duties required of the school principal. The vital instructional phases of his duties are sometimes not comprehended by teachers. They see and comprehend merely the routine duties. They misconceive or fail to see the major role that the law imposes upon the principal—that of being the "professional head of the school."

Teachers who regard the work of the principal as largely clerical in nature look upon administration, not as the necessary means to accomplish the school's purposes, but as largely routine business. They make the unfortunate distinction between administration and teaching. Such a notion stems in part from the conception, based on first-hand experience, that the job of the school principal is one primarily of mechanics, with most of his working day consumed by the application of this technique or that device to specific tasks and situations. The concept held is that of the principal being guided by a "recipe" book to which he turns for answers.

Too often employees have been witnesses to or participants in "futile conferences" or "meetings packed with trivia." The principal gave the employees the impression that he believed all activities were important and that the principal must be "in action" regarding all of them.

When the real duty of the principal is clear to teachers, they more readily see the need for a different budget of time. They see that the task of the school administrator is that of helping school employees carry out the educational will of the state legislature.

## The Teacher's Job Assignment

Teachers may be assigned to a particular position or grade level with Principal X. Later on, the principal may be called upon to inform a teacher that the position no longer exists and that the work load as previously outlined needs modification.

If the changed assignment for the teacher is one for which he is qualified, and if it does not materially affect the working conditions, the courts have held that the new assignment will be considered reasonable. It must be accepted by the employee, since job assignment is within the discretion of school officials who are charged by law to provide as efficient an instructional program as they know how.

Incidentally, in some localities the teacher is still selected by local authorities, not primarily on the advice and approval of the principal. Sometimes there is pressure on the principal to see that a teacher is employed who does not altogether meet the state standards governing such employment.

**Programs of Instruction**

The statutes of the several states say much about the program of instruction of the public schools. The responsibility for the "on the job" program of instructional improvement rests with the principal. It must be organized and conducted along lines approved by the school-system superintendent. The superintendent usually has charge of the over-all inservice program together with the meetings of principals, supervisors, and teachers that the program demands. Principals and employees are supposed to assist in the conduct of the work as they may be directed. Usually a teacher must attend inservice classes and help prepare materials that may be requested.

The principal is usually asked to hold, at regular intervals, meetings of the teachers for the discussion of educational matters. These are in addition to required attendance at the regular conferences and special meetings called by the superintendent. No excuse for absence from such meetings is usually allowed other than that which justifies absence from regular teaching sessions.

The principal's credential ordinarily stipulates that he is qualified to devote his professional energies to the supervision of instruction in the school, doing actual teaching when necessary. The principal who is not, or cannot be, aware of some of the limitations of teachers regarding improvement of instruction falls short of his legal duty as the school principal. In fact, teachers presume the principal knows appropriate methods of instruction. Teachers can expect the principal to help them discover and use new knowledge.

The principal is supposed to discuss with teachers the teaching he has observed, offering constructive criticism. It is often the responsibility of a teacher, following a supervisory visit, to consult with the principal concerning the nature of the supervisor's report. Whenever requested, the teacher is supposed to confer with the supervisor also.

Teachers have the duty to cooperate with the school principal in order to explore effective methods of instruction, school organization, and school government. They have the legal duty to teach all the required subjects as well as their teaching competency permits. Daily Bible reading may be required of teachers, as it is in some states. Where such statutes are operative, the school principal must see that regular reports are submitted showing that such provision of the state school law has been complied with. The principal is sometimes asked to supervise the activity to see that it is carried out properly.

Teachers are obliged not to replace basal books with those appearing on a supplementary list or lists. Choices as far as teachers go are limited to the textbooks adopted by the state board of education (or comparable body) which have been placed on approved lists in the school office. A teacher is supposed to display in the classroom, on appropriate days, placards of temperance and "law and order." In the City of Baltimore, Maryland, teachers should plan "appropriate patriotic exercises" as a part of the general opening exercises of the school or the class.[1] In a "deep-South" state, teachers are to plan special exercises to observe special days. Ranging from Uncle Remus Day to the birthday of Crawford W. Long (a pioneer in anesthesia research), nine days in all are to be observed by appropriate exercises.[2]

Any sectarian propaganda of whatever nature is debarred from being used in the public schools. Any teacher who directly or indirectly, in any manner whatever, attempts to disseminate propaganda within the school is liable to dismissal after a hearing and trial finding him guilty of the act.

[1] *Rules of the Board of School Commissioners* (Revised to September 1, 1944), Department of Education, Baltimore, Maryland, p. 111.

[2] Eugene Cook (ed.), *Georgia School Laws* (Atlanta: State Department of Education, 1955), p. 72. Part III, entitled "School Year, Scholastic Month, and Special Days," includes Title 32-1503 of the School Code which stipulates what special days are to be observed by the "law abiding teacher."

## Records and Record Keeping

Besides the areas of teacher assignment and the program of instruction, a third category of responsibility involves the teaching employee in legal relationships with the principal. This category is the keeping of accurate school records, an obligation which neither the employee nor the principal can legally shed. For his own protection and professional well-being, a teacher should know that the school principal must submit required reports periodically. Many are requested of the principal by the superintendent, his associates, and supervisors of instructional areas and special services.

For his part, a teacher must keep accurately all types of records required of him by the building principal. He is obliged to abide by regulations of the board regarding reporting and to follow directions from the principal about proper completion of printed forms. Oftentimes this noninstructional chore consumes much time and effort.

Quite specific duties concerning records and reports fall to the principal at the time of the opening and organization of a new term. However, in many of the "paper work" details, teachers and principals must share responsibility for completion. One such "joint task" is the preparation of instructions for new employees regarding school routine. Others include reporting of class size on appropriate blanks, reporting of homeroom or grade enrollments, and tallying of pupils who live outside the school district for compilation of tuition fees. Assignment of clothing space, of groups to the appropriate lunch period, and of assembly seats are tasks accomplished by the office with teacher assistance.

Teachers usually assist in preparing requests for room or grade changes. They often help prepare grade lists or schedule cards. They also help to check health records for vaccination certificates and birth records.

At the start of a new school term, the principal needs from teachers requests for textbooks, equipment for class use, and supplies. Before the term has progressed very far, the principal's office has need of "residence data" about each pupil enrolled. Seating charts for grades and class sections should be available so that supply teachers can have a basis for making reports in a teacher's absence. In a school of appreciable size, instructions must be prepared regarding traffic flow, "excused absences," and "lost and found" articles.

The permanent record of attendance must be maintained at least on a weekly basis if error is to be checked easily. Usually teachers must transfer daily attendance data to the permanent record at the close or beginning of each school week. Accuracy here is vital. In addition to their use as a basis for the district's procuring financial aid from the state, the attendance reports are legally admissible as evidence in court. Individual reports from teachers are combined and used by the principal to make the master report to the superintendent's office.

Teachers help to enforce the state compulsory school laws when they make their report of violators to the office of the principal. In extreme instances, teachers would notify the parent or guardian of a pupil who is truant. Notification is sometimes required to be in writing. The case can then be picked up by the attendance officer.

Teachers must keep a record of the scholastic standing of pupils under their instruction. From such records they are required to report, at stipulated intervals, to parents of the pupils. At other times the principal may require special notices from teachers to "go home" to the parents. A teacher must see to it that pupil personnel records are returned to the appropriate files after being consulted.

A teacher has a duty, along with the principal, to keep the kind of records about pupils that support a plan of guidance. With accurate data available, a teacher has "proof" of the presence of academic and personal problems. Such records may indicate to the principal the need for organization of special classes with the school system. The statutes of some states require teachers to make a report to the principal of pupils the teachers consider "not educable" or "feeble-minded." The superintendent can then refer such pupils to appropriate welfare agencies.

Unquestionably, the principal and employee should get information to "the public" about the amount of money involved in education locally and state-wide. All adult citizens who are employed or "earning dividends" pay some taxes. Employees should be able to tell where school funds come from, how they are spent, and why the local school district makes the financial effort that it does. They must have "the facts" for such explanation. They can learn about the costs of operating the schools today as compared with even a decade ago, about the costs involved in comparable systems, and about the amount of money that is expended for "instructional costs."

The need for the collection and accounting of moneys taken up during the school day (and night, too) can be understood better by the teacher if he has such a background and if he is aware of some of the varieties of funds that prevail in the average public school. In a school with the "average number" of out-of-class activities going on, teachers must spend considerable time and effort in taking up money. The office may receive funds from fifteen or twenty different sources, such as:

cafeteria and teachers' lunchroom;
school drives;
nonresident fees;
school store;
publications;
athletics;
library fines and contributions;
school accessories;
workbooks and other supplies;
school trips;
book replacements;
social activities;
insurance for pupils;
pictures;
saving stamp program;
school bank;
P.T.A. funds;
commencement funds;
awards;
postage;
professional dues.

Both teachers and principal need to maintain a careful accounting of all funds by means of some receipt system. Some additional sources of school moneys are:

fines;
gifts;
cotton or corn or strawberry picking;
P.T.A.;
taxes;
musicals and school plays;
carnivals;
athletic events;

vending machines;
lunchroom;
fees;
school store;
school sales (pictures, paper, and so on).

To keep track of funds and not permit "bookkeeping" alone to swamp the school, employees and principal should see that all funds collected by the school are deposited in one or at most two accounts. The teacher in charge of a special activity should receive a receipt for money deposited in the name of the club or activity. Payments for bona fide charges are made by check so that strict accounting of public funds is possible.

"Petty cash" funds are usually not permitted. Such funds are made up of loose cash, from which selected personnel may draw to cover miscellaneous expenditures as those connected with instructional or welfare activities. To be on the "safe" side regarding school funds, employees and principal should agree on some total-school bookkeeping system. The school treasurer should be bonded. A reputable agency should audit the "books" periodically to provide protection and give evidence of "good faith."

In the last analysis, it is the principal who is charged with accurate reporting of school moneys. He must use prescribed forms and proceed according to instructions laid down by the business department of the central office. Care must be exercised all the way to see that "no waste" occurs where tax funds are involved. The board assures the public that proper accounting is made whether funds are derived from taxes directly or from special drives or nonclass activities. All such funds are school funds—state funds.

Another obligation which employees share with the principal is care of school property. The board imposes upon the principal responsibility for the proper care and use of school facilities. The teacher's duty is to urge pupils to protect property so that the need for repairs will be kept at a minimum. All employees can assist in clean-up campaigns on desks, rooms, and locker spaces to reduce the hazard of fire and disease and thereby comply with state codes and local ordinances.

Before the time for renewal of contracts, the principal has the duty to make reports regarding the professional performance of teachers. The "rating" reports serve as one basis for contract renewal or nonrenewal. The record determines in part whether tenure is to be earned. Also, the record provides "evidence" at a hearing in case a tenure teacher is charged with incompetency.

Evaluation of teaching performance depends upon the keeping of adequate records. Details regarding the probationary period of the teacher are governed by policies of the board. The mechanics are generally the responsibility of the superintendent who is controlled by those policies.

Where rules and regulations require that a teacher be given "notice" of his rating, there would appear to be no problem. However, the phrase, "as the law requires," is capable of misinterpretation. The area of teacher evaluation is one laden with emotional implications rather than legal guides.

Record-keeping duties occur at the close of school also. Teachers must prepare lists of probable school failures, dropouts, transfers, and graduates. Records must be consulted to help determine the recipients of awards. Grade norms and class standings must be computed. Supply lists for the ensuing year must be prepared. Book lists and repair lists must be put in order. Pupil account books must be audited and filed away. Bills against pupils must be forwarded and collected. Mailing addresses of employees must be compiled. The book-check and other inventories must be completed. Diplomas and attendance certificates must be prepared. Teachers must check their official registers, straighten out other records and reports, and submit annual reports to the principal before they are officially "off for the year."

A list appears below of "typical" reports required of teachers in a Midwest high school:

1. A teacher must make out grade slips for the pupils in his classes and for the pupils in each homeroom represented in his classes.
2. He must fill out his daily schedule in triplicate, recording classes, number of pupils in each, grade level, average daily recitations, average number of pupils each day.
3. Four times a year he is required to fill out forms for each pupil in his homeroom whose parent or guardian works or lives on federal property.
4. Each semester he must fill out for the central office file a card for each pupil in his homeroom, giving the pupil's complete school schedule, his age, and the address, telephone number, and occupation of his parent.

5. Each semester he must fill out for the local P.T.A. a card for each homeroom pupil, furnishing the same information except the schedule.

6. He must collect and keep books on money turned in by pupils in his homeroom whose parents join the P.T.A., and turn in a form with each membership. He must transfer the data from these forms to a master form.

7. At the close of each semester, he must turn in to the central office a pass-fail report, on which is listed the number of boys and girls in each of his classes, the number that failed, and the percentage of failures in each sex in each class.

8. Approximately a month before the close of each semester, he must turn in to the office a tentative failure report similar to the final pass-fail report.

9. Each month he must count and sort the sales-tax stamps turned in by the students in his homeroom and fill out a form giving the number of stamps of each denomination and the total amount.

10. He must fill out a residence form for each homeroom pupil, which is to be checked against school boundaries for purposes of determining whether a tuition payment is due.

11. He must issue lunch-permit blanks to each pupil in his homeroom. These blanks are signed by the teacher and parent, then returned to the teacher, who must compile all the information on a master form. He must fill out lunch-permit cards, with a different color for each period, for individual students.

12. At the close of each semester he must compile information about lost books, giving the name of the book, its number, the pupil's name, and the money collected. He is required to keep this record up to date during the semester and is responsible for the money collected.

13. He must make out grade cards for each pupil in his homeroom.

14. He must keep daily attendance records in his homeroom.

15. He must fill out an enumeration report on a long office form, giving the pupil's name, sex, address, and parent's name.

16. He must fill out an age-grade distribution report on a long office form, giving the pupil's birthday, address, and parent's name.

17. He must fill out a new-pupil report on an office form.

18. He must collect money for gifts for needy families at Thanksgiving and Christmas.

19. He must fill out honor-roll certificates and perfect-attendance reports.

20. Each six weeks he must fill out reports on individual pupils to be submitted to a local service club.

21. He must make survey reports for redistricting of school boundaries.

22. He must fill out an absence-excuse form for a pupil when he

returns to school. Each class teacher is required to initial the excuse form as the pupil comes to his class. The excuse is returned to the homeroom teacher, who files it for future reference.

23. At the start of each semester he must fill out a form for each pupil in his homeroom who owes shop or art fees, collect the fees, and turn them in, together with a master form, to the office.

24. He must fill out a monthly report, giving the number of boys and girls in his homeroom, the numbers withdrawn and entered.

25. In the middle of each semester, when reorganization for the next semester is begun, he must fill out a form for each pupil in his homeroom, giving his complete schedule of subjects and the subjects he desires for the next semester. The teacher then tallies this information on a master form.

26. At the end of each semester, he must write in duplicate the complete schedule of each pupil for the new semester.

27. At the end of each semester, he must enter in ink on permanent record cards the grades, credits, and attendance record of each pupil in his homeroom.

28. Midway in each semester, he must fill out a permanent record of each pupil's personality and character traits and his out-of-class activities.

29. The teacher of a graduating homeroom has additional tasks: he must collect senior dues, fees for caps and gowns, and money for miscellaneous senior functions. These necessitate elaborate record keeping.[3]

## Rules and Regulations

Printed by-laws, rules, and regulations of a board of education of necessity cover many subjects pertaining to employee-principal relations. With little exception, regulations exist (1) regarding when employee is to report for duty, (2) describing what "faithfulness" to duty means, (3) prescribing care of pupils, (4) providing for discipline, (5) permitting or prohibiting use of corporal punishment, (6) regarding use of detention, (7) completing records and reports, (8) attending meetings and conferences, (9) notifying principal of anticipated absence from duty, (10) providing for leaving school during working hours, (11) specifying excuses

[3] Robert E. Jewett, "Why the Able Public-School Teacher Is Dissatisfied," *Educational Research Bulletin*, Vol. XXXVI, No. 7, College of Education, The Ohio State University, 1957, pp. 223-228.

needed for tardiness or absence, and (12) barring sectarian teaching in the classroom.

Information regarding such obligations can be obtained in several ways. Obviously, a teacher who can get to a copy of the board rules and regulations can read them. The principal can keep an up-to-date loose-leaf file in the office where sheets can be inserted regarding new regulations and from which old material can be removed when no longer applicable. At staff and at community meetings also, employees and principal can plan for discussions that show the essential role board rules and regulations play in giving rise to possible court action.

Despite access to "printed" rules and regulations, most persons, including employees and principal, need to be reminded of the weight of authority of local rules. Where statutes of the state are silent, the local rules and regulations are binding. Recall that the legislature may delegate to the local district the power to make rules and regulations. These legal prescriptions, resulting from the exercise of discretionary power, have the force and the effect of law. They are valid in every respect and must be kept in mind if legal involvement is to be avoided.

The duties, responsibilities, and restrictions seem quite formidable. Here will be considered only those rules which are the immediate concern to the school employee and his principal. In other words, leaves of absence for illness, bereavement, or for professional advancement are ordinarily beyond the scope of authority of the principal and employee. In addition, each has little real influence on such matters as pay during illness, salary deductions, or qualifications required for certain types of school jobs.

Many matters, though, impinge upon employee and principal in a direct way. Both he and the principal are to see that denominational propaganda of whatever nature is barred from the instructional program sponsored by the school, whether such activity occurs within the classroom or outside of it. A teacher who directly, or indirectly, disseminates such propaganda as a part of the school program subjects himself to dismissal, after a hearing wherein the teacher is found guilty of such act.

A teacher is not to tutor, coach, or teach any pupil for pay during the regular school term when such instruction is part of the regular school offerings. A teacher has the duty, according to most local policies, to consult with the principal concerning off-campus visits and to confer with other school personnel as designated by the principal. A teacher may be asked to submit any excuses for absence or tardiness (beyond a minimum number of minutes) that occurs in connection with school duties.

The requirement is usually in force that an employee is not to leave the school grounds before completion of his work-day without first notifying the principal. In some large school systems, a teacher must enter on the daily report blank that he has left the building before dismissal time. The principal is asked to record the reason for the early leaving. When a teacher expects to be absent from school duty for any reason, he is to contact the principal beforehand about the contemplated absence.

Even though the school program may be organized informally, a teacher is expected to participate in scheduled inservice programs of instruction. Such programs may be organized and conducted by the principal with or without approval from the superintendent. He must prepare such written comments as requested. A teacher may be required to attend all regular and called meetings and conferences. Excuses for absence from such meetings are allowed on the same bases that would justify absence from regular school sessions.

Sometimes the local regulations stipulate that detention of pupils in the elementary grades for more than thirty minutes after dismissal of school is not permitted except by written consent of the parent. A pupil in the high school who is not doing satisfactory work may be detained longer, usually for the length of one class period, in order that such pupil may receive help from the subject teacher. For disciplinary purposes, a pupil may be detained up to two periods after dismissal or may be required to report to the school for conference at a time set by the discretion of the principal and teacher. Teachers have the obligation to keep an accurate and permanent record of the attendance and scholastic standing of pupils under their instruction and shall make such special reports to the parent or guardian as may be necessary.[4]

Teachers are called upon to exercise a vigilant care over the conduct of pupils in the classroom, on the playground, on school-

[4] *By-Laws, Rules and Regulations of the Board of Education* (Atlanta, Georgia: Revised under Direction of the Rules Committee, November 11, 1952), p. 41.

connected trips, and, so far as is possible, while pupils are going to and returning home from school. A teacher is expected to supervise play periods. He is not to keep a child in from recess unattended without reporting such to the principal. A teacher is expected to act civilly to his pupils, requiring from them politeness, courtesy, and obedience to reasonable rules. A teacher is usually directed to aim at such discipline in the classroom as would be exercised by a judicious parent. He is not to engage in controversy and attempt disciplinary measures directed at one or several while in the presence of the whole class. In difficult cases, a teacher is to seek out the principal for advice and direction. Corporal punishment is permitted unless the local regulations or state statutes expressly prevent its use. In those systems where such punishment is not permitted, a teacher may employ it ordinarily when the parent or guardian of the child to be punished gives consent.

Whatever the means of punishment used, a teacher is cautioned against acting in anger. He must be fair and not inflict what the courts will say is "permanent injury." When trouble persists, the principal has the power to suspend a pupil from school. If a teacher complains of a pupil's persistent violation of school regulations, the pupil can be kept from attending school altogether. However, a pupil cannot be removed from school or suspended indefinitely without approval of the superintendent. Regulations usually require that notices of suspension be in writing, a copy going to the home and to the superintendent.

Yes, a teacher has the legal duty to maintain "good order and discipline" along with the principal. A teacher stands *in loco parentis* during the time the pupil is under the direct supervision of the school. This concept means that a teacher and principal do not need the consent of parent or guardian to mete out reasonable punishment upon the pupil for infractions of reasonable regulations.

In North Carolina, for instance, the School Code states that the teacher has the duty

> . . . to maintain good order and discipline in the school, to encourage temperance, morality, industry, and neatness; to promote health by frequent periods of recreation and exercise and to supervise play activities during recess.[5]

[5] Sections 115-144 of the *North Carolina School Code,* 1953.

The principal has the duty to see that teachers devote themselves exclusively to such duties—to instruction and care of pupils. A teacher is obliged to abide by rules made and enforced by the principal even though not necessarily adopted by the board of education. Any refusal by a teacher to accept duties that are connected with the program of the school may provide grounds for dismissal.

Besides management problems, a teacher has the duty to abide by the health regulations to protect children and associates. He must submit a health certificate before employment, usually through the principal's office. He is expected to make the minimum physical examination of each pupil at stated intervals and to enter data on appropriate medical records.

There are regulations affecting a teacher pertaining to the duplication of copyrighted materials. The principal is under some obligation to inform teachers about the legal danger involved in such a practice. A teacher can be helped to see that the term "book" in the copyright law includes bound volumes, pamphlets, leaflets, and even single sheets. The copyrighted materials are the exclusive possession of the owner, who decides what to reproduce, publish, and sell, and in what form.

Regulations and rules pertaining to use of school facilities and the building in general sometimes cause the principal and teacher some embarrassment. Principal and teacher should be familiar with any stipulations that may have been adopted by the board of education concerning the use of school facilities by outside groups. It is well, for each school, to have prepared a calendar of activities that are scheduled for the school year. After each activity has been entered, dates for recreational activities can be arranged. To these can be added requests from church and other community groups for after-school use of the building. Finally, there will be a few dates available on which to schedule events sponsored by "outsiders." If teacher or principal is confronted with a request from an "unknown" source, the school office can delay any response and schedule a school event before calling back to inform the party that the night requested is not available.

Rules and regulations govern teacher and principal. There is no escape. Employees do not have reason to be familiar with the details of many regulations. However, unless they know general policies, they act aimlessly and grope for answers to queries. A teacher should know the age at which a child may legally enter the public school and that a "shopping tour with mother" is not a good enough reason for absence. Employees should understand that a parent needs to telephone about illness and that visits from the attendance officer are warranted. A teacher should know the regulations about work permits, the age for lawful quitting of school, and what a "continuation" school is.[6]

## "Chain of Command" Concept

In terms of legal responsibility, the "chain of command" idea refers to the scope of authority exercised by persons in the series of positions that make up the educational "hierarchy." It refers to the kind and amount of authority—the right to command the actions of others—that can be exerted by "superiors" over "inferiors." In a typical local situation, the "chain" would be made up of these persons, listing them in the order of legal powers and duties: board of education (where members must act in concert), the superintendent of schools, school committee (if any), the principals, teachers, and the pupils.

The principal exerts legal authority over employees in many different ways. He exercises controls by means of (1) certain management or executive functions, (2) procedures, (3) activities pertaining to the instructional program, and (4) relations involving the school organization and other community agencies. To illustrate, the principal exerts authority by means of all the acts or processes required to make policies and procedures effective. He influences an employee when he permits decisions and behavior of persons to help accomplish the objectives of the school. He is the means by which pressure comes to teachers regarding instructional purposes, the range of activities for the curriculum, diagnostic services, instructional aids and methods. He must help employees keep perspective regarding the many auxiliary activities now directed by the public school and the demands made by agencies or authorities for other services.

[6] Ward G. Reeder, *The Fundamentals of Public School Administration* (New York: The Macmillan Company, 1951), chap. XIX.

## Position of the Principal

A question often arises that involves a teacher's right or his freedom to teach without being under the control of the principal. Can a teacher escape from being on the receiving end of the "chain of command"? It seems clear that the legal authority of the school principal extends over teachers in the classroom, to the extent that both the content and methods of instruction may be controlled.

From a purely legal viewpoint, a teacher may be cited by the principal for insubordination and be subject to dismissal by the board of education if he refuses to comply with reasonable requests of the principal. In legal theory, the principal is responsible for the total school program. It is he who must require that certain instruction be given in order to comply with local and state regulations. The courts have held rigidly to the theory that the type of control exercised by the principal over teachers must be both reasonable and necessary to the best interests of the school. His actions, at least visibly, must be without malice or bad faith.

Whether the principal acts in an authoritative manner, suggested by the "line" concept, and makes all assignments himself, or whether he employs a cooperative plan, the legal relationships between the principal and employee are the same. Regardless of the "method" of getting things done, the principal cannot relieve himself of the legal responsibility his position entails. Those duties which are implied by virtue of his position are "his" despite a temporary sharing of them with other personnel. He can be relieved of legal duties only on approval of the board of education through the superintendent. For example, the principal retains the responsibility for establishing and enforcing safety rules even though a teacher is assigned to carry out the provisions by setting up procedures by which pupil and teacher are to abide.

Whether the principal is merely the directing head of the school with full-time teaching duties or a full-time administrator, the legal relationship between principal and school employee is little different. The principal has been charged by the board of education, through the office of the superintendent, to carry out certain prescribed duties and assume responsibility in certain areas. He has the implied legal power to carry out these obligations. In theory, the principal stands in relation to the single school unit much as the superintendent does to the total school system.

The "chain of command" concept is real. The school principal can be asked by the superintendent to be in attendance at the schoolhouse at some given hour before other employees and pupils arrive. The principal is ordinarily requested to remain "on duty" throughout the total school day. He must notify the appropriate "central office" official if he leaves his post during regular school hours. The principal must comply with and follow detailed instructions regarding local school matters that come from the "Office of the Superintendent of Schools." The principal has little discretion when it comes to reporting to the proper authorities all matters requiring or deserving attention. He is the immediate and direct supervisor (or should be) of the custodian and his assistants.

## Position of the Teacher

It may appear, from a glance at the range of authority of the school principal, that the "poor" teacher is at the mercy of the principal and that he could be compelled to behave as the principal dictated. Of course, this is not the case. In fact, this description is rather far from the facts. A teacher is not held to be guilty of insubordination unless he actually fails to obey authority that is duly constituted.

A teacher can exclude a pupil from his classroom and refuse to instruct him if he is unruly and a menace to the welfare of other pupils and to the safety of the teacher's person. The courts have held that a teacher has this right even though the school principal feels otherwise. A teacher is thus protected legally, despite the fact that it is the principal who must formulate general rules for the discipline and the efficiency of the "learning environment" in the school.

In matters of general school control teachers are in a subordinate position to the principal. However, they are individuals with their own legal duties and responsibilities. When difficulties arise for teachers, it is the usual practice for the principal to come to the support and defense of the acts of teachers, at least before the patrons. However, the acts of a teacher are his own legal responsibility. Under no circumstances can he use as a defense that the principal or the board of education has sanctioned his conduct.

A teacher's place in the administrative hierarchy is one that precludes his working directly with the board of education. His contacts are indirect. All requests should be channeled through the office of the building principal, who in turn submits them to the superintendent for consideration. This dictum is sound regardless of the size of the school system or of the degree of familiarity between any one teacher and the superintendent. A teacher must not take upon himself the authority for managing the school. The responsibility is upon the principal's shoulders, placed there by the board of education. Teachers have been given no authority, either expressly or impliedly, to interfere with school management by the board of education or superintendent. The courts will not "imply" such a right. They will construe the duties of a teacher not to include meddling at the "top level" with the management responsibilities of school administrators.

Do not conclude from the foregoing discussion that the relationship of employer to employee exists between principal and other school employees. This is just clearly not the case. A teacher is subject to many supervisory controls by the principal, but he is still free in his professional status. A teacher acts without binding the school officials. A teacher is customarily an employee of the state in which he teaches, performing his teaching duties under authority granted him by the state by means of his license to practice his profession. He does not get his authority to teach or to discipline from the school principal, the superintendent, members of the board of education, or from the parents of the children he instructs. His authority stems from the state that issues him a teaching certificate.

## Merits of Delegation

Certain powers are delegated to the principal by the board through the superintendent. The principal retains the responsibility for seeing that the functions are carried out even though they have been "delegated." When the delegation of responsibility carries with it authority commensurate to do the job, legal pitfalls will be fewer and results superior.

The "chain of command" is the means of getting a job done. The hierarchy of positions enables persons and things to be organized so that purposes may be accomplished effectively but within the legal framework provided.

# ETHICAL ASPECTS

A discussion of ethical aspects of the relationship between school employees and principal is fraught with difficulty—for several reasons. First, there seems to be little distinction made in the literature and in practice between matters that are clearly ethical in nature—based on moral considerations—and those related to the professional competency of the employee.

The professional abilities of a teacher or principal should not depend on ethics. Competency should be approached through pre-service and inservice educational activities. Sometimes it is difficult to label a specific improper action the result of ignorance, immaturity, carelessness and indifference, or poor judgment. The stress in this section will be upon those actions of a teacher and principal which result from doing less than is needed and expected when professional insight in and of itself is not the basic point in question.

Just as competency itself is hardly within the realm of ethics, as such, the decisions of a teacher and principal about better ways of accomplishing educational goals are hardly within the province of ethics but in the realm of educational philosophy. A board of education may prescribe, within a code of ethics, that the school system should build its own philosophy and then insist that the philosophy be democratic or otherwise. Would this not indicate merely inconsistency? There seems to be no evidence of "unethical" conduct. Again, to require the principal to adopt personnel practices that he may dislike seems to violate principles of sound educational administration. The requirement does not, however, seem to indicate any failure to uphold the standards of ethics.

A second reason for difficulty in examining the ethical aspects of a teacher-principal relationship is that much has been said and written in contention about what *is* or *is not* included within the scope of "professional ethics." A teacher and principal have little tangible ground for agreement, should serious trouble arise. For some, untidy personal appearance is an ethical problem. For others, ethics treats more properly of the nature of human actions in terms of their moral implications.

Third, some discussions of what the "ethical" teacher or administrator is like amount to little more than "sentimental noise." The exhortations, admonitions, and lists of seraphic behaviors and wholesome attitudes make one "real glad" that he is just "an ordinary kind of guy" with at least one parking ticket to his credit.

Within these limitations, or despite them, ethical relationships between teacher and principal exist and persist. The categories for discussion are: (1) exercise of leadership, with some emphasis upon participation by teachers in school government and other factors contributing to high morale; (2) misconceptions of the principal's role with emphasis upon behaviors "typical" of an ineffective teacher; (3) the matter of disloyalty; and (4) problems of recommendations of a teacher by the principal.

## Exercise of Leadership

The principal is the key person of the "school team" since it is he, and not board members nor superintendent, who should support a teacher in his important task of instruction. The "big sister" and "buddy" arrangements are essentially devices for assisting the principal to help a teacher enter upon his teaching responsibilities with a minimum number of tension-provoking episodes. Orientation to teaching and continued professional support of the experienced teacher are responsibilities of the principal.

### Creating a Climate of Understanding

The school climate in which a teacher works depends, to some considerable degree, upon the principal's way of perceiving his job. If, for example, the principal believes and acts on the premise that a teacher and he have joint responsibilities for raising the quality of school offerings (all learning activities), a teacher would tend to be encouraged to seek out the counsel of the school leader on professional and even personal matters. Teachers thus have the opportunity to develop into personal and professional assets of their neighborhoods and school systems as their principals ask questions about the many problems facing teachers, always directing attention away from personalities, focusing on the immediate problem at hand.

Evidence of understanding of teachers' concerns, both professional and personal, *and* extending help will provide the principal
with "tools" for helping teachers over rough spots. Such thoughtful-
ness tends to build confidence within a teacher regarding his capa-
bilities. The principal with this view of his role as leader may well
be instrumental in keeping within the teaching ranks those who,
without such access to encouragement, might find "going it alone"
too difficult a job. If he has maintained a close contact with a
content area as well as deep interest in the broad problems of
school administration, the principal can speak the language of a
teacher and communicate in terms of specific and timely illustrations. This kind of leader will be sought out for "thinking things
through" with a teacher.

An additional perception of the effective school leader would
undoubtedly be that of the importance of helping a teacher clarify
his notions of the function of knowledge and of the ways in which
humans change their behaviors. The principal would be anxious to
help produce an "atmosphere" on the job in which it would not be
difficult for a teacher to employ devices of instruction that are more
nearly consistent with the purposes of the school than some
already "much in vogue." Using varied classroom procedures is
but one element. A teacher who accepts the sponsorship of a student council where pupils are chosen by their classmates and faculty
to participate in school government could help pupils realize that
"democratic procedures" involve clear-headed choices among alternatives, not going in any one direction merely because a majority
voted its support.

The exercise of leadership—with all that this concept embraces—
has as its goal the finding of opportunities for teacher and principal
to develop the educational environment. The principal who plans
for such accomplishment will have to divide labor, to make assignments wisely so that no one employee is overburdened or saddled
with activities unsuited to him. His office will have to be cleared of
some of the daily procession of well-meaning persons who knock on
his door. He must plan for wise use of employee school hours.

The school leader generally earns tax dollars over and above those
of a teacher, and in return he is to help himself and the staff visualize
the purposes for which the public school exists. He performs this

service in order that the public which "foots the bill" gets what it thinks it is purchasing.

## Importance of Operating Procedures

A teacher deserves to work in a school where the leader has mastered the purely technical matters of organization and the processes of administration. It is then, and only then, that the school principal is actually able to offer assistance to teachers who have the obligation to help children solve their school and nonschool problems. Such a principal can be depended upon to have the time and energies for building rapport with teachers. He is more likely to make pertinent suggestions to teachers when trivia are under control, so that they can grasp the organization of the school unit and the system itself. A teacher would thus be encouraged and reciprocate by suggesting ways and means of carrying out school duties.

The principal who exerts such leadership will, as a part of his obligation, help a teacher understand the rules and regulations that affect teachers—because he is a teacher. Of course, teachers have the moral obligation to see that the regulations are abided by openly and fairly. Teachers should seek no special favors of the administration so that in effect some colleagues are discriminated against.

A regulation generally in force is one against outsiders' contacting teachers during school hours to solicit nonschool-connected business. Such a policy may seem onerous, but actually it is devised to protect teachers from pressures that could result in private advantage for the outsider. A teacher should scrupulously help the principal maintain the policy of refusing permission to anyone who wants to speak with a school employee on school premises, except on business directly pertaining to the school or to the personal problems of a teacher that result from his employment as a teacher. At such times, a little patience goes a long way in helping others see the "whys and wherefores" of school policies.

## Defining Professional Conduct

The principal and teacher should include in their concept of "supervision" the matter of distinguishing scrupulous from unscrupulous professional conduct. Surely, a teacher shoulders the burden of acting wisely and making sensible choices among alternatives. However, the school leader must help a teacher interpret problems as situations arise. He can delegate to no other the responsibility for perceiving in a clear manner the differences between unethical and ethical behavior, between unprofessional and professional conduct. With considered attention, both teacher and principal will be able to evolve a guideline whereby the incompetent performance of the teacher can be separated in discussions from the acts that may not be "professionally right and befitting."

A teacher and principal need also to seek out differences between conduct that falls below "ethical" standards as such and that which should be described merely as "not desirable." Should a violation of an ethical precept by a teacher justify the meting out of penalties? If so, why exactly? By whom or what? Where?

A teacher and principal operating within the "code of ethics" have the task of creating professional climate in the community. A teacher needs the professional support of the principal. However, they and the public must understand what support entails and under what conditions it may have to be withheld. A code should assume agreement between teacher, principal, and the "taxpayer" regarding the basic policy and main purposes of "their school system." Otherwise, only confusion results from varied interpretations as to what is meant by such comments as "He wasn't professional," or "She didn't act properly in that situation." Should a teacher expect protection from the administrator against adverse but perhaps unjustified judgments by parents, community or business leaders, or other members of the profession.

At the very minimum, a code of ethics should commit teacher and principal to the broadest concern for pupils, to loyalty to the board of education and its employees, and to one's own professional insights. The code should act as an important element in upholding morale, in committing human resources to advantages gained from having carefully planned goals, and to gaining cooperation with nonschool groups to provide improved conditions of living for children and adults.

### Teacher Participation in Policy-Making

Evidence of the performance of a "good leader" (who perceives leadership as "helping to get a teacher wholesomely concerned with improvement of instruction") is the measure and level of participation by a teacher with the principal in arriving at decisions about things that matter a great deal. Usually, "way down deep," a teacher earnestly wants to work in a school where the faculty member shares wisely in formulating local policies.

The rewards of participation, even when not as fruitful as would be desired, include reduced frustrations and diminished feelings of resentment. A teacher has a chance to "shine" and demonstrate skills and points of view that may contribute substantially to school betterment. Friction is lessened when teacher and principal have established understandings, in terms of a working agreement, about the kinds of policy decisions that should be those solely of teachers, those which should be largely within the province of the administration (for accepted reasons), and those which should lie within the realm where joint action by teacher and administration is feasible and desirable.

Policies and their consequences are not "ethical matters" as such. However, the policies themselves are only secondary; it is arrival at understanding through participation in decision-making that is first in importance. This is not to say that the decision itself can be ignored, but that the quality of decisions reached about policy can and will be raised when those involved lay stress upon the means as well as the ends. Even lesser ends may be justified when those who participate in decisions know all will take them honestly and seriously.

Chances are good that a teacher who has confidence in the skills and judgment of the principal regarding his job will give wholehearted support to "school projects." For him, faculty meetings become opportunities for himself and others to solve professional problems. Occasional "griping" may well be limited, under such circumstances, to the lounge and for times when the teacher "just wants to let off steam." A teacher who "pulls rather than pushes" is likely to believe in "his school" and say so to all who will tarry long enough to listen.

For many reasons, then, a teacher who is extended the chance to take a regular and active part in formulating school policies tends to be a booster of the school and the system and of teaching. He is "professionally minded," seeking out opportunities for raising and sustaining morale. He is a part of the school, with first-hand knowledge of plans and problems, successes and failures.

Within a school where a teacher is welcomed as a partner in making decisions affecting the welfare of teachers, the "teachers' club" can flourish and contribute much. It can be a "safety valve," through which a teacher in one school can be provided with the opportunity to speak frankly about "the administration" of other schools. Properly organized and managed, such an organization of teachers can help provide teacher satisfactions and by-products that pervade many facets of teacher-principal relationships.

## Teacher Morale

Evidence of the performance of a "good leader" was the level and measure of teacher participation in the decision-making process of school administration. When morale is noticeably high, teachers have responded well to the exercise of leadership by the principal. A teacher participates willingly in jobs facing "our school" when morale is high.

The school where teacher morale is high is clearly distinguishable from one where morale is low by the opportunities provided for teachers to share in shaping significant decisions that are within the province of the individual school unit to control. There seems to be ample evidence that teachers want to assume professional responsibility.[7] In reports of research, effective teachers encouraged their principals, not only to formulate statements of teaching effectiveness, but also to defend these in terms of definite and understandable ideas. Teachers are reported to have requested that the principal keep a folder of materials to point up the administrator's evaluation of the teachers' effectiveness as professional workers.

Stated in other terms, there is an exceedingly close connection between a teacher's judgment of the leadership exerted by the principal and the extent of a teacher's satisfaction in working in the

[7] This proposition is supported by studies undertaken by the Cooperative Project in Educational Administration, supported by the Kellogg Foundation.

given school and system. When the principal is considered to be "a fellow worker," the teacher tends to have his expectations fulfilled. His morale soars. When disappointed, teacher morale takes a "nose dive." [8]

A teacher's very professional existence depends upon high morale. A professionally alive teacher believes that it is within the scope of responsibility of the principal to raise the level of group operation, to stimulate attainment of ideals, to promote the unity and the solidarity of the teaching corps. Then, what is "morale"?

The term means many different things. To one it is a mental attitude of an employee that leads him to subordinate his personal desires when the good of the school seems to ask for it. To another it is a disposition on the part of school personnel to behave in ways that contribute to the progress for which the school exists.[9]

However its definition may be worded, morale is a vital force enabling teacher and principal to reckon with the "two-way interest" of which Tead speaks.[10] One interest involves the person's integrity or selfhood. The second pertains to the person's effective relation to his total surroundings. Tead stresses the fact that these two fundamental concerns are closely interdependent. As a human being, a teacher desires to stand well in his own eyes and also in the eyes of those whose approval he values.

Thus, satisfactions for teachers are being sought in two directions simultaneously—the inner and the outer. The choices made in terms of each direction and the balance effected must differ, of course, from person to person, from one situation to another. For example, the artist, the recluse, or the individualist teacher may tend to place higher value on his subjective experiences when asked to make a decision than would the more outgoing person. Whatever the wellsprings of action, teachers possess a selfhood for which they feel solely accountable and which they must strive to cherish, defend, and build. When this inner integrity is supported by social sanction and the commendation of others, teachers possess

[8] Francis S. Chase, "Professional Leadership and Teacher Morale," a Midwest Administration Center Study in *The Administrator's Notebook,* Vol. I, No. 8, 1953.

[9] American Association of School Administrators, *Staff Relations* (Washington, D.C.: National Education Association, Thirtieth Yearbook, 1955), p. 15.

[10] Ordway Tead, *The Art of Administration* (New York: McGraw-Hill Book Company, Inc., 1951), p. 45.

a high measure of well-being. The "morale" is at a truly high level. / Further evidence of high morale within a school are the com-/ments of a teacher who supports school decisions and policies outside of school as well as inside. There is no "blind" loyalty but a predisposition to help others "see" school conditions and problems and to make intelligent allowances for shortcomings. The teacher is careful to save "gripes" for staff meetings inside the school where teacher, colleagues, and principal can analyze and weigh points and adopt a course of action that will solve rather than produce problems.

The typical working day of a "high-morale" teacher is characterized by a willingness to support school rules and regulations. He believes that enforcement of general school rules is his responsibility, whether in the corridors, lunchroom, and playgrounds or in class periods. He submits reports on time, based on data that are not "doctored up" to appear to be something they are not. Such an employee requisitions school supplies and equipment with a definite need in mind.

Defined operationally, duty imposes upon a teacher the obligation of conducting school business through proper channels. He shows that he understands "line organization" to be his pattern, channeling the flow of control through the school office. The thoughtful teacher transacts his school business with the principal when this procedure is at all possible. He contacts the principal first because on his shoulders rest different kinds and degrees of responsibility and authority. He is "one notch" above on the line. A teacher speaks first with the principal about affairs affecting a pupil because it is right to do so. A teacher would hardly ever go directly to the superintendent or to a parent about a serious problem without first attempting at least to get support from the principal. A teacher cooperates with the superintendent and board best when he first seeks out the help of the principal with whom he has been officially assigned to work.

Duty thus conceived and carried into practice will find a teacher saying that "Our principal is understanding and fair. He listens to our problems." Or, "The principal is aware of my work. . . . He understands children and teaching problems." It is likely to be deemed a privilege by a teacher and the administrator to work in a school where "best efforts" count for something.

### Some Misconceptions Concerning Leadership

Several thousand teachers in one state, it has been alleged, quit the teaching profession one year. One survey seemed to indicate that inadequate salaries and overwork headed the list of teachers' reasons for not returning to the classroom. In addition, the teachers added that too many demands were made on their out-of-class time, that too many after-school meetings were held, and that too-heavy teaching loads were required of them. However, the third most frequently listed reason for quitting teaching, as stated in the replies, was attitudes between the administrator and teacher resulting in friction. Especially scored as "typical" attitudes were those described by such words as dictatorial, undemocratic, insincere, and "busybody."

### The "Authoritative" Administrator

A "directive-writing" administrator may insist, for complex and related reasons, that he alone must adjust the program of teachers when he spots trouble and that he alone must change the school schedule when things "aren't going smoothly." In this climate teachers labor under tension that militates against the achievement of even minimum mental health aims. A teacher is literally caught between adhering unthinkingly to rules promulgated by the administrator or suffering the torment that accompanies not knowing "just what's coming next."

A principal who conceives of his job of administration as "running the show" will be dubbed many things by many people. In addition to the burden such an "operator" adds to the load of all teachers in the school, he is unprofessional and unethical. If his manner and attitude suggest that things are fine as they are and that "you leave if you think you'd be happier someplace else," the principal is not fulfilling his job at even the minimum level of professional standards. Even worse, he may be the very person who is most critical of a teacher who "doesn't provide for individual differences."

The dictatorial administrator may even talk democratic procedures while acting on the premise that the opinions of teachers are naive at best. A committee assignment for a teacher is then mere "window dressing." A teacher is duped, together with the public, since the work of committees can lead to no change in policy under such a "system." A teacher must be confused when asked to give up energy and time for meetings when he knows that the principal has decisions "in the bag" before the committee even has its first meeting scheduled.

Under such circumstances a teacher gets a false picture of what the function of a principal is, of where leadership actually begins, and of how staff morale can be built so that professional obligations —rights and privileges—are accepted as normal procedure by members of the school team.

A teacher who feels that professional competence depends, at least in part, on feelings of security and satisfaction in his work must be critical of a principal who literally operates at the level of the "superdisciplinarian." Persistent thwarting of the will to be recognized as important and "worth something" is one factor for a teacher's falling into attitudes and habits deemed by the principal as unethical. When ability is not recognized, much less capitalized upon, the attitude of "it's no use" catches hold quickly.

A teacher with such an administrator has a "problem principal" on his hands—or, more correctly, a principal with problems. For, to the principal, threat to the teacher is imaginary. A mental hygienist would tell him that the importance of threat cannot be overemphasized. Some authorities have seen threat as *the* basic factor in maladjustment.[11] According to this view, the maladjusted teacher is he who is attempting to deal with threatening perceptions. "And the most threatening perceptions with which people must deal are those which relate to their concepts of themselves." [12]

A teacher who has to work with a principal who acts as though he were happy only when suggestions coincide with his perceptions, and who knows what is good "for all people, at all times, and in all places," will find opportunities to retaliate against the "headmaster." Not only will any spark of interest be extinguished, but teachers

[11] D. Snygg and A. W. Combs, *Individual Behavior* (New York: Harper and Brothers, Publishers, 1949).

[12] Robert E. Bills, *About People and Teaching* (Lexington: College of Education, University of Kentucky, Bulletin of the Bureau of School Service, 1955), p. 11.

will "get back at" the principal in a hundred and one ways. Not ethical? Of course not!

If interest in teaching (as the principal defines it) should wane, unethical conduct will not necessarily result. Continued frustration, however, may produce an atmosphere in which unethical acts may develop. The first little irritations may eventually loom large to both teacher and principal. A teacher may become the victim of an administrator who "stalks about the building" with his "small black book," noting his impressions of unwise use of instructional time, of neglect of duty, or of misdeeds, trespasses of the code, and insubordination. A conference is doomed to failure under such tactics. The concepts "unethical" or "unreasonable" can mean little save what one says they shall mean.

Aggression may beget aggression. A teacher may receive a memorandum in which the charge of "unprofessional conduct" is made by the principal. As a reprisal, the teacher may be forbidden to see parents during school time or to accept an office, the principal hoping that he can thereby contain the "ambitious" employee. Feelings against such a principal accumulate and a teacher "gets sympathy" outside of school. Such negativism can and does damage teacher effectiveness and the cause of education generally.

## Support of Groups or Organizations

In addition, there are subtler ways in which a teacher can be made to suffer as a result of poor leadership. A teacher may have pressure put on him to join this or that organization. If only inadvertently, the "we're a 100 per cent" administrator must trample upon some pretty important values. Perhaps a teacher who cares not to join a particular professional group should be charged with unethical conduct only when membership is considered, by board policy, to be a professional responsibility of all employed teachers.

A teacher and principal may be at odds regarding what groups or organizations their particular school should encourage or support by making teacher or parent leaders and facilities available. A hands-off attitude is bad. However, the "first come, first served" policy may help to encourage an unwieldy number of organizations to seek resources, eventually strangling the school program and dissipating staff time and energies.

A teacher and principal ought not support or favor one group over another unless such support is official board policy. A teacher must be careful that he does not encourage the principal to give support to secret or exclusive societies. There will be persons who allege that the attitudes and behaviors fostered by the groups are inimical to the values that the public school should champion. An obligation of both teacher and principal is to work out an out-of-class program that strengthens the purposes of the school and that is balanced as far as variety of pupil interests goes.

A teacher can expect that the principal will not misrepresent any condition within the school to him, a patron, or others. The principal's letters, reports, or other communications (oral and written) must be scrupulously fair. A substitute teacher, acting in this spirit, must desist from volunteering information to the principal that could possibly reflect upon the competence of the teacher for whom he acted as a substitute.

Loyalty to a faction, heightened by a bungling administrator, consumes the energies of teacher and principal who should use what resources they possess to help children solve the many problems each child faces daily.

The total "school situation"—tasks, groups, organization, and leader—appears to shape and color attitudes of teachers, which in turn affect morale. The tendency to engage in practices deemed unethical, whether by teacher or administrator, is enforced by the environment in the school rather than by differences among persons as such. According to recent studies, the one almost incontrovertible fact is that teachers must work with more ineffective than effective principals. The poor leadership stems largely from limitations in the realm of staff relations.

## The Unprofessional Teacher

No honest person would attribute all problems of teachers to "poor leadership" of the principal. A teacher may cause trouble for himself, other teachers, and the principal by coming to school or to meetings when he pleases. A teacher may be indifferent to attending professional meetings because "all that stuff is so much hokum."

Perhaps a teacher may look for excuses not to accept responsibilities for carrying out the program of activities sponsored by the school.

## The Eccentric

Specifically, a teacher who is a habitual "office runner," who insists that the principal must be involved in each encounter with a pupil, hurts himself and pupils and other teachers and the principal, as well as the patrons' faith in the teaching corps generally. A teacher becomes a source of trouble when he steals the show at staff meetings with prolonged treatises on his pet topics. A teacher is a party to unprofessional conduct when he seeks to be or permits himself to become a member of the "office guard" who gets to know things "first" and who then encourages the flourishing of the "grapevine" type of communication.

A teacher who speaks openly about "too much committee work" and who drops disparaging remarks about this person or that situation may be a person who is lonely and unhappy. Nonetheless, it is clear that he is not one who practices the basic ethics of his chosen work. Without listening too carefully, one can hear a teacher who says that "the principal around here ought to do what he's supposed to and let us teach." Such a teacher may collar a substitute teacher and a student teacher to complain about the "stupid P.T.A.," or the "windy speeches" at the state teachers' meetings. He'll never go to a Saturday meeting or a summer workshop, "not on your life!"

A teacher may feel that he should be scheduled to work only with the superior pupils. He may advertise freely that a considerable number of the pupils in his classes "don't make the grade." Or, he may give the impression that his pupils "really know what work means."

A teacher may be careless in his personal habits. His dress may leave something to be desired. Whether the teacher has actually "violated" ethical standards is debatable, depending upon how broadly one defines "professional conduct becoming a teacher." Perhaps certain practices or habits do offend others. The principal may feel that the careless teacher actually causes trouble among the staff members. This, however, is not a problem of ethics as such but one of taste and personal judgment.

### Improper Bids for Personal Gain

A teacher is a violator of ethics if he applies for a teaching position at a school where he has not been told by the principal about a specific job opening. When an application is made, there should be no "deals" about working fewer hours and for less money than the salary schedule stipulates. A teacher should avoid making comments that would tend to undermine the work of teachers at the school. A teacher should not misrepresent his qualifications by padding or passing over direct questions about particular aspects of his professional background. A teacher ought to refrain from talking with a principal about a teaching position with the sole purpose of using an offer to get through an increase in salary on the old job. He should not make promises that are against the best interests of pupils, fellow teachers, and the administrator.

A teacher violates ethics when he attempts to influence the principal in selection of applicants for positions that are available, or uses his influence to gain favorable ground for one teacher over another.

A teacher must avoid soliciting and selling products to his associates on school time and premises. Good judgment demands that activities for private gain be pursued outside of school hours. If a teacher persists, he runs counter to the principal's obligation to protect teacher and pupil from such outside pressures.

### Authority of Principal and Chain of Command

A teacher must respect the position of the principal to the extent that he does not direct what instruction shall be given in the school. When a teacher makes use in the classroom of textbooks not approved by the board, he embarrasses the principal and demonstrates an inability or unwillingness to attack problems on a professional plane. A teacher is obliged to use textbooks from the approved lists. However, the use of supplementary materials should be left to the discretion of teachers with no pressure being exerted from the principal to use this or that device. It is not ethical for a teacher to be partisan in class presentations so that the furtive and concealed "message" cannot be subjected to critical analysis by the pupils or the administrator. A teacher should be willing to follow the suggestions of the principal regarding what kinds of problems may embroil a neighborhood and reflect badly upon school personnel.

Much friction develops in a school organization by a teacher's failure to recognize the "chain of command." Perhaps the reason is that there is much fuzzy thinking about rights and privileges of all under a democracy. Most major problems need to be planned for and attacked cooperatively. However, the principal is an executive head of the school, as far as the teacher is concerned.

A teacher respects the "chain" concept when he works only indirectly with the board of education members. All requests should be channeled through the principal's office and thence to that of the superintendent. A teacher does all a disservice when he interferes with the measure of authority and responsibility placed upon the shoulders of the principal.

A teacher should keep in mind that the management of the public schools—with all that this concept embraces—is the direct responsibility of the principal, who acts under the supervision of the superintendent, who, in turn, is employed by the board of education. The teacher must remember that he reaches the board of education as a corporate body only through the principal, in matters that deal with professional problems and personal problems connected with employment in the school system. Even though the principal appears indifferent to requests from teachers, they should avoid "going around" him to the superintendent or board member.

A teacher must remember that the board of education is a unit as far as educational policy is concerned. Even though individual members comprise the board, it is their corporate and joint action that enables the board to function. A teacher should avoid "getting favors" by contacting individual members. They, in turn, should discourage teachers from seeking them out for "private conferences." If taken seriously, the following advice would be one sure way of damaging the relationships between the employee who followed it and the principal:

> The excellent teacher works with, not against, his board. He thanks each member for his help. He keeps his requests to the board reasonable. He establishes dignified, businesslike relations with the board. . . . He knows the members of the school board personally and shows them due deference. . . . He plays no fa-

vorites with members of the school board at any time. He takes time, on leaving at the end of the year, to say good-bye to the school board members and to other friends. . . .[13]

The advice quoted applied to a situation and a time when the administration of schools was quite different from what it is today. There was no hierarchy or "chain of command" to speak of because none was needed. Yet, practices of yesterday sometimes continue when situations have changed radically.

Sometimes a teacher gets into "hot water" with the administration and may cause extra headaches for the principal if he engages in outside employment of the kind that "lowers the status of the teaching profession" in the eyes of the employer and other influential members of the community. Or, a teacher may fail to "conduct school business through proper channels," thus violating a standard of conduct usually held up as desirable. An unthinking teacher may deem it merely a device of administrators "to choke off criticism" of the administration.

The "chain of command" must have teeth to deal effectively with a teacher who feels no compunction about flouting administrative superiors or community mores. The failure of a teacher to recognize authority in the office of the school principal, regardless of the virtues or limitations of the one performing the duties at the time, is a clear violation of the ethics of his profession. Sometimes a private admonition to a teacher will persuade him that his personal opinion, no matter how valid, cannot serve as the basis for the principal's decisions. If violation of ethics continues to be a serious matter and impairs a teacher's efficiency, the principal may have to refer the matter to his superior. There may be instances where a violation of ethics requires action by a local, state, or national committee. This may entail loss of the teaching certificate of the offender, or even dismissal from the profession, making employment elsewhere difficult if not impossible.

Can a teacher incur community disapproval and the enmity of the principal but still be an effective teacher? As yet there is no answer. The real point here is that the teaching-learning act is so complex that any rupture in relations between parts is bound to affect the whole. If a teacher is "kept on" who cares little or nothing

[13] Joseph E. Avent, *The Excellent Teacher* (Knoxville, Tenn.: Joseph E. Avent, 1931), pp. 422-23.

about interpersonal relations and "what the community thinks," another teacher sooner or later will think he has the go-ahead. His conception of taste and sense of responsibility may cut deeply into the values the school wishes to uphold. Such a person may care little or nothing about his colleagues, the principal, or the status of teaching and teachers. He may think of teaching only as a commodity—merchandise—to be sold and bargained with to make a little money.

## The "Disloyal" Employee

What constitutes "loyalty" or "disloyalty" quite clearly depends upon who is using the term and for what purposes. A teacher may be disloyal, as far as a principal goes, if and when the teacher questions what he has ordered. On the other hand, the state must rightly be concerned with keeping "undesirables" out of the classroom.

It is agreed that "disloyalty," however defined, whether involving the individual school or system or the state, violates ethical principles. The problem is, what precisely does the concept include or exclude? What must a teacher do or feel or say to be labeled disloyal? Is there a clear distinction between "disloyalty" and "disrespect"? Is there a difference between a teacher's rights and obligations to be a teacher and a leader, and emphasis upon conformity by the administration?

One is faced with the fact that even the formulation of a legal definition is fraught with peril. Quite regularly one can read in the press about a school board that has dismissed a teacher solely on the ground that the board believed the teacher had invoked his right under the federal Constitution not to answer a query. By so doing, the teacher, at least in some jurisdictions, is rendered unfit for the position of teacher.

A teacher may be branded as disloyal by the administration in certain states as the result of legislation passed by state governments in the wake of the division on the "Segregation" cases. It is disloyal, in some jurisdictions, for the teacher to advocate the teaching of mixed classes or even "to think that the idea is a good one." In some states at present, such a teacher can be dropped from the teaching rolls. Morally, a teacher ought to abide by and support the law. But what law must he obey if he is to be a good citizen? How can one practice that which he cannot be permitted to teach?

## Teacher Recommendations

There is some disagreement over whether the code of ethics excludes an incompetent teacher from being a member of the profession. One of the problems is the indifference or laxity with which a teacher's professional papers are prepared by principals in previous places of work. One teacher can have little or nothing stated in his folder concerning "poor work." Another teacher may receive lukewarm endorsements for "failing to cooperate."

What constitutes a misrepresentation of professional qualifications? And, who in the school system should be authorized to receive confidential information about a teacher? Under what conditions? For what reasons? These are not idle questions, of course.

Forms for rating of teachers vary, as do the efforts and insights of the raters. A statement of strengths and weaknesses of a teacher is desirable. However, it is no easy matter to get at accurate data even when relations between teacher and principal are cordial. However, the principal usually has the duty to turn in comments about teachers at stated intervals. He is supposed to report what he knows and feels as well as he is able. The recommendation of one principal serves as a basis for future employment within the system and will influence other prospective employers in the years ahead.

A teacher should expect the principal not to include in his set of recommendations unwarranted reservations concerning the quality of work. If a teacher is anxious to work elsewhere, he has a right to expect to be recommended without hedging on the part of the administration. "Go, but we'll do all we can to keep you" ought to be the attitude. The principal must be honest. For him to single out a petty or inconsequential shortcoming to cast a reflection upon a teacher is a violation of ethics.

What nonprofessional criteria can a principal use in failing to recommend the employment of a teacher? Surely, this depends upon the principal. However, matters pertaining to the private life of a teacher have no place within the recommendations unless those matters touch clearly upon his professional competence. A teacher has a right to expect that only his professional work is within the scrutiny of an employer, within the public domain, to be discussed, investigated if need be, and written about. The teacher must be ready, able, and willing to place his teaching out so that it can be praised or damned.

Unless a teacher commits a crime or runs for political office while under contract, his private life must remain his own. It should not properly come within the purview of the principal, or anybody else for that matter. Not only does a teacher have the right to defend his privacy—social, religious, financial, or other—but the public has the obligation to do so since one man's liberty must stop at exactly the point where the next man's begins.

Candid information, stated in such fashion that misunderstanding is reduced to a minimum, should form the basis of a teacher's professional papers. When doubts arise, perhaps a teacher needs to be given the benefit of those doubts. It would be professionally dishonest, on the other hand, for a teacher's papers to contain no mention of difficulty when a teacher had encountered teaching difficulty of some magnitude. The administrator should talk over with the teacher the general nature of the trouble before he includes any mention of it in written form.

## QUESTIONS FOR STUDY

1. Does the principal of a school supervise instruction because he wants to or because it is a duty imposed upon him by law?
2. Must "state-adopted" textbooks be used for all pupils, regardless of their mental ability?
3. To what extent is "record keeping" the business of the principal? If he assigns such work, has he "pushed off" clerical tasks upon the teacher in order to free himself for more desirable duties?
4. Exactly what regulations is it the teacher's duty to enforce?
5. What is the legal definition of maintaining "good order and discipline" within the classroom?
6. To what extent is the teacher legally bound to abide by regulations promulgated by the school principal?
7. Under what circumstances can the teacher "take matters into his own hands" regarding the punishing of an unruly child?
8. Does the *"in loco parentis"* standing of the teacher confer any protection upon him in his performance of teaching obligations?

9. Does the teacher enjoy any direct contact with the board of education that excludes the principal?

10. Can the principal delegate to a teacher the duty to formulate rules for fire drills and hold him responsible for their proper enforcement?

11. What is meant by the statement that "you have a moral obligation to tell him so"?

12. What factors breed "unethical conduct"?

13. What must a teacher do to be called guilty of a violation of ethics?

14. What is disobedience? What is an "insubordinate" act?

## SUGGESTED READINGS

*American Law Reports,* Second Series. Under "Schools," see paragraphs 30-48, dealing with Teachers and Principals.

*American Jurisprudence,* Vol. 47, "Schools." See paragraphs 108-145 for Teachers and Other Employees; paragraphs 146-188 for Pupils: Administration, Discipline, and Punishment; paragraphs 189-199 for Health Regulations; and paragraphs 200-207 for Courses of Instruction, Textbooks, and Supplies.

*Corpus Juris Secundum,* Vols. 78, 79, "Schools and School Districts." See paragraphs 154-238 for Teachers, Principals, and Superintendents; paragraphs 445-508 for Pupils, and Conduct and Discipline of Schools.

Edwards, Newton, *The Courts and the Public Schools* (Chicago: University of Chicago Press, 1955), chap. XVII, "Administration of the Teaching Personnel."

Greider, Calvin, and William E. Rosenstengel, *Public School Administration* (New York: Ronald Press Co., 1954), Part III, "Instructional Leadership."

Hamilton, Robert R., *Legal Rights and Liabilities of Teachers* (Laramie, Wyoming: School Law Publications, 1956), chap. III, "Liability of Teachers."

Moehlman, Arthur B., *School Administration* (Boston: Houghton Mifflin Company, 1951), chap. 13, "Executive Activity: Instruction."

Reeder, Ward G., *The Fundamentals of Public School Administration* (New York: The Macmillan Company, 1951), chap. IX, "Evaluating Teacher Efficiency"; chap. XXIV, "Administration of the Curriculum"; chap. XXV, "Administration of Extracurricular Activities"; and chap. XXVI, "Administration of Textbooks."

Remmlein, Madaline Kinter, *School Law* (New York: McGraw-Hill Book Co., Inc., 1950), Part II, "Problems of Pupil Personnel"; Appendixes B, "How to Find School Law," C, "Glossary of Legal Terms," and D, "Selected Bibliography."

# Supervisor-Personnel Relationships

## 5

### PROBLEM SITUATIONS

What would you do in each of the following situations? Analyze each in terms of questions raised at the beginning of Chapter 3 (page 56).

CASE A

Several pupils at Maple School started a petition to have Miss X dismissed as an instructor of English. Ten parents signed the paper as framed by the pupils. A teacher on the faculty of the school saw the petition and reported the matter to the principal.

Miss *H*, an instructional supervisor in the school system, was contacted by the principal. She turned over to the principal notes she had made on her impressions of the effectiveness of Miss X. During a conversation between Miss X and school officials, it was revealed that neither the principal nor the supervisor had spoken previously with the teacher about any of the comments contained in the supervisor's notes. In other words, the supervisor had merely kept a record of her impressions for use by the principal.

CASE B

Mr. *H*, a retired college professor, came to Plains High School to teach eighth grade. He was assigned two classes of arithmetic and two of geography. All pupils in three classes seemed to be making fair progress. According to Mr. *H* one class was "terrible." This group was composed mostly of pupils from Mrs. *S*'s homeroom. It seemed that a small number of girls retained in the eighth grade arithmetic class was causing the difficulty by "getting out of control." At a staff meeting the supervisor volunteered that it would have been better had the girls been promoted. Two teachers objected strenuously and said that "those girls ought to stay in the grade until they can do what the others do." One

151

muttered something about a supervisor talking "big" with no real responsibilities anyhow.

Mrs. S said later that the girls had behaved well in her room. Three other teachers reported to the principal the following week that they did not wish to teach pupils the next year who had been in Mrs. S's homeroom.

The lack of control in the one class of Mr. H became more noticeable. Pupils in the other three classes started "to act up." On the next visit of the supervisor, two teachers across the hall from Mr. H told the supervisor "in strictest confidence" that she ought to do something "pretty quick."

CASE C

As principal of Blackacre School, you have the responsibility for management of the school lunchroom. The cafeteria head has brought to your attention that many of the seventh graders have refused to eat the foods in the regular "plate lunch." For the most part, stated the manager of the cafeteria, the foods not being eaten are those supplied under the federal government's surplus commodity program.

In a room directly off the cafeteria the principal, the instructional supervisor, and two teachers were talking. This conversation was interrupted by Miss C who reported that 40 out of the 65 seventh graders had brought their lunch to school that day.

On hearing this, the supervisor walked past Miss C at the doorway and went to the tables where the "food strikers" were consuming their sack lunches. The supervisor looked squarely at two of the bigger boys who were sitting apart from the rest and said, "If you were in my class, you'd eat what's put in front of you!" The supervisor then turned about and approached the cafeteria manager. In a voice loud enough for children and teachers to hear, she stated, "Perhaps the children wouldn't dislike the lima bean soup so much if it didn't look so much like dishwater."

CASE D

Miss B has taught children in the elementary grades for 24 years. Her husband now has a job with a publishing company and is a close friend of the school superintendent.

Two weeks ago a mother became irate over what she alleged to be persecution of her child by Miss B. In fact the mother became so disturbed that she started a campaign to have the teacher removed from the school. She enlisted the sympathy of a group of class mothers. Together they visited the principal. He brushed off their complaints as "unimportant" and something that Miss G, the supervisor, could straighten out "in no time at all."

The group paid a visit to the supervisor's office. The supervisor listened quietly to the charges of "favoritism," of "ridiculing pupils," and of the teacher's "prolonged absence" as a result of which some of the pupils would get out of hand. The supervisor concluded by stating that she could make no promises to the mothers but assured them that she would speak with the principal and teacher involved. She stopped to tell the irate mother that she would call her by telephone within a few days.

The supervisor asked permission of the principal to speak with the teacher about a Christmas play. When she saw the teacher, she attempted to get to the bottom of the trouble by skilful questioning. After a careful search of the data she had compiled right after the meeting, the supervisor seemed to think that there was little to go on.

The principal stated later that he would take no action but felt that the usefulness of the teacher to the school had been seriously impaired. The supervisor was told, in a conference with the superintendent, that the ringleaders of the mothers' group were "all crackpots." The supervisor knew she had to make a telephone call before long. Above all else, she wanted to keep the respect of the teacher and the administrative personnel. Could she recommend that Miss *B* be employed in the school for another year?

In all probability the classroom work of teachers is "watched over" or supervised by one or more persons called "specialists." In no (or at least very few) school organizations do teachers actually have sole responsibility for instruction. In larger systems, where there is emphasis on formal arrangements, specialists make regular visits to teachers to "coordinate" the program. In smaller systems, with little emphasis upon formal "chain-of-command" procedures, the principal may be the only supervisor. Whoever he is, the "supervisor" has the job of helping teachers plan those activities of the school curriculum (those relating primarily to the classroom rather than nonclass) which in the judgment of school employees will provide the opportunities for desirable growth or behavior change.

The role of the specialist or supervisor is consequently one of great importance to teachers, for the supervisor can help a teacher improve the level of instruction or can place mental obstacles in his way by his noneffective behaviors. A teacher should try to consider the supervisor as an indispensable part of his school program and not merely as someone representing administrative authority.

This need—to have teacher and supervisor be members of a school team—has been stressed at considerable length in publications dealing with the professional problems of the teacher.[1] Con-

[1] For example, Harold E. Moore and Newell B. Walters, *Personnel Administration in Education* (New York: Harper and Brothers, Publishers, 1955).

sidering these numerous guideposts, and the stress being laid constantly on the "professional" approach to solving problems, teachers could well expect that relationships between themselves and the supervisor would be rather well defined and have commonly accepted patterns of procedure. As teachers know, this is not the actual situation today in these United States, at least in most schools. In fact, more honest study should be directed to finding out how firm and wholesome relationships between teacher and supervisor can best be established and maintained.

## LEGAL ASPECTS

### The Supervisor as a Teacher

There seems to be no single well-defined principle to express the precise relationship in law that one employee bears to an employee called a supervisor. Both are employees of a board of education. But what are the lines and working spheres of authority?

Because of many different patterns of school organization, and the varied arrangements for use of the supervisor's services, it is difficult for a teacher to understand what the job of the supervisor is. In some states the term "supervisor" has been placed in the school codes along with the principal and superintendent when duties are prescribed. In other states it has been left up to state departments of education to set up "supervisory" positions. Quite frequently, state school laws give the state (or a district supervisor) the power to inspect, report, and recommend regarding changes to be made in practices in the schools. In some county and city school systems the supervisor appears in the pattern of organization as an intermediate "line" employee between the top executive and the school principal.

When the position or authority of the supervisor has been challenged in the courts, it has been said in general that the board of education has the power to use its discretion (its power of free decision and judgment) in the employment of "special teachers." Of course, a special teacher or supervisor must usually be qualified specifically in the field of his major interest or specialty. In addition, a supervisor is required to hold a valid teaching certificate. The contractual and assignment privileges of a regular teacher and a supervisor are very similar, if not identical.

In short, the supervisor is classified as a teacher. The fact that the position of supervisor has been filled by Miss X for a number of years does not prevent a board of education from assigning Miss X to a classroom, *providing* (and this point is essential) that such change in Miss X's duties does not reduce the salary earned. The principle involved here is that when changes in the school staff are deemed necessary, an employee under "tenure" may not be required to accept less pay nor may he be required to assume work radically different from his area of competence.

## Line and Staff Employees

It will be recalled that teachers are usually considered in school organization as "line" employees, as distinguished from "staff" employees. Despite certain exceptions (mostly in larger school systems), a supervisor is not "in the line" of authority but occupies the position of a "staff" employee. This means that he is a specialist attached to some one person in the line who performs services different from those of a classroom teacher. The person who is a staff employee does not have administrative authority except, of course, over the personnel in his own office.

To expand this concept further, teacher and supervisor bear different relationships to the principal. As a line person, a teacher is directly responsible to a building principal for complying with and supporting board policy. A supervisor who visits on occasion has indirect responsibilities to the principal. The principal is not the "boss" of the supervisor. Unlike a classroom teacher, a supervisor is generally not assigned to *a* particular school. His "home base" of operation is in some central office, whether in a separate structure within the school district or in one room in the "administrative wing" of the secondary school.

On occasion, the supervisor may perform "line" type duties. When he is a teacher who teaches a class, he is directly responsible to the principal. When the supervisor is called upon to prepare reports for use by an immediate superior, he is performing, at that time, a "line function." In other words, the supervisor is not advising (performing staff functions).

A classroom teacher and the supervisor can vie with each other for authority, or each can accept as "a fact of life" that some organization of a school is necessary and can try to work effectively within the framework. The working relations will perhaps be better when each knows and accepts the advantages of the "line" concept and each realizes its inherent obstacles. Where straight "line-staff" delegation is practiced, the line or flow of authority is from the superintendent, to assistants, to the building principals, and then to the teachers.

It is the superintendent as chief executive of the board who is directly responsible for all management phases of school operation. Supervisors are employed to assist line employees (teachers) to help improve instruction. But, a superintendent and his assistants handle their jobs in terms of the "chain" also. So must teachers. They are confused about the line concept when they complain to the principal that their authority has been challenged by a supervisor who offers suggestions for changing classroom procedures. This is his job! When, of course, a supervisor orders and directs, he has stepped beyond his own sphere and arrogated to himself the position of principal. We are speaking here of the legal relationship. The line employee has legal authority over those in lesser positions of responsibility. How wisely authority is used depends mainly upon nonlegal considerations.

In general, school personnel charged by law with authority to operate the public schools are the "line" personnel. Their authority is delegated to them, with minor exceptions, "down the line" from the board through the office of superintendent. Because of this plan of operation, a teacher cannot decide what instruction shall be given certain pupils or what textbooks shall be used. A teacher gets such information from the office of the principal. Understanding this necessary plan of operation, a teacher would not make requests of a supervisor to talk to individual board members either for legitimate requests or for personal favors.

The unclear perceptions as to the supervisor's role in the complex educational hierarchy (the scale of positions from superintendent to classroom teacher) are a major source of trouble within school systems. In addition, the whole theory of line-and-staff has been and continues to be under attack. Nonetheless, several rather well-defined principles support the line idea and help to explain the

legal relationship of supervisor to other school personnel. What
follows is not a presentation of arguments pro or con in terms of the
line idea, but a statement of principles that help explain the
success of organizations in terms of external arrangement.

A first principle is this: of necessity, authority is centralized in
a school system in the legally appointed (or elected) person who
then becomes the "head" of the organization. In other terms, it is
the superintendent who is legally responsible for the excellence of
the instructional program of the school system. Teachers are employed by the board (presumably on the recommendation of the
superintendent since he is charged with the end result) to help carry
out the program of instruction. Teachers receive help from principal
*and* supervisor. It is obvious that nonlegal factors can and do
militate against the amount and quality of aid received.

A second principle: authority *and* responsibility held by the
superintendent may be delegated to (temporarily shared with) "inferior" personnel in the line of authority. The one to whom the
authority has been delegated is invested with it for as long a time as
the "superior" line employee may choose.

A third principle: the lines or channels through which delegation
of authority and responsibility must be accomplished (or through
which delegated power will flow) must be sharply and clearly
defined. There are numerous practical limitations to a realization
of this concept. However, teachers should be working under conditions in which they receive suggestions about one matter from only
one person.

Two other principles should be mentioned. The fourth is that the
duties and activities pertaining to one person must be assigned
"down through the line of authority." The fifth and last one is that
staff personnel are the instructional experts and consultants. The
supervisor provides help when called upon to do so by principal
and teacher. To repeat, a teacher cannot be "coerced" by the supervisor through any exercise of authority to do a particular thing. As
far as a teacher is concerned, the supervisor possesses no executive
power.[2]

[2] John A. Rorer in his *Principles of Democratic Supervision* (New York:
Bureau of Publications, Teachers College, Columbia University, 1942), pp.
124-250, makes an important distinction between principles of external organization and those of internal organization. He points out that the former deal
with the machinery and the personnel of a school system, and the latter with

To make use of such principles of administration, which attempt to make clear legal relationships between school personnel, teachers should urge that lists of general duties be prepared in an effort to determine and settle upon those best performed by teachers and those best fulfilled by the supervisor (and other employees for that matter). The aim should be the elimination of unnecessary overlap which results in friction, confusion, and sheer waste, both human and material. Besides the preparation of such lists to clarify areas of responsibility, teachers should encourage the formation of councils, committees, and the like that have broad representation. Conferences with broad representation may partially correct the weaknesses of line-staff organization.

## Who Is a Supervisor?

In any one school system a teacher may discover many or few persons designated as supervisors. They may be identified by such titles as "Supervisor of Instruction," "Supervisor of Student Welfare," and "Supervisor of Buildings and Grounds." Some areas represented by the titles are recognized as teaching fields while others are not. Rarely if ever does the nonteaching supervisor come into direct contact with a teacher. Our attention here is limited to the relationships between teacher and "special teacher" as supervisor.

## What Does a Supervisor Do?

A teacher, as noted above, performs work different from that of an instructional supervisor. A teacher has his "locus" of operation confined to planning the activities within one building. A teacher confines his duties to the building to which he has been assigned and works directly with one principal. (A principal may, on the other hand, have direct responsibility for two school faculties.) Even when there is a chairman of a grade or several grades or a head of a

the functioning of that machinery. For additional comments see William H. Burton and Leo J. Brueckner, *Supervision; a Social Process,* 3rd ed. (New York: Appleton-Century-Crofts, Inc., 1955), p. 102.

The strength of the conventional line-and-staff organization is its provision for clear assignments of duties, which lends itself to specialization. The weaknesses grow out of these very strengths. Cooperation between the teacher and supervisor, for example, may actually be impaired by too careful differentiation and overspecialization. Here lies the real objection, not that the system of organization resembles big business or the military.

department, a teacher helps plan and implement policy under authority and responsibility residing in the principal.

The supervisor is a helper, a catalyst, a stimulator, and one who should induce in the teacher "wholesome concern" for improving instructional practices. If a teacher is to do his job effectively, the supervisor must direct his own efforts through the person or office of the principal. The supervisor is obligated to talk over plans with the principal, who then is able to share in their formulation. By such behavior the supervisor has recognized the legal relationship between teachers and principal. The supervisor has observed "channels." A teacher should realize that an effective supervisor advises only. A division of authority referred to above is not thereby deepened.

## How Did the Supervisor's Job Originate?

As the size of schools grew and larger building units were erected, the practice developed of employing specialized personnel. Supervisors were teachers not assigned to any particular classroom. Along with the increase in physical facilities and more complex organization came the idea that the program of instruction should be broadened—that teaching should be improved by giving attention to the special fields of instruction. Classroom teachers were not competent in all the areas contemplated. So the special teacher was employed to assist in the teaching, or to teach the special subjects.

Teachers thus employed to assist came to be called supervisors. Employed by boards of education to teach special subjects, supervisors helped with this development after the 1870's. When the extension of the program gained momentum, problems of teacher and supervisor multiplied. The special teacher traveled from building to building to give instruction in the new subjects. Relations between teacher and "traveling teacher" depended—then as now —upon insights of the persons involved rather than upon any particular patterns of organization.

School systems began to grow in size after the 1900's so that one elementary school could use the services of a full-time teacher in a special subject field, especially in music and art. The traveling specialist thus became the local teacher responsible to the building principal. Because of the very nature of the work, the newly created specialist had both administrative and "supervisory" duties. The supervisor from the central office engaged in both types of duties. One result was that the teacher and the supervisor grew to see each other's roles less clearly.

At first, special subjects came under the jurisdiction of the supervisor. Then the supervisor from the central office began to oversee the "academic" areas as well. Over the years the supervisor of a department was created in secondary schools. This expanded the number of persons who were involved in "supervisory" activities. The development of specialists eventually led to the state of affairs that still exists today, where the teacher and supervisor are not sure of the legal ground on which each rests.

One factor that has complicated the picture is that the function of the school principal changed markedly between 1900 and 1940. The teacher's role and relationships were thus altered. Administrative duties that had come to be associated with the principalship were gradually supplemented by activities associated with the supervision of instruction. Since the principal was strategically situated to offer help to teachers in the building, the sphere of activity of the special teacher grew to be more and more limited. Acceptance of the idea—though gradual—that the principal was instructional head of the school led to friction between principal and supervisor. The teacher came out, second best, somewhere between the two contenders.

### Present Legal Status of the Supervisor

The primary legal question in supervisor-personnel relations is the measure of authority over personnel that the supervisor is able to exercise under the local board policies, state board regulations, and state statutes. Such regulations must be understood by teachers, the principal, and the supervisor if better schools are the common aim of all.

It is recognized by most teachers that authority of one school employee over another stems from the authority that rests in the board of education itself. Fundamentally, control over education is exercised only by the state. The state shares its authority over education with the local school board. The board has the duty to establish the relationships it desires so far as personnel and their work go, so long as procedures are consistent with school laws. Courts will not interfere with board discretion unless arrangements decided upon are deemed to be unreasonable or arbitrary or to show evidence of malice.

Organization-wise, in the simplest plan the principal assumes the responsibility of general supervisor. A teacher works directly with a principal as supervisor or the superintendent, where the system is small. Sometimes a teacher is supervised by a building principal who is given the duty of supervisor of arithmetic for all elementary schools. So designated, the principal would be a supervisor in relation to the building principals of schools he visits.

In another plan a teacher is met by a supervisor who comes into the school at the call of the principal or the teacher himself to assist in solving instructional problems. Indirect assistance to the teacher is stressed so that the teacher and principal will trust and depend upon each other. In this plan the bulk of everyday classroom supervision of the teacher is assumed by the principal.

In larger systems the teacher may be visited by several supervisors, each of whom has the responsibility for a large segment of the school program. A teacher may get help from each in specific subject areas. Also, a subject teacher can act as supervisor and a grade teacher may serve either the "lower" or "middle" or "upper" level classes.

Patterns of operation may vary between two extremes. In one situation a teacher flatly refuses to comply with instructions of a supervisor who possesses "line" authority. Here such employee could well be "guilty of insubordination" as far as the board is concerned. The board could press for the dismissal of the employee on that ground alone. At the opposite extreme may be the situation where a teacher actually calls the supervisor into his classroom by specific invitation. Under such circumstances, the supervisor serves as legal assistant to the teacher if and when the teacher so wishes. The teacher may or may not choose to follow the supervisor's suggestions. Here the supervisor does not differ in his authority from any regularly appointed teacher as far as supervisor-personnel relationships are concerned. Both are directly and equally responsible to an administrative "superior."

## ETHICAL ASPECTS

Teachers should be specialists in directing pupil learning activities. Supervisors should be too. Herein lies the basis for trouble. A
classroom teacher may think of the supervisor as an "outsider" and
a "poacher" on his territory. Both need reminders that their duty is
to serve others by professional conduct.

### Undesirable Behavior Patterns

Perhaps it is not unkind to state that the negative attitudes of an
employee toward the idea of supervision—whether the idea be im-
plemented by supervisor or principal—is the one major factor
militating against the effectiveness supervision might achieve.

On close examination some of the qualms of employees concerning supervision do not actually pertain to the process itself. They
result from the accidents and mistakes and good intentions of
bungling persons engaged in the supervision of employees. In other
words, the employee who balks at the very mention of supervision
and screams "outside interference" is erroneously judging supervision—the concept—by the specific acts of an incompetent supervisor. Here, the term "incompetence" refers not to professional
limitations as such, but to the behaviors of one who acts unreasonably and unjustly in dealing with employees.

There is general but not specific agreement concerning the manner
in which the supervisor ought to conduct himself while in another's
classroom. However, certain behaviors clearly smack of unprofessional conduct. At Old Bemish School Miss *B* was helping some
sixth graders work out misunderstandings regarding the cancella-
tion process in fractions they were multiplying. Billy was at the
side chalkboard. The front door of the classroom was opened by
Mrs. *H*, a supervisor in the system. She walked past the science
corner and then stood quietly at the rear of the room for several
minutes with her arms folded. Miss *B* asked the supervisor whether
she would like to quiz some of the children about arithmetic
language. The supervisor declined. The lesson continued, with Billy
showing on the board that he had failed to divide both parts of

the fraction by the same number. The supervisor walked over to the window side of the room and picked up some notebooks that were piled there. She hurriedly glanced through several of them and then placed two under her arm. Billy took his seat. After a moment or so, the supervisor went to the desk of one of the pupils and picked up her arithmetic book. She asked Mary something about why she had placed a certain answer on her homework paper. Miss B tried to go right on with the lesson in fractions. It is obvious that more is needed to remedy this situation than "pie-in-the-sky" platitudes about judgment or consideration.

Unfortunately, a teacher will remember the visits and *faux pas* of such a supervisor, forgetting the visits and pleasant conference periods spent with perceptive supervisors. Surely a teacher is in error if he permits his attitudes to be unduly influenced by one such incident. But teachers are apt to take the thoughtful supervisor for granted; the "sore thumb" sticks out in one's consciousness and the return visit of the "goof-ball" will be dreaded by both teacher and pupils.

On many faculties can be found a teacher who seems to be uncooperative and disagreeable—one who insists on going it alone, whatever the cost in animosities created and frustration built up. There is little need to talk of common objectives, for this teacher knows precisely what is required. She has had success without supervisory interferences. Along with the uncooperative employee, the supervisor will of course meet the indolent, the unappealing, and the colorless employee—all part of school personnel.

It is the job of the supervisor to help all workers to perform effectively. There is no one simple route, and chances are legion for misunderstandings to develop and grow. If success is to come, conflicts that are created must be handled with patience and understanding. Neither a teacher nor a supervisor can afford to develop "undesirable" behavior patterns. Then either may attempt to resolve the trouble on a personal rather than on a professional basis.

## Some Variations in Supervision

Until the 1930's—the decade of the Great Depression—the patterns of supervision to which teachers were subjected could be characterized by the terms "paternalism" and "domination." Essentially, teachers were told "what was right" without too much regard for professional etiquette. They received "packaged answers" accompanied by little thought about the usefulness of the exhortations and platitudes to the person involved. (Surely, there must have been many exceptions to the stereotype of a supervisor just described.)

The 1950's have produced, at least up to writing time, no panacea for ending even some of the ills of authoritarian supervision. Teacher and supervisor carry on their activities within administrative structures that are based on the concept of insistence upon arbitrary standards of behavior. The "just-because-I-hold-the-idea, it-must-be-good" philosophy is perhaps a too prevalent basis for working "for or to" people and not "with" them.

A teacher may well feel and show this is pure "manipulation." Or, teacher and supervisor may be "diplomatic" in their objections to thoughts and feelings that do not seem to square with their own. They may have learned to behave in a fashion that indicates recognition and acceptance of the concept of individual differences as an operational principle.

There was, of course, no *one* person or act or happening that served as *the* stimulus to focus attention away from "traditional" concepts of teacher-supervisor relationships and toward the importance of "getting along." The studies relating to supervision pursued by schools, industry, and business, which had gained momentum prior to World War II, have stated the importance of basic attitudes to create wholesome work climate and help provide the foundations on which confidence depends. A common thread in studies reported seems to be that the task of supervising a group of people, no matter what the reason, is "at least 75 per cent dealing with people and their strange behavior towards each other." [3] The one item *know how to get along with people* is now rated as the most important among supervisory practices that appear in check lists.

Increased attention is being directed to the study of human

---

[3] Ayer, *Fundamentals of Instructional Supervision*, p. 165. See also Leo M. Chamberlain and Leslie W. Kindred, *The Teacher and School Organization*, 3rd ed. (Englewood Cliffs, N.J.: Prentice-Hall, Inc., 1958), chap. 11, "Working with Supervisors."

beings and "what makes them tick." Teacher and supervisor are becoming acquainted with the meaning and application of the "imposing lists of principles" dealing with child development and growth. Each is beginning to see that time taken to study how adults behave as well as children is time profitably spent. Although the supervisor's role is now that of assistant instead of inspector, attitudes will continue to range from "the other fellow should be cared for and I will decide to what extent" to "the other fellow is capable of being far more than he is, and it is my responsibility as supervisor to help him develop to his optimum."

## Problems of "Scientific" Supervision

Teachers and supervisors have been urged to "professionalize" themselves. Advancement often has depended upon taking courses at colleges and universities, where "standards of performance" have been outlined without reference to the job to be done or the persons to do it. Stress has been laid upon "incentives and rewards" and upon "time schedules."

As teacher and supervisor have sought self-improvement, the stress on being "objective" has, in some instances at least, made relationships between teacher and supervisor more taut and strained. This evil has arisen, in part, from a misunderstanding of what is meant by "striving for objective results" or "setting standards." With neither teacher nor supervisor giving careful scrutiny to "evaluation jargon," misunderstandings have multiplied and the gulf between teacher and supervisor has been widened and deepened.

Some have used the term "scientific" to describe supervision that lays stress on measurement of objective results by various paper-and-pencil tests. Much of this effort has been to the good. However, scientific supervision does not have to imply the uncritical or un-imaginative, or even bungling, use of scientific tools by either teacher or supervisor. When it does, a teacher will seek out ways and means of "getting even" with a supervisor who relates that Miss X does not seem to stress "fundamentals" since test scores for her children are low in comparison with other teachers. If either teacher or supervisor puts emphasis upon quickly achieved and narrowly construed goals, conduct may tend to become arbitrary, partial, and destructive of the morale without which leadership takes a "nose dive."

Two writers on supervision caution against "justifying" grades or marks earned in terms of "normal curve" thinking. They say:

> An ignorant enthusiasm for the science of education and for scientific method [by either teacher or supervisor] seems to make some persons harsh, arrogant, and dogmatic. Similarly unbalanced emphasis on democracy and freedom seems to send some dancing among the daffodils when they should be attending to the spring plowing.[4]

Teacher and supervisor can lean too far in believing that "scientific" means new or current or modern. Each can act as though "a change" is good in and of itself. Teacher and supervisor may agree on what "the latest device is," go into operation with some freshly named but loosely thought-out principles, and fail to come to grips at all with the fundamental problems of the learning process. The use of a novel device with an authoritative name may blind one to the fact that he is tilting at windmills.

A teacher who needs help will be short-changed by a supervisor who wanders about the school and classroom merely mouthing the results of research, as he sees them, which are conceived as no more definite than the typical P.T.A. yearly theme. Such a supervisor might better simply "scatter sunshine" wherever he goes, since some good at least might result.

So, actions by teacher and supervisor that are based on "latest trends" uncritically accepted are likely to do little else than win easy popularity with other advocates. Efforts at help will center on generalizations and sentimentalities. The awful result, as mentioned before, is that the teacher who needs help will be deluded and accept "pat" answers. He may be led and lead himself to believe that the results of a few "latest studies" are a substitute for honest study of his own strengths and weaknesses. The teacher-and-supervisor relationship, under such circumstances, will deteriorate.

The scrupulous professional worker is not content to let words stand for thoughts. He goes behind the symbols and builds his behavior patterns on his notions about desirable conduct. Scientific supervision then is an ally to program improvement. The teacher and supervisor reject the "help" of him who operates with a "kit of

[4] Burton and Brueckner, *Supervision; a Social Process*, p. 83.

latest gadgets" to solve problems that are current. They reject the concept that scientific supervision must be synonymous with lack of critical evaluation of tools. They are rightly wary of the teacher or supervisor who conceives his job as that of "casting a general influence for good" within the class or school and of "stimulating a general glow of optimism" among colleagues by commending all on their degree of understanding of learning problems.

## The Realities of "Super-Vision"

The teacher who has the opportunity of working with a colleague who possesses "super-vision"—which is vision above and beyond that required of a teacher—can enjoy working in an environment that has comparatively few fear-producing and tension-provoking elements in it. This means that teacher and supervisor can have the chance to pull rather than being pushed. They recognize certain limitations and restraints and accomplish their tasks within these boundaries.

Where the supervisor is perceptive of others' problems, a teacher gets more than a pat on the back, more than a welcome ear, more than easy agreement about what is best or what to do next. The supervisor here described—too rare, indeed—knows that the needs of the teacher vary. This notion lies at the very core of his efforts and accounts for his achievements in helping the teacher.

In laying plans for establishing wholesome relations with a teacher, this kind of worker realizes that behind differences in the bearing and behaviors of the teachers are differences in beliefs, in perceptions of self, and in concepts of what others think about their personalities. A teacher can be helped to see that such differences offer challenges, not obstacles. Each person has opportunities for growth. A teacher who recognizes the worth of the "supervision" supervisor can capitalize on this understanding. He can' speak freely without fear of reprisals or demerits being recorded. He can rest assured that he is getting leadership.

A teacher who seeks out the aid of the superior supervisor can be helped to see the immensity of the problems involved in human relationships. He will see how imperative it is that teacher and supervisor plan their work on the basis of considering the personality structure of the persons involved and the means by which "each person may best learn and grow." [5] A teacher and supervisor may, at different times and in different situations, be combinations of the "self-directive" person, the "adaptive" person, and "submissive" person, the "defiant" person, and the "unadjusted" person.

What is "right" to do in a given situation or what is the "professional" thing to do are influenced by factors other than personality variations. The determiners of action, in addition to personality structure, may be the realities "of the situation" as perceived by the parties involved. These include economic differences, status conceptions, physical vigor, prejudices, facilities, and other ingredients.

A sound relationship results if a teacher sees that differences within and differences without are considered by the supervisor in his contacts with the teacher. It results from a deep concern by the supervisor himself with the individual needs of teachers. These needs vary considerably. But recognition that they exist and that they help explain why a teacher or supervisor acts as he does is vital to a successful relationship.

Teacher problems stem from a complexity of factors. Maladjustments can be traceable perhaps to a form of rejection, by self or others. Considerateness in getting near "causes" means much. Reflection of attitudes may be the wise procedure, wiser than the supervisor's prescribing a remedy for an ill that is loosely and carelessly defined.

Much has been written about the value of employing the "techniques of group process" in helping an adult get insight into why he acts the way he does and why others are the way they are. One caution needs to be mentioned. It is that neither teacher nor supervisor must get so "worried" over his own or another's mental health so that he becomes the patient rather than the doctor.

A teacher and supervisor should together understand and use the resources available to get a better picture of how people really are. Each must accept responsibility. The teacher can then place faith and trust in the suggestions of the supervisor. The supervisor directs his efforts towards getting the teacher to act—to act differently from the way he has acted previously. The teacher uses his new insights and changed perceptions to work differently with

---

[5] Harold P. Adams and Frank G. Dickey, *Basic Principles of Supervision* (New York: American Book Company, 1953), p. 75.

children. The principal must back up the teacher and supervisor. Meetings and conferences will be "their" responsibilities, not opportunities for the school leader to "take a powder" to sort cards or count equipment.

Under the ideal circumstances being described, a teacher helps to secure support for the policies he and the supervisor formulate. He assists the supervisor in experimentation. He serves on committees and helps in devising curriculum changes. When a teacher notes points wherein he thinks the class and program of activities could be improved, the supervisor has performed the responsibility entrusted to him. When the supervisor encourages the teacher to study the effectiveness of his instruction, the supervisor is doing his professional duty.

The considerate acts of the supervisor, even of those with little or no "super-vision," help build up the morale without which no person or organization can accomplish much. A teacher feels at ease because he recognizes that the supervisor "practices what he preaches," operates on the basis of principles. The encouragement of the thoughtful supervisor can melt away fear and distrust and build up a wholesome concept of the supervisor's role.

A teacher can see, through good example, that supervision is participation in activities with the help of the supervisor. A teacher's confidence in the supervisor and the idea of supervision grows because he realizes that his weaknesses are considered as opportunities for improvement, not as limitations for which the teacher will be "rated down."

Some recent research seems to point out that leadership "takes the place of authority derived from the status person" when teacher, supervisor, principal, and other personnel participate in the formulation of school policy. Authority grows out of the particular situation. Cooperative exchange of significant ideas buttresses rather than interferes with legally constituted authority. All help to create a "concern for improvement."

This kind of a notion means that good supervision is teacher-activated rather than supervisor-oriented. It may mean that the effective teacher remains because "working conditions are good." He consciously recognizes that he is willing and anxious to give forth his best to achieve the purposes of the school program. The supervisor aids the principal in helping the teacher see that his first obligation must be toward the "opportunity and challenge of the job."

Under these circumstances, a teacher believes that he ought to "give before he can get." He realizes that he first learns and can then teach considerateness. His high morale is a by-product of a good program of supervision. He will know, from personal experience, that to teach kindness, it is first necessary to be kind; to teach humility, to be humble; to teach integrity, to be genuine; and to teach democracy, to be democratic.[6]

Besides the notion that the needs of a teacher are of paramount importance, there is the growing recognition that the principal is the one person best situated for accomplishing the aims of supervision. He can be alert to antagonisms and words or actions of disloyalty. He can see whether the subject-matter teacher feels he knows more than the supervisor. He will, if he is alert, know how well or how badly relationships between teacher and supervisor are going.

The preparation programs of secondary school teachers will have to be modified considerably and relationships better defined among teacher, supervisor, and principal before effective supervision will be widespread at the high school level.

## Employee Orientation

The supervisor can be of much help immediately after a new teacher has been employed. The teacher has many adjustments to make and new relationships to establish. The writers on this topic say that "however emotionally stable a young teacher may be, there are problems which arise in adjusting to a new job situation that are exceedingly baffling."[7] The initiative for orienting a new teacher resides with the superintendent, who usually delegates this task to an assistant or a committee. In any arrangement, the supervisor is a key person. If he chooses, he can lend sympathetic aid and muster help of associates within the system and in the immediate school neighborhood. The supervisor can point out the variety of religious, fraternal, service, political, and labor organiza-

[6] Ayer, *Fundamentals of Instructional Supervision*, p. 167.
[7] Elsbree and Reutter, *Staff Personnel Relations*, p. 115.

tions that hold opportunities for helping the new teacher become settled in his new community.

Providing personal help in making social adjustments is just a good beginning. If the school staff accepts its responsibility, it will make the new teacher an integral part of the staff from the very time he has been given assurance of his appointment. One of the first duties of a supervisor, after making the teacher feel wanted, is to help the teacher get complete knowledge of his conditions of employment, those items not specifically covered in his contract. The teacher can become informed about the numerous regulations concerning school attendance, which are not always understood even by experienced teachers. The supervisor can see that the teacher knows the function of the regulations and why each is necessary.

The supervisor can then help give the teacher a feeling of confidence in his work. Closely related is a responsibility to give the teacher a feeling of pride in his new assignment. That this does always not run smoothly is quite clear. Status differences among employees within the school and system sometimes constitute a barrier to effective work. One new teacher put it this way:

> Being a new teacher in the system, I expected to do some dirty work, but not all of it. The pets in this system never have an extra duty. The only thing you have to do around here to get out of work is to be a friend of the principal.[8]

The supervisor-teacher relationship would be much improved if both started out at the very beginning to see the new job as it is supposed to be. Perhaps this is just a dream.

## Teacher Evaluation

The evaluation of the effectiveness of a teacher has probably been surrounded by more bitterness and confusion as to purpose and worth-whileness than has any other aspect of educational endeavor. One source of trouble has been the place and method of evaluation of teaching, or teacher rating.

Fear of a visit from a supervisor is not difficult to understand when it is related to the topic of rating of the teacher. It need only

---

[8] Kimball Wiles, *Supervision for Better Schools* (Englewood Cliffs, N.J.: Prentice-Hall, Inc., 1955), p. 47.

be remembered that in some systems the teacher must receive a high rating or score from the supervisor in order to win a raise in salary or promotion in rank. Admittedly, rating scales and check lists of behaviors have constructive uses. These devices are favored by school administrators. However, when used unwisely, they are serious disturbers of the morale of the teacher.

In some school systems the supervisor is purposely kept from dealing with problems like rating, promotions, and transfer. These are deemed to be administrative concerns. This practice is believed to encourage the teacher to feel more free to request help from the supervisor.

Use of scales and case histories plays an important part in teacher evaluation. A chief argument against the use of a rating device by a supervisor is that he generally does not have sufficient time for the extended observation believed to be essential to competent judgment of the teacher.

The problem of ethics, of professional conduct of a teacher and supervisor, will not be a major one if and when the supervisor can promote self-evaluation, within the staff. The supervisor can develop within the teacher a desire for the practice of constant re-evaluation as he gets the teacher concerned with his own improvement, helps him to define what he is trying to do, offers suggestions on ways of collecting data, and helps him make judgments and plan ways of improvement.[9] It is easy for the supervisor, in extending this help, to be considerate of the strong teacher or even to praise the virtues of the weak teacher. How to be both understanding and effective with the obvious faults of the weak teacher calls for strategy of the highest order.

The supervisor can do more *with* and *for* an excellent teacher who is receptive to new ideas and is truly interested in the improvement of his teaching than with the teacher who is far less able and is also indifferent to improvement. A competent supervisor will overlook minor mistakes of any teacher. However, it would be the height of folly for him to condone major faults in teaching.

The teacher is entitled to consideration from the supervisor. Considerateness is not all kindly regard for his feelings, however. It includes also reflection concerning consequences. Sympathy, tolera-

[9] Wiles, *Supervision for Better Schools*, p. 266.

tion, and conciliation are desirable traits in anyone. Complacency and indolence must be treated definitely and positively.

In conclusion, a fundamental question is: Which is the more important for the supervisor—keeping records, sending out questionnaires, rating teachers, writing bulletins and courses of study, or helping the teacher to grow and so improve his quality of teaching? The answer lies in the latter. Thoughtful kindness and well-advised regard form the cornerstone of sound relationships for the teacher and the supervisor. If the supervisor is capable of sober reflection, a regard for circumstances or consequences, he is considerate. When he is capable of observance of the rights and feelings of others— has a kindly regard for others—he is in a position to extend help to others.

The supervisor should show confidence and respect for the teacher; avoid being critical in the presence of a third party; and make evaluations of work to the teacher—not reports to superiors about the teacher. The literature dealing with the supervisor-learner relations, whether it be in business or in education, stresses the importance of consideration of all personnel, whether white- or dark-collar workers. It suggests that the greatest shortcoming of administration has been its lack of understanding of human needs, of human problems of the worker, and of the people who have to supervise that worker.

## QUESTIONS FOR STUDY

1. Who in your school system is called a supervisor? Why?
2. Are supervisors teachers? Should they be?
3. What type of authority does a supervisor possess? To what extent does the supervisor "have the right" to command action from the teacher?
4. If the teacher is "in the line" regarding authority, how can the supervisor influence the teacher's actions?
5. When the teacher and supervisor are in a classroom, who has the legal responsibility for pupil behavior? Why?
6. What do you feel are the real stumbling blocks to an effective supervisory program?
7. Because of his position is the supervisor inclined to be less ethical in his relationships than is the teacher? Why do you think so?

8. Can the "democratic" teacher and the "authoritarian" supervisor get along?

9. Should a teacher engage in an activity suggested by a supervisor for which the teacher has no "professional stomach"?

10. Describe the difference between a teacher who acts thoughtlessly to hurt another and one who is arrogant for "good cause."

## SUGGESTED READINGS

The topic of the legal relationships of the teacher and supervisor is missing in the literature. One reason to account for it is that the supervisor and teacher are considered as "one and the same."

The readings on the general nature of the relationships between the teacher and supervisor are legion. Some are:

Adams, Harold P., and Frank G. Dickey, *Basic Principles of Supervision* (New York: American Book Company, 1953), chap. VI, "Supervision Through Observational Visits," and chap. VII, "Supervision Through Individual Conferences."

Bartky, John A., *Supervision As Human Relations* (New York: D. C. Heath & Company, 1953), chap. 3, "The Supervisor," chap. 4, "Teacher Personality Treated Synthetically," chap. 5, "Teacher Personality Treated Analytically," and chap. 15, "Supervision and School System Organization."

Burton, William H., and Leo J. Brueckner, *Supervision; a Social Process* (New York: Appleton-Century-Crofts, Inc., 1955), Part I, "The Definition and Organization of Modern Supervision."

Cook, Lloyd, and Elaine Cook, *School Problems in Human Relations* (New York: McGraw-Hill Book Company, Inc., 1957), Part Two, "Solving School Problems."

Griffiths, Daniel E., *Human Relations in School Administration* (New York: Appleton-Century-Crofts, Inc., 1956), Part Three, "Case Studies."

Overstreet, Harry, and Bonaro Overstreet, *The Mind Alive* (New York: W. W. Norton & Company, Inc., 1954), chap. 4, "Accepting Ourselves," chap. 12, "Letting People Be Themselves," and chap. 15, "Creative Handling of Conflict."

Wiles, Kimball, *Supervision for Better Schools* (Englewood Cliffs, N. J.: Prentice-Hall, Inc., 1955), Part Four, "Supervision as Skill in Personnel Administration," including chaps. 11 and 12.

# Teacher-Teacher
# Relationships

## 6

### PROBLEM SITUATIONS

What would you do in each of the following situations? Analyze each in terms of the questions raised at the beginning of Chapter 3 (page 56).

CASE A
Several pupils in the eighth grade at —————— School will reach their sixteenth birthday before school closes in June. The boys do poor classwork and are "discipline" problems in the school and on the grounds. They don't seem to care about failing since they "plan to quit soon anyway."

One teacher has encouraged the pupils to remain in school—to "stick it out." One homeroom teacher has resented the interferences.

CASE B
Herb was being discussed again over coffee in the teachers' lounge after school. One teacher reported that he and two others had been caught walking over the tops of classroom desks with their wet and soiled overshoes. Mr. S, a social studies teacher, said that he knew that "a couple of licks in the Army would straighten Herb out all right," and that he didn't mind letting all know how he felt. For him, Herb was a "wise punk" who excused himself out of every situation.

"But Fred," said Miss J, "Herb needs our help. He cuts up because he can't be the lawyer or the doctor his brothers are no matter how hard he tries. He needs to find himself."

"Ya, that sounds like you, Fay. I've talked about Herb and his problems to everyone I know. What he needs I'm ready to give him right now."

CASE C
A seventh grade girl wrote an "obscene" story about the "Married Life of Mrs. J." She had illustrated it with "appropriate pictures." Mrs. J, the teacher, took the story to the principal. The girl's mother was a

175

third grade teacher in the same school. She called the principal for a "showdown" for tormenting her daughter.

CASE D

By means of the grapevine, the principal of City Elementary School hears that one of the teachers is becoming "very attached" to a few of the children. She has been taking the children where they want to go, it is alleged. She spends a great deal of time with them. She seems anxious for all the children to like her. She tries to be a "pal" to them. She encourages them to talk with her as they would someone at their own age level.

The principal knows this teacher is trying to help the children in many ways and that the teacher is anxious to have a child of her own. Yet, the "pal" attitude is causing discipline problems in the rooms of the other teachers.

CASE E

Bill *M*, president-elect of the Hi-Y, president of the junior class, manager of the football team, and candidate for state officer in the Beta Club, was involved in a "gang activity" in the community. The group was alleged to have moved porch furniture, started two grass fires in vacant lots, and moved a teacher's car three blocks from her home.

Two teachers have gone to the principal to "demand" that Bill be removed from all school offices held. At least one other teacher has "stood up for Bill." This teacher has remarked that the so-called "offenses" are merely childish pranks that "some teachers would be willing and ready to do if they only could seize the chance."

The systems of one-teacher schools of past decades generally did not present problems to teachers insofar as getting along with other teachers was concerned. One teacher was seldom in contact with others, except that on occasion he may have attended a "Teachers' Institute" at the county seat under the direction of the County Superintendent or County Commissioner of Education. There was no problem in such schools involving common purposes, division of labor, or class load. The lone teacher did everything that had to be done in the realm of the educational program, and his ideas never came into conflict with those of another teacher who may not have seen things just as he did. To some teachers today this arrangement may appear to have been sheer "Utopia."

As one-room schools grew into two-room schools, and two-room schools into ten- and twelve-room schools (and in the larger cities even thirty-room schools), and as consolidation progressed in rural areas, school organization changed too. Today, instead of one lone teacher going to the schoolhouse each morning and ringing a bell or crying "books, books" to bring the children in from play, teachers enter large and frequently ugly buildings to find their way through a maze of uninteresting corridors to particular classrooms with a number above the door and a lock that requires a particular key. To obtain this key and report arrival at school, a teacher usually reaches his classroom by way of the principal's office.

## The Teacher in the Large School

Today a teacher finds himself a part of a large city or county organization. A teacher in the large school sees other teachers as he walks down the hall to get keys and sign the attendance roster on his way to his classroom. The teachers he sees each day are those with rooms adjoining or close to his room. At recess, the halfway mark between school opening and lunch, a teacher may take his turn at minding the children at play. If another teacher assists, he may have a brief opportunity to exchange a few words of greeting with his co-worker. Teachers not assigned to recess duty may be found so very busy trying to catch up with classroom chores that they barely find themselves able to get to the classroom door to receive the children as they return from play.

The next chance a teacher has to see a fellow teacher is during the lunch hour. However, in some large schools the children must be supervised in the cafeteria. Sometimes a teacher eats with the pupils in his class to "insure good behavior." Then, if time remains for the children to play, he may escort them to the playground where he supervises their activities until the bell marks the return to classroom duties. During the brief lunch period, contacts with other teachers may be limited to a few words of greeting and a mutual complaint about the weather or the behavior of one or two particular "charges."

The next break in the school day is signaled by the afternoon dismissal bell. The children must be made ready to go home with all their wraps, homework, and last word of caution about care in crossing streets and going directly home or cooperating with the bus driver. Teachers then must go through the final chores of the day—straightening of the desks, adjusting shades, storing loose instructional materials, and packing into a brief case the papers and notebooks that must be appraised. Each teacher then emerges from his classroom, turns the key if the custodian has not yet arrived to sweep the room, proceeds down the corridor to replace his key on the rack, signs the check-out report, and leaves for the day. There is the possibility that he will meet other teachers doing the same things and will call a "good-bye" to them. Teachers may glance toward the bulletin board before they leave. It is possible that the principal has called a meeting. However, each scans the board with a feeling of relief as he realizes that he can depart safely.

The above account of a teacher's day in a large school shows that he is not alone like a teacher in a one-room school. He is in contact with other teachers. He is part of a big, throbbing, live organization made up of a thousand children and thirty classroom teachers. He has come into contact with other teachers at least three times during the day and perhaps has had short conversations with several of his neighbors up and down the hall. To be sure, he recognizes the names of the remaining twenty-three or twenty-four because they were introduced at the first faculty meeting. With these teachers on the second floor, or in the west wing, or on the north side, or in different grade levels, most teachers have very little in common.

If this picture of the larger school is accurate, it might be concluded that it is little different from that of the one-room school so far as teacher-teacher relationships are concerned. Each teacher in the large school is still a lone worker. Whether he teaches a grade or a subject, he is very much on his own.

## LEGAL ASPECTS

A teacher is generally not concerned with the legal nature of his relationships with other teachers. Ordinarily there is no need. Seldom does a teacher have any contractual relationships with other teachers as teachers that would cause any questions to arise other than those pertaining to citizens in general. Seldom does one teacher bring another into court to answer charges of libel or slander even though there may be just cause to do so. Seldom does a teacher violate copyright laws and have to answer charges of plagiarism.

There are proper legal procedures for teachers who violate their contracts and for boards of education who exceed their authority in their contractual relations with teachers. Although action in a court of law is not the appropriate remedy for the solution of many of the problems that arise between teachers, there are some occasions when it must be so.

A teacher as such has no legal rights that another teacher can infringe upon that he does not already possess as a citizen. His license to practice his profession is a legal right conferred upon him by the state through his certificate to teach, and it can be taken away from him only by the authority of the state. No teacher can deprive another teacher of his right to teach school. No teacher can deprive another teacher of his legal rights and responsibilities to carry out his professional responsibilities.

### Slander as a Civil Action

Slander is the utterance by one person of words about another person in the presence of a third party or parties that will damage the character or reputation of the person about whom the words are spoken.

> The speaking of words which are base and defamatory tending to prejudice another in his reputation, office, trade, business, or means of livelihood constitutes a slander.[1]

Any words tending to harm a teacher's reputation so as to lower him in the estimation of the community or to deter teachers and others from associating with him are defamatory words. Under certain circumstances words form the basis for a suit in which the person "injured" seeks damages and the clearing of his reputation. Defamation may be a statement of fact, as "Miss $X$ did thus and so." It may be the expression of a derogatory opinion based upon facts known, assumed, or disclosed, as "I think Miss $X$ should be fired for the betterment of the school."[2]

[1] All persons are civilly liable for damages which may occur through their spoken words unless the law protects them through immunity legislation or they have immunity under the common law. The teacher is not immune.

[2] See Madaline K. Remmlein, *School Law* (New York: McGraw-Hill Book Company, Inc., 1950), p. 165.

Any statement to a parent, another teacher, or to pupils in a class or to the custodian, that is detrimental to a teacher and will cause him personal harm, may be cause for action of slander. It may not be necessary to prove malice on the part of the person uttering the words, but it is necessary for the plaintiff (the one who commences a suit) to prove that he has been injured by the words uttered. Since teachers have professional reputations to uphold, any statement regarding competence may be damaging professionally even though it does not damage character per se.

Slanderous words can be communicated under "privileged" circumstances. A teacher whose line of duty requires him to make confidential reports regarding other employees may claim immunity for such oral reports. In such situations the law extends to a teacher a special legal prerogative, a protection from suit which is not enjoyed by his colleagues. His remarks are "qualifiedly" privileged.

When careless statements made by one teacher regarding the competence of another go unchallenged, one might ask the reason why. The answer can be sought in two factors: (1) the school teacher's extreme antipathy toward getting involved in court action, and (2) the lack of financial vulnerability of teachers. Though a judgment can be secured, a teacher's wages in most states cannot be garnished. The cost of the suit could more than offset the possibility of collecting damages. Thus, the suit would become more punitive to the defendant than rewarding to the plaintiff. If this condition should change, teachers might need to take heed of the possibility of action in slander by another teacher.

### Libel as a Legal Action

The same general principles apply in the action of libel, except, of course, that libel consists of words printed or written and caused to be read by one or more third (disinterested) parties. Again, there is some measure of legal immunity where the words are written "in the line of duty" as a confidential report. The best example of this kind of communication is one wherein a teacher is asked to write a professional reference about another and the words written are untrue. Even though the teacher concerned later finds out about the false statements, and even though the teacher is injured professionally and personally, such knowledge cannot be used as a basis for a charge of libel. The report in which the words appear is a confidential report and therefore qualifiedly privileged.

On the other hand, if a teacher writes a statement about another teacher to a third party, such as a parent, a colleague, or even a pupil, that puts the other teacher up to ridicule and challenges his professional reputation, the teacher has just cause for an action of libel.

### Protection of Personal Property

Sometimes a teacher may copy from another teacher or use material or services that another teacher has created for his own use. The question arises: Is there a legal remedy for the teacher whose apparent rights are thus violated? The only right a citizen has to inventions or writings that he may have created is obtained through the patent and copyright laws. If a teacher copies and uses some material that has been thus protected, he can be sued for plagiarism. Frequently publishing companies give teachers the right to reproduce copyrighted material. If such permission is not extended, teachers should not reproduce for their own use such protected material.

## ETHICAL ASPECTS

The human body has many related parts to help make it an effective organism. So has the modern school many interrelated parts. A teacher should be conscious of the degree to which his efforts are a part of the total efforts of other employees. The relationships between employees obviously are not controlled by law. They are governed by the general rules of behavior that a group of people adopt as they attempt to work out problems for the common good. These rules are found in codes of ethics, written or spoken, well defined or indefinite.

The behavior of some teachers can be pointed out as plainly unprofessional since it militates against accomplishment of the job to be done. Behaviors include that of a teacher who carries around the attitude, "It won't work anyway, so why try it." A teacher may, in conversations that are general and social, talk of school problems that involve other teachers. Another teacher may cherish "his clique" and help make others feel as outsiders in the group. Another may "ride the fence" on every issue before the teacher group. None of these behaviors is difficult to spot in most schools.

However, there are questions involving teacher-teacher contacts of an ethical nature that are not so easily tagged. Is the "Do unto others . . ." dictum an unqualifiedly sound principle of ethics for the teacher? What should be or usually is included in the admonition "not to act improperly" so as to embarrass the group? Is a teacher helped to be aware of the difference between behaviors that are short of ethical and those that are "incompetent?" How can a code of ethics help a teacher to distinguish between the unethical and the merely undesirable conduct of a colleague? Should a violation of the provisions of an "accepted code" justify penalties against a colleague who has committed some infraction?

Equally troublesome queries are these: whether a teacher should be ethically bound not to testify to the quality of work performed by another teacher; whether a teacher can tell the difference between scrupulous and unscrupulous professional conduct; and whether "academic racketeering" is too strong a term to use to describe a teacher who sells his creations to other teachers for a profit.

Following are sections dealing with various aspects of ethics in teacher-teacher relationships. They include "Causes of Friction Between Teachers," "Attitudes Toward New Staff Members," "Supporting Associates," and "Relationships in Staff Meetings and Committees."

## Causes of Friction Between Teachers

Frequently just a casual remark or some bodily movement at a particular time may be a symptom of unprofessional attitudes between teachers. They may indicate poor human relations. For example, one need not go far to overhear a teacher "snipe" about the "band leader's easy job," or see a teacher who incurs ill-will from colleagues because he somehow "gets out of" his share of playground or hall duty.

Sometimes the causes for friction lie much deeper. The professional worker tends to resent a colleague who plays the role "I'm going to the principal first with this so he'll find out from me." A teacher may have reason to gripe about the "coach" who draws three study halls because of after-school duties. A teacher builds up resentment against a colleague who receives more pay for a similar class load, who has "free time" during the school day, and who is freed from accepting responsibility to sponsor student activities after the last class period is over.

Parts of the causes for the "deeper" kind of friction result from the many differences within and among teachers themselves. The differences—physical, emotional, intellectual, social, singly or in combination—give rise to conflict. If, for example, one teacher must "pinch-hit" two days prior to a performance by seventh graders because his colleague was hospitalized for ulcers, the substitute believes the patient has played "a mean trick." A teacher with a heart ailment is often willing to work beyond his strength. Sometimes he gathers more and more "jobs." If his heart fails under the pressure, the staff is left with the task of protecting a semi-invalid. Other teachers resent the fact, then, that the handicapped one is not able to accept out-of-class duties. Perhaps the supervision of the school newspaper or playground duties must be assumed by another teacher who feels overburdened already.

The posture of a teacher, his expression, voice, and other externals sometimes lie at the root of the biases of co-workers.[3] Once they are established, the biases tend to persist in all future relations between teachers. The bickering between two teachers of English at Madison High on the "Our Miss Brooks" radio and television shows illustrates, with much exaggeration, similar situations that exist in all schools, in all places where people see one another day after day.

If a teacher has social position and status in the community, his behavior toward the librarian or toward his department head may have a tone of authority and confidence that cannot be mustered by a teacher with less social prestige. With incomes above associates, some teachers can afford to be more generous with children than other colleagues dare be. A teacher with a cultural upbring-

---

[3] The writer is indebted for ideas in these paragraphs to the work of John A. Bartky, in his volume *Supervision as Human Relations* (New York: D. C. Heath & Company, 1953).

ing reflecting less privilege may be biased toward his more privileged associate. When a common problem faces these two teachers, the latter, conditioned by his former experiences, is likely to be convinced that his ways are highly desirable ways of solving all social problems and meeting life situations. He opposes his associate, perhaps unconsciously, because it is difficult for him even to tolerate ways of living different from his own.

Jessup found in his study[4] that "disparaging remarks and harping criticisms" was topmost in frequency of the ten most violated standards of the ethical code. Unfortunately, remarks of this sort are frequently made about a predecessor or colleague, sometimes in the presence of a disinterested third party. If the report is accurate, a serious indictment of members of the teaching profession is in order. Invariably the "habit" thus indulged in does more damage to the "talker" and the profession than to the one talked about. Excuses are made for disparagers on the basis that it is natural to gossip or that petty jealousies cannot be avoided. Whatever the reason for the vicious habit, it can be ill afforded and must be condemned in the strongest terms one can discreetly muster.

There may be those in the teaching profession who have developed a feeling of insecurity to the point where they can find security only in attacking others. Their outlook on life has so warped their perspective that they find no good in others. Pangs of jealousy may have impaired their judgment. To say to them, "The behavior you exhibit is not ethical," would have little effect. There is a remedy, however. It is to refuse to listen! For every cruel remark uttered about a fellow teacher there must be one who listened. A teacher who listens to loose talk is an accessory to the act. He must refuse to listen so that the one compelled to gossip will find no pleasure as his audience ceases to be. For, to listen, even though not interested, is to encourage the practice and is unethical.

Comment upon all the differences that influence teachers' relations is impossible. Highlights can be suggested. It has been pointed out that teachers differ in many respects and that differences, when emphasized and dwelt upon, cause cleavages. Teachers differ to an even greater degree, possibly, than do children because they

[4] John H. Jessup, "Violations of Ethical Standards," *Phi Delta Kappan,* Vol. XXIX (November, 1947), p. 170.

have had a longer time to acquire their biological, cultural, and psychological characteristics and quirks.

Again, teacher participation in school policy formation sometimes causes friction within the faculty group. The "in group" and the "out group" carry on unofficial warfare. In such a situation teachers tend to behave as members of a clique, muttering disapproval of suggestions from the "opposing camp" or, as the case may be, applauding loudly when an opinion is expressed by one of the sympathizers. A voice of protest must be raised against such practices. Professional ethics demand that no comment be made that is detrimental to the efforts of all. Support must be general to policies that further the interests of boys and girls. Honest criticism must be voiced openly at meetings, or carried to responsible school personnel. When there is division within the ranks, principles of ethics properly observed can help to solidify the group. All teachers must understand that the important factor is not maintaining the identity of "groups" but accepting certain rules of behavior so that the whole staff can get the best solutions to common problems.

## Attitudes Toward New Staff Members

As a rule, as each new school term begins in September new members are added to the school staff. Much has been written regarding the need for orienting new teachers to their jobs. The suggestions place the responsibility for proper orientation on the shoulders of the principal and superintendent. The principal is usually charged with the duty of informing teachers about school policies, textbooks, supplies, and the general procedure of organization within the school. A popular plan today is for the principal to appoint one of the experienced members of the staff to serve as a "buddy" to a new teacher.

Any plan of orientation brings new teachers into direct relation, eventually, with all staff members and with community members. Depending upon how well they are conceived and carried out, orientation efforts may help or hinder a new teacher's first months. Sometimes he is left after the first week of "being buddied" to fend for himself. Or, he may well feel that the school is cold and hostile because the teacher selected to help him has accepted the task in a most perfunctory fashion. He may express the attitude that "You'll find out soon enough," or, "Let me give you a little of the low-down on this place."

The attitude of other teachers toward their school and their work is undoubtedly the most powerful single influence for good or ill in the life of a new teacher in the beginning months of his work. These first impressions a new teacher gets are frequently lasting ones, even though they prove to be limited or incorrect.

It is the professional duty of each teacher to assist a new teacher to get that "feeling of belonging" to the staff. It is his obligation to show the new member that the teachers are loyal to their school and profession and that they are anxious to share with him any information that will make his work easier and more effective. Each must discourage the passing of "destructive and carping criticism" so that ears unaccustomed to such talk will not be called upon to make judgments they cannot and should not make.

A new teacher may be "made or destroyed" by his first experiences in the early days of his career. Ethics and plain common sense demand a loyalty to the profession of teaching that guarantees to the novice the most wholesome working conditions. The task ahead for the beginner is difficult enough without placing obstacles in his professional path.

Numerous student teachers tend to "complain" about the teacher who, perhaps inadvertently, has given them a feeling that "you surely picked the wrong thing if you're out for an honest buck." The regular teacher who makes such a comment, even in jest, is showing poor manners and judgment too. What alternative is left for the student teacher but to "run as fast as he can in the opposite direction" to escape getting into a profession whose members think it so lowly.

## Supporting One's Associates

Even though the positive approach to the solution of problems is emphasized time and again, it seems easier to accentuate the negative. There are few teachers who do not know at least one within the ranks who fails to support his colleagues, who, instead, tries to "knock" and "tear down." This kind of person sometimes attempts to bring pressure to bear on others to think and act as he does. If one with such ideas of ethics attempts to "poison" a new teacher or a student teacher by his onslaughts, his conduct is especially reprehensible.

There are teachers on many school staffs who, in terms of the street, "double-cross" a colleague by agreeing on a policy or procedure and then, to make a better showing for themselves, violate the agreement. There is the teacher who undermines rather than supports his associates by withholding plans for a program, trips to be made, or contests to be entered. He may even impose the pledge of secrecy upon pupils. Then, when the plan is unveiled, the teacher can have the satisfaction of surprising and surpassing his colleagues. These few teachers fall into a pattern of thinking in terms of their own excellence instead of having as their goal the very best program for boys and girls. They fail to recognize that it is unprofessional for them to struggle to excel at the expense of other teachers, other pupils, and the whole school program.

There are practices resorted to by teachers to undermine an associate that may involve passing most complimentary remarks. The fox of the well-known fable obtained from the unsuspecting crow a piece of cheese by telling him what a beautiful voice he possessed. Flattery may be one means of gaining advantage over another who, in turn, is hurt by it. For a veteran teacher to shirk responsibility by inveigling an inexperienced teacher to assume it is professionally dishonorable. The upright approach would be for the experienced teacher to solicit the interest and help of the younger faculty member through a frank discussion of the importance of the venture.

It is appropriate now "to accentuate the positive." To indicate in any detail *the* desirable attitudes a teacher should possess enabling him to support his colleagues in their mutual effort is a well-nigh impossible task. However, despite limitations in phrasing and in meaning, the following suggestions have merit. A teacher who encourages and fosters these attitudes performs a valuable service to other teachers, children, himself, and the profession. These predispositions to action include: active friendliness; cooperation with both new and experienced teachers; recognition of performance of quality work; willingness to learn from others; sportsmanship; the "booster" spirit.

To the extent that a teacher engages in the following kinds of activities he will be supporting the efforts of his associates and helping materially to improve relations between teachers:

> Helping other teachers locate and remove difficulties;
> Maintaining wholesome relations by guarding language;
> Conferring with teachers about school regulations;
> Securing advice and assistance from other teachers;
> Assisting new teachers in their orientation;
> Assisting in schedule-making;
> Sharing committee work;
> Sharing plans with substitute teacher and successors;
> Cooperating with teachers in testing programs;
> Cooperating in making out daily and quarterly reports;
> Cooperating in keeping pupil and other school records;
> Advising about room and corridor displays.

As a classroom teacher, are you able to answer "yes" to each of the following questions? Do you:

1. Support associates in conversation in and outside of school?
2. Seek ways to give and receive constructive ideas?
3. Give recognition for achievements of others?
4. Give recognition for help others give you?
5. Help associates secure merited promotions?
6. Avoid interference in the classroom affairs of associates?
7. Shoulder responsibility for actions, rather than shifting it to an associate?
8. Hold inviolate confidential information about associates?
9. See to it that a substitute (or successor) finds materials in good working order? Has access to data and other records? Finds information necessary to carry on the work of the class?

Think of a specific instance within the past few days where you behaved as indicated above. Be able to tell yourself the who, what, where, when, how, and the why.

Fundamental to the American ideal is belief in and respect for the worth of each individual. The principle of mutual respect as it applies here means more than that respect which one owes to another because he is a human being. The mutual respect of one teacher toward another is inherent in the profession of teaching. This means that as teachers work together they respect each other as members of a great profession, and that they never knowingly act in any way that would cast reflection on a fellow teacher and upon the profession. The fifth principle in the code of ethics of the National Education Association states: "The teaching profession is distinguished from many other occupations by the uniqueness and quality of the professional relationships among all teachers. Community support and respect are influenced by standards of teachers and their attitudes toward teaching and other teachers."

How does the above principle apply to a classroom teacher in his relation to other teachers? There are at least two kinds of contacts teachers have which are frequently overlooked. For want of better terminology, we may speak of horizontal relationships and vertical relationships, thinking of work with teachers within a grade or subject level and with teachers at all levels from kindergarten through the college program.

When teachers are working in the same grade level or subject area, they must guard against competing for favored assignments. A teacher respects his colleagues in his own department or grade unit when he avoids saying, "You may be able to get away with poor spelling in Miss Brown's class, but you surely won't in my class." He helps to improve the atmosphere of the whole school as he avoids repeating to a parent an incident that involved another teacher. He would not say, for instance, "I surely would have handled Johnny differently," or, "I wouldn't have made him write those poetry verses." Perhaps a youngster is fortunate to be in one second grade rather than another. However, the wise teacher helps the parent see the good points in all teachers.

Without thought, perhaps, a teacher will compare "his" pupils with those of another grade or course. If he mentions scores made on tests or honors won by pupils under his supervision so as to indicate a "better" quality of work, he is forgetting about the principle of mutual respect.

A teacher may think of himself as an individualist and have little regard for the other teachers in the same building or in other schools who are working with either younger or more mature pupils. However, since the lives of children touch each other intimately, they cannot grasp the full significance of community living unless the school sets a pattern of harmonious group living. The tensions and discords of teachers, whether they are within a school or between schools, are seldom concealed from the children.

## Relationships in Staff Meetings and Committees

The type of staff meeting held in a single school unit depends almost entirely upon the leadership ability of the principal. He may use the meeting as a means of disseminating administrative information about policies, reports, and the means of obtaining materials. Or, on the other hand, the principal may conceive of the staff meeting as the opportunity for planning many phases of the program of the school. If the meeting is one of the former kind, there will be few new contacts for teachers as a result and little chance for new insights to be developed or old ones to be deepened. If the meeting is a true planning session, the teachers are active participants, helping to make decisions about schedules, materials used, curriculum organization, and various matters of pupil welfare. Some school staffs study better methods of evaluation, and a definition of the purpose of education. Other faculties tackle such problems as the planning and design of school buildings and salary schedule for their school system.

As staff meetings begin to shift from the principal-dominated to the teacher-planned type, certain relationships develop which may heighten professional interest of the teachers. Working together closely brings into focus some kinds of problems that would otherwise not be obvious. Individual drives, desires, and opinions come more clearly into view and play a part in decisions made about school affairs. The more opinionated and dominating teacher has the opportunity to "jockey" for the limelight and so lose sight of the reason for meeting together. He can force group discussion at almost every opportunity around to his own problems, creating rather than solving problems. He is brash, not brave. His contrariness is akin to pleasure at shocking or being in a tiny minority. He seems to "enjoy" the onslaughts of his fellows in order to feel sorry for himself in order, in turn, to feel superior. Unless such a teacher can be helped, the result must be serious impairment within the school staff.

The purposes and procedures of general meetings will seldom be concurred in by each and every member. However, a teacher who objects loudly and often to plans agreed upon impairs seriously the effectiveness of himself and of the total group. For example, consistent and belligerent refusal to promote policies, decided by the majority to best serve the interests of the school program, can and will prevent the building of a public opinion that will demand better schools. Differences can be expressed in open discussion and through the appropriate channels of communication. Only when dissatisfaction takes the turn of destructive criticism, or of underhanded tactics to harm the program, or of personal attacks upon the principal and other staff members, does it destroy. Persistent behavior of this sort must be labeled in bold letters what it is—unethical conduct, unbecoming to a member of the profession of teaching.

Some teachers have not developed such clear-cut opinions, negative or positive. They have no particular drives and follow the lines of least resistance whenever possible, not wishing to be burdened with challenges or with decisions to be made. One such teacher may say: "Why should we deal with this problem? That's the principal's job. What's he paid for anyway!" Somewhere in between the two extremes are the teachers who are willing and ready to work cooperatively on school problems for the best interests of the pupils, themselves, and the community of which they are a part. It is this group of teachers who can effect changes in the school program. It is they who develop their perceptions so that they can work together easily and well.

Quite frequently, a member of a faculty is selected as chairman of a committee. It is his function then to get the members to express their opinions about what is to be done and how, direct them in research, and lead in the development of a committee report. Hundreds of committees in schools over the land function well. However, on occasion a chairman senses that the report taking shape will not be a popular one with school authorities. He is "sincere" in everything he says and yet takes care not to present a report that may disconcert potential supporters. He will give the impression that group action is proceeding but alters the report, sometimes with the knowledge and help of another, to make it "coincide with the popular idea." The final report is then drafted with literally no consent of the members of the committee. It happens that a chairman may say to the members, "It is not necessary for us to meet. I'll take care of this report without troubling you." He takes it upon himself to "do all the work."

In either case, the action of the chairman borders on deception. It is unethical and violates basic principles of democratic solution to problems. Such action misrepresents the facts and falsifies the opinions of other committee members. Whether a report is written or oral, the chairman is charged with the responsibility of seeing to it that it represents the consensus. If it does not, or cannot, the chairman should insist upon the drafting of a minority statement by the dissenters to the report.

Surely other committee members besides the chairman sometimes engage in conduct not above reproach. For motives unknown or suppressed, a member may attempt to hamper the assigned job of the group by engaging in various types of obstructionist tactics. He may introduce extraneous issues so as to cloud the main one. He can obstruct cooperative effort by introducing irrelevant material, wasting the time of other members.

Tactics of clouding the main issue, of wasting time purposely, and of generally hampering committee effort, are not uncommon in political and labor meetings and even in some legal circles. In the profession of teaching, though, where best results are achieved when the whole educational team plays the game together according to the accepted rules, there seems to be little to justify such maneuverings. Deep differences there are in and between people which become evident as they struggle to work successfully together. However, the rules of the game call for putting forth the best efforts to plan constructively for change. If the rules are not abided by, changes will occur, but they tend to become progressively more detrimental to everyone involved.

## QUESTIONS FOR STUDY

1. What assumptions are made when one terms the "one-room school" organization a "Utopia"?
2. Do you agree that today the "typical" teacher finds himself in a situation not unlike that of his colleague of the "one-room" school?
3. For what reasons are teachers generally not concerned with the legal nature of their relationships?
4. Does a certificate to teach confer on the holder legal rights above and beyond those he possesses as a citizen? Explain your answer.
5. What are "defamatory" words?

6. What is meant by a "qualifiedly privileged" remark?
7. What are considered to be "just causes" for an action for libel?
8. What is included in the phrase, "the ethics of teacher-teacher relations"?
9. Upon what basis do school relationships rest?
10. Does "concern for the other fellow" necessarily mean reduced prestige or status for the individual?
11. What factors sometimes lie at the root of teacher biases?
12. What standards of ethics are most often violated by teachers?
13. Is the act of "listening" always beneficial or sound from the standpoint of ethics?
14. What is the meaning of the fifth principle in the code of ethics of the National Education Association?
15. Describe situations where a teacher demonstrates the "principle of mutual respect" for colleagues.
16. Why will the first experiences of the new teacher "make or break" him?
17. Describe the behavior of a committee chairman who is deceptive.

### SUGGESTED READINGS

Chandler, B. J., and Paul V. Petty, *Personnel Management in School Administration* (Yonkers, N.Y.: World Book Company, 1955), chap. 18, "Communication Within the School Organization."

Elsbree, Willard S., and Harold J. McNally, *Elementary School Administration and Supervision* (New York: American Book Company, 1951), chap. VII, "Organizing the Staff for School Improvement."

————, and E. Edmund Reutter, Jr., *Staff Personnel in the Public schools* (Englewood Cliffs, N. J.: Prentice-Hall, Inc., 1954), chap. 11, "Morale," and chap. 15, "Professional Ethics."

Grieder, Calvin, and William E. Rosenstengel, *Public School Administration* (New York: Ronald Press Co., 1954), chap. 10, "Improving the Instructional Program" (contains subtopics on morale and organization).

Hepburn, William M., *Cases on The Law of Torts* (St. Paul, Minn.: The West Publishing Company, 1954), chap. 7, "Defamation."

Moore, Harold W., and Newell B. Walters, *Personnel Administration in Education* (New York: Harper and Brothers, Publishers, 1955), chap. 3, "Morale Factors and Leadership in Personnel Administration."

Remmlein, Madaline Kinter, *School Law* (New York: McGraw-Hill Book Company Inc., 1950), chap. 9, "Defamation of Character."

————, *The Law of Local Public School Administration* (New York: McGraw-Hill Book Company, Inc., 1954), chap. 6, "Personnel Administration" (contains six selected references at the end of the chapter).

Yeager, William A., *Administration and the Teacher* (New York: Harper and Brothers, Publishers, 1954), chap. 2, "Teachers and Their Characteristics," and chap. 19, "Administration of the School as a Cooperative Group Enterprise."

# Nonteacher-Other Personnel Relationships

## PROBLEM SITUATIONS

What would you do in each of the following situations? Analyze each in terms of the questions raised at the beginning of Chapter 3 (page 56).

### CASE A

Mrs. *J*, an eighth grade teacher of English at City High School, was having much trouble with Jane. It all started when Jane reported on a book that "everyone knows is too strong for young minds." Mrs. *J* let it be known that she couldn't accept the book report and that Jane's reading should be "on a higher level."

In the cafeteria at the teachers' table, Mrs. *J* told a "small group" how shocked she was. Mrs. *K*, a supply teacher for the day, remarked that she had seen one of the maids "passing picture cards" to Jane right inside of the girls' toilet. Mrs. *J* left her sandwich and carrot sticks to "share a piece of her mind" with the custodial staff at City High.

### CASE B

Some of the pupils at ——————— School had developed the habit of going to the basement boiler room between bells for a smoke. Sam, the custodian, had rigged up a couch and several chairs for the students' comfort. On occasion he would share some of his "special blend" tobacco with Bill *S*, who, allegedly, visited Sam after school.

### CASE C

Miss *T* was relieved from teaching one class in English in order to coach dramatics. She apparently used the time to take pupils out of class to discuss their failings. She had made demands upon the time of the office staff during the coaching period.

The principal reminded Miss *T* that she should remain in her classroom.

However, she not only continues to disturb the office routine but quite regularly goes to the cafeteria to complain about the "starchy and unattractive food" served her. The cafeteria manager told her recently, "Get away from my territory or else!"

A teacher, as a matter of course, must associate with other teachers in and outside the classroom. However, the fact that a teacher also comes into daily contact with other workers associated with the school who have different duties from teachers is often taken for granted, if not actually overlooked.

The very nature of the school enterprise requires that many nonteaching and noncertified personnel be employed by the board of education. The relationships between teacher and nonteacher are important and affect directly the success of the school program.

In the school office, for instance, where the clerk meets the public, one finds relations vital to the entire school system being cemented or damaged. The assignments of nonteachers are sometimes as crucial in influence as are the professional ones. This is so despite the fact that one could maintain a school without clerks and dietitians but not without pupils and teachers. Many principals assert that "they would far rather lose the best teacher in their school than lose their best custodian." [1]

Increasingly, good teaching depends upon the work of a school "team" whose members work together in making school decisions —policies concerning a multitude of matters daily touching the lives of children in and out of school. The ability of a teacher to work well with members of the school team who are classified as the "nonteachers" is a significant factor in a teacher's success in the classroom.

In the school where cooperative effort is a distinguishing mark, the school principal is the leader of a team of teacher and nonteacher. It is he who logically must bear the burden of establishing the "working climate." He bears the same relationship to the whole staff—the team—as a teacher does to the class. It is the obligation of the school principal to help bring the skills of individual members of both the instructional and service staffs to their fullest development.

[1] Henry H. Linn and others, *The School Custodian's Housekeeping Handbook* (New York: Bureau of Publications, Teachers College, Columbia University, 1948), p. 8.

## Nonteachers and Noncertified Personnel

The workers on the school team who are not teachers have been identified by various terms. To understand the meaning of personnel classifications such as "certified" or "nonteaching," one needs to divide each into more familiar categories. The certified personnel are professional persons and include classroom teachers, principals, supervisory staff members, and any others who require special preparation and certification for their work. Clinicians, nurses, and psychologists are included in this group, although they are not considered teachers.

The nonteaching personnel—ordinarily the noncertified or nonprofessional—are the operating, maintenance, clerical, and service employees of the school system. The operating employees are those associated with the operation and management of the school plant —the custodians, engineers, watchmen, and bus drivers. Maintenance employees are those charged with the responsibility for the upkeep of the school plant and equipment. They include carpenters, plumbers, electricians, and mechanics. Clerical employees are those with responsibilities for immediate public relations and record keeping in the school offices. Service employees are assigned to such duties as food preparation.

The nonteaching personnel are sometimes called the "noncertified" personnel. Some deliberately avoid using the term, since within the group are some who hold qualifications for employment and are actually licensed or rated before they can be hired. When the designation "noncertified" is used, it includes custodians, maintenance workers, gardeners, lunchroom workers, bus drivers, attendants in special schools, and clerks.

It is difficult to think of certain school personnel as belonging either to the group of professional educators or to the group of nonteaching personnel. Included in this "in-between" category are physicians, dentists, nurses, recreation workers, architects, auditors, public relations directors, and TV and radio technicians. In addition to the personnel in the categories of professional educator and nonteaching personnel, therefore, there are workers in a third category who are in "professional services" auxiliary to education.

None of these breakdowns is totally convenient. Personnel of the public schools will be classified, however, in this section into two general types: the professional or certified personnel, and the non-teaching personnel. The workers who merely assist in the educational enterprise will be thought of as the "nonteaching" workers. Those included perform work essential to maintaining and operating the school system. They may be professional, in some cases, and some are certified as are teachers.

Classification of personnel, based upon functions performed, is not meant to imply the assignment of importance or priority rank to any type of worker. It represents, rather, a convenient basis for the discussion of legal and ethical relationships. Discussion will center on the legal and ethical concerns of personnel but in relation to (1) the custodian and his staff, (2) the food service workers, (3) the office workers, and (4) health personnel.

## Legal Aspects in General

### Mutual Employees of the State

The personnel serving the public schools is a body of public employees. The legal relationship of the teacher to "the school personnel" is that of mutual employees of the state.

Employment by a branch of government is analogous to employment by a private employer. The relationship between employer and employee is a contractual one. The employee, whether teacher or engineer, has only the rights and obligations contained in his employment contract. All "school employees" are civil servants and are thus solely "employees" of government. As such, teacher and nonteacher have only the legal status that the law generally accords to all employees. The relationship of the teacher as an employee of the state to the nonteacher is not different from that of a relationship between private employees. In the absence in state statutes or local rules and regulations of provisions to the contrary, the board of education, as an arm of the government, has the same discretion with regard to the appointment and dismissal of teachers and nonteacher personnel that any private employer has.

For a teacher, the relationship of the teaching to the nonteaching areas is one of achievement of purposes (teaching) through the services afforded by the personnel in the nonteaching areas. Teachers must be acquainted at least with the nonteaching functions and responsibilities. With the help of the principal, teachers can very quickly learn to distinguish between the services of instruction and those services connected with operation.

As public employees, school personnel are limited and controlled, to a very considerable degree, by state laws and local regulations. As individuals and as members of a professional or vocational group, they are controlled by the voluntary prescriptions of their respective groups. This dual regulation, though not in and of itself creating conflict, helps to create the conditions whereby coordination of the work of the school is made more difficult.

School officials who do hiring should be diligent about observing local and state regulations. Failure to adhere to them might subject them to heavy penalty. Even more important, failure to observe rules might make school officials liable under laws of negligence, should an accident occur.

## Importance of Job Classification

Systematic job classification does not avoid personal liability for injury. Such classification and job description will, however, go a long way in clarifying the relations between the nonteacher and other personnel within the school system. A complete classification of nonteaching positions in the system would indicate the duties and qualifications for each class of positions. Such a plan would include the personnel authorized by the board of education and the nature of the duties expected of persons working in those positions.

The minimum qualifications and the special training requirements for appointments to each class of positions would be stated in the classification. Such a procedure would aid personnel immeasurably in their understanding of areas of responsibility. Sound relationships between the nonteaching personnel and others rest upon such understandings. A teacher would be aided in working with nonteachers on the staff by having available to him statements of policy by the school board with respect to nonteaching personnel.

If teacher and nonteacher are to appreciate one another's role, each must understand many facets including those of job security and areas of responsibility. Each needs to know the differences in the purpose of retirement plans. The objectives of social security and of local retirement plans are usually similar for all personnel but may vary in some details. To understand these means less likelihood of misunderstandings and litigation.

## Ethical Aspects in General

Of much importance to the school program is the nonteacher's associations with pupils and other workers. Within the school, teachers come in contact with many nonteaching employees every working day. Some teachers become "well known" to nonteachers. Relationships then may tend to become "routine" and seem cool and formal.

However, "when the compliments are passed out, the man in overalls and the woman in apron should not be forgotten." [2] Surely, the considerate attitude of a teacher toward the auxiliary workers and their services helps them take pride in "their school." Wholesome relationships between teachers and the worker "who comes and goes" may be difficult to develop owing to the temporary nature of assignments. The specialized nature of the work to be performed within a school system tends to disunite the total employee group. One of the characteristics of personnel in the public schools is the high rate of turnover, particularly in the nonteaching group.

The total school employee group is quite diverse in skills and functions. Services performed require wide differences in ability. Other than teachers, the "employee" as such is drawn from a number of fields. Generally, the workers have had little or no background in school work before entering the employ of the local board and may not "act properly" as far as teachers are concerned.

## Concern for the Common Goal

It is recognized that a teacher can promote increased understanding on the part of nonteaching staff members by suggesting, when suitable, the educational task and broad responsibility

[2] John T. Wahlquist, *et al.*, *The Administration of Public Education* (New York: The Ronald Press Company, 1952), p. 249.

of schools. The best chance to achieve an "employee team" is through establishing interest in and concern for the common goal —admittedly an enormous task. The diverse interests and tasks militate against setting up the ways and means of coordinating the various efforts of personnel. Bases for misunderstandings are thereby laid.

The class stratification in school ranks is due to such factors as rank, salary, authority (power), social position, and the like. Obviously these are serious obstacles to the effective coordination of a total program. When a teacher, or other worker, discriminates against school personnel because he feels, and perhaps believes, that they are of a "lower class," that teacher is hardly a representative of American ideals in practice. Plainly, a teacher should not be a party to the perpetuation of discrimination, whatever its bases. When a teacher "looks down his nose" at the secretary and cafeteria manager because he thinks of them as "hired help," he damages the delicate fabric holding the staff together. He literally punctures the protective wall and allows "poison" to seep in. Whether this comes from dishonesty, incompetence, or ignorance, the net result is the same—a poorer school environment for the children of that community. It should go without saying that a teacher is actually obligated to treat all school personnel with equal courtesy, regardless of whether they are a "deHabersham" or a plain "John Doe."

### Emotional Stresses and Courtesy

Constant relationship with the public, often in exacting and very personal situations, creates emotional stresses within the personnel of the school. These tensions sometimes prevent those involved from remembering always to act and speak courteously toward others. In addition to the dictates of good judgment, all members of the staff need to refrain from doing anything or saying anything that later may cause embarrassment. Loyalty to the pupils, the staff, the principal, and the system requires this minimum level of consideration.

Members of the staff who are nonteachers may at times slacken their pace just like teachers. At that time, a teacher may want to hint or make an outright statement about such matters. It is hoped the employee will take the hint and make the effort to adjust that which seems to be bothersome before real complications arise. Sometimes it would be better if a teacher called attention of the matter to the principal, with just enough details to enable him to speak at an appropriate time and place with the employee and his immediate superior. A teacher's role does not include telling others what their job is.

A teacher who unintentionally commits a breach of good judgment should apologize just as promptly and sincerely whether the person involved is the custodian, lunchroom manager, or secretary. A genuine effort to be thoughtful and considerate of all employees at all times is the best insurance against a misunderstood act. It has been stated often and in many places that courtesy costs absolutely no dollars, yet it pays huge dividends. In few relationships does this maxim hold as true as in contacts between a teacher and nonteacher where each is engaged in the business of education.

Attending to personal affairs during working hours—seeing friends, talking over the telephone, or addressing personal letters —uses improperly the time of the employee for which the board is paying. Telephone service is paid for by the board of education and should at all times be available for school business, emergency and routine. School calls may be missed and needed help delayed when an employee uses the telephone for a personal call. No employee has the right to charge personal calls to the school, or to use school stationery and school stamps for sending personal letters. Dishonest conduct is involved here, not only unethical actions.

## CUSTODIAN-PERSONNEL RELATIONSHIPS

### Legal Aspects

The responsibility for providing healthful and sanitary surroundings for pupil and teacher belongs to the board of education. It must furnish such custodial care as will insure good working conditions, for a teacher has no responsibility for the actual performance of custodial acts. For example, the courts have held that a teacher is justified in refusing to teach in an unheated room where the temperature is below that deemed necessary for good health, and in refusing to teach in unsanitary surroundings. It is true that a teacher may be charged with the task of seeing to it that good conditions are ever present insofar as it is within his power to do so.

## Function of the School Custodian

It is clear that the function of a teacher is "to teach." It is not always absolutely clear as to what the function means. However, it was decided fairly early by the courts that teaching did not include building fires, sweeping floors, and performing general janitorial duties on the school premises. The development of this limited concept of teaching brought into the school system the personnel whose chief function it was to provide for the custodial care of the classrooms and the immediate school environment. These persons were referred to as school janitors and, more recently, as school custodians.

A teacher should realize, despite the development of the concept of the custodian for schools, that the custodian ordinarily has no professional status as such. The public school operational personnel—the group charged with the upkeep of the physical plant —is that body of nonteaching employees whose responsibility it is to keep the school plant and other auxiliary operating services (pupil transportation and delivery services) functioning so that the educational purpose of the school may be achieved. Teachers and principal must understand the need to define and delegate duties and responsibilities of the custodian. A teacher should be helped by the principal to understand the functions of the custodian just as clearly as a teacher understands his own duties and responsibilities.

## Custodian's Responsibility to the Principal

It is important for a teacher to know that, within the building, the principal delegates to the custodian the duties and responsibilities essential to the successful performance of his work. Rarely does the administration of a school system provide that the custodian be in any way responsible to teachers for his work. As a matter of fact, in most school systems the custodian is responsible both to the principal of the building in which he is hired and to the superintendent of schools or an assistant. The employment, pay, and policies of supervision of the custodian are the responsibility of the employing body—the board—which ordinarily delegates the actual work to the superintendent or an assistant. The immediate direction and control of his work are obligations of the building principal. In turn, the principal is responsible to the superintendent for the proper operation and maintenance of the school building in which he works.

In brief then, the principal and not the teacher directs and supervises the work of the custodian. The custodian is directly responsible to the principal and a central office person. The assistant to the superintendent usually helps the principal in improving the custodian's skill and in facilitating the accomplishment of his work.

The custodian cannot be asked by teachers, under any circumstances, to assume the responsibility for supervising pupils. A teacher can expect, though, that the custodian will cooperate with him and the principal in the enforcement of school rules and regulations.

### Ethical Aspects

The very nature of the "operating" jobs within the school system and the background of the employee who is ordinarily available for the jobs make it difficult at times for a teacher to "see" beyond teaching. This myopia may bring with it problems that are ethical in nature rather than legal.

### Recognition of Custodian's Heavy Duties

A teacher knows of course that the tasks of the school custodian are many and most varied. His working day is long. In most instances, he is assigned more work than he can attend to properly, even with adequate training and minimum experience. A teacher should realize that upon the custodian, and such assistants as may be furnished him by the board, falls the duty of maintaining all the external conditions necessary to effective learning. For example, the custodian must attempt to keep rooms at an even and proper temperature, despite a teacher who sticks a letter-opener in the thermostat to "bring up the heat," only to throw open the windows some moments later to "cool things off."

More seriously, in a typical school (outside of large urban areas), the custodian is responsible for the operation and maintenance of the heating and ventilating systems, all cleaning, sweeping, dusting, and scrubbing, plus a large amount of minor repair work. In the smaller schools, the custodian is the engineer, the maintenance man, the truck driver, the general repairman, and the holder of other "positions" found among the service personnel in larger school systems. He must sweep and maintain the floors, dust walls and furniture, clean windows, keep toilet bowls and rooms in sanitary condition, care for lawns, shrubbery, and "school gardens," clean chalkboards and erasers, repair window blinds and shades, paint and varnish furniture and woodwork, repair plumbing and electrical fixtures, run errands, cooperate with the principal in the enforcement of rules, and assist teachers with dozens of tasks that they cannot or should not do.

## Teachers' Requests for Extra Services

In addition, a teacher may want extra things done in his room and may feel no compunction in turning to the custodian for help. Strictly speaking, a teacher should not turn to the custodian for his "services" because extra duties are just what the term implies. When a teacher requests the custodian to perform work out of his line of service to the school, that teacher—unwittingly, perhaps— is impairing the level of service the whole staff expects from the custodian. A teacher need only remember how many working hours there are in a day and that two hands, even with modern gadgets, can do only one or two things at a time.

A teacher who shows consideration for the custodian will not only refrain from requesting "extras" for his room but will avoid getting the custodian to construct animal cages, record cases, or book racks. Carpentry work of this kind is not among the duties of the custodian, although a teacher can be led to believe so because there are some custodians who do such tasks for some teachers. There are custodians who regularly abandon their scheduled duties, and who work after hours without any extra compensation, to complete the "projects" that have been requested by a well-intentioned but thoughtless teacher.

The teacher who respects the rights and duties of the custodian will refrain from such requests and from telling him what to do concerning teaching jobs. A teacher will need only to think of the position of the custodian in the school structure to realize that he is not, and can never be, the personal servant of every teacher.

## Custodian's Influence in the Community

Whether the custodian be illiterate and untrained for his job or a college graduate with preparation comparable to that of a teacher, he is a vital part of the school staff family. Teachers require his assistance if they are to perform well the task of teaching. Frequently, the custodian is a resident of long standing in the school community and enjoys a status to be reckoned with. This is true despite one description of the typical janitor as "just an ordinary individual, unskilled in any line of work, ignorant of sanitary standards and of educational needs, sometimes grouchy, sometimes pigheaded, but usually quite human, amenable to kind treatment, and willing to do about what seems to him as fair and reasonable for the pay he receives, and not much more."

The modern custodian is more often than not familiar with community mores and traditions. He is sensitive to its interests, customs, and prejudices. When he is a respected worker in the community, his opinion of teachers and the school is likely to carry much weight with important citizens. His influence can be almost as great as that of a teacher, principal, or superintendent.

## Necessity for Avoiding Gossip

Employees must take extreme care and engage in conversation with the custodian about no matters that cause injury to others. A teacher should not fall into the habit of gossiping with the custodian about the problems of children, of teachers, of the principal, or of parents. School information a teacher possesses is always confidential. To share any of it with the custodian, consciously or through carelessness, is a breach of faith. It can do little good and may hurt others.

Comments about poor housekeeping performance should be reserved for the principal, not the custodian. Comments of a teacher about what the custodian does or leaves undone, if directed to the principal, help him to maintain a satisfactory building. A teacher should encourage the custodian to see that the program of the school will be strengthened if he shares bits of information with the principal rather than with teachers. There is the ever-present temptation to listen to "news" that one seems to want to divulge in the belief that it will be helpful for all concerned.

A teacher may himself be the victim of gossip if and when the custodian reports on the shortcomings, as he sees them, of a teacher. Teachers can avoid trouble if they refrain from complaining at all about the limitations of other personnel. If a person's sense of status, security, or prestige with a group becomes dependent upon his being able to recount each day fresh news about a fellow staff member, then that person needs the help of a trained analyst.

A teacher with insight into the principles of organization and operation can readily grasp the sound interrelationships between custodial service and teaching. He will have little difficulty in seeing to what extent the activities of pupils and teachers are affected by the work of the custodian.

## Cooperation with the Custodian

If the relationship between teacher and custodian is such that it engenders a spirit of cooperation and consideration, the work of both will be more effective in aiding pupils. It is important that the custodian hold the opinion that teacher and principal are professional workers interested, first of all, in seeing that the schoolhouse is as good a place for children to work and play in as it can possibly be.

In this task, a teacher is expected to help at all times by recognizing that the school plant and its equipment are maintained and operated solely to facilitate the school program. Care on a teacher's part to commend good work is important as is his cooperation with the clean-up schedules. On the other hand, a teacher may be justly irritated if the custodian fails to keep his schedule and barges in to clean a classroom before teacher and pupils have completed their work. Strict rules cannot cover each situation. As in many other areas, good judgment and good will of the parties must operate.

Teacher and pupils can do much to make the work of cleaning lighter, thereby helping the custodian to keep his schedules. If care is exercised in using materials, the after-school clean-up is not a chore. With paste removed from table and desk tops, with paper and chalk and crayons off the floor, and with books and objects back on shelves, the custodian can devote his limited time to caring for the floor properly and to general tidying up.

Quite a different kind of problem, but one that touches the relationships between custodian and other personnel, concerns attendance of nonteachers at staff meetings. There is general agreement that when certain problems face the staff, the contributions of the custodian may be helpful. Should he be invited to attend? Should he come if so invited? Also, should he be extended an invitation to attend one or several of the social gatherings of the staff? Should the hospitality committee request that the custodian contribute to the "sunshine fund" in order that he be remembered by the group when occasion warrants? This topic of social relations of all staff members—teachers and nonteachers—merits considerable attention. Morale is related to the "pulling togetherness" of all members of the school team. The workers "backstage" are an integral part of this total group.

## SERVICE PERSONNEL RELATIONSHIPS

### Legal Aspects

The service personnel within public schools comprise a growing group of employees, chiefly cafeteria and lunchroom workers. In recent years schools have paid increasing attention to phases of general health and welfare of pupils. Since the school day is generally six or seven hours long, pupils must have a break for lunch. Because of school consolidation and other factors bringing children in from some distances, it is impossible or impractical for them to return home for the noon-hour break.

Of course, in an earlier day, the pupil carried his lunch. Eating was looked forward to with anticipation. An hour was generally devoted to eating the lunch. The teacher seldom participated either in eating with the pupils or in playing "anthony over." If a teacher brought his lunch, he ate it within the building giving little thought or concern to what the pupils ate or how they ate it. Any supervision along this line was not considered to be the obligation of teachers. In legal theory, there is little evidence to show that instruction included observation of what pupils ate, how they ate, or where they ate. If a pupil had no lunch at all, a teacher might be concerned from a purely humanitarian point of view. Such concern was not, however, any part of his legal responsibility.

Out of the early simple lunch program has grown the present school cafeteria. It is found, with varying degrees of development, in most schools today. The interest in school "hot" lunches was stimulated by the federal government, which gave the program real impetus during the years of the Great Depression.

## Relation of Food Service to Instruction

In legal theory, it would seem that furnishing pupils with a "hot" lunch does not come within the meaning of the concept "to teach." The relation of teacher to this activity is incidental, not fundamental. It follows that the relationship of a teacher to those persons who furnish the food service is an incidental and not a fundamental one. Cafeteria employees are not teachers, and in no way do they have an "instructional" function in terms of the statutes' usual definition of instruction.

Much has been said about the school's concern for the "whole" child. This philosophy helped boards of education to see the need to include cafeterias as integral parts of school buildings. So rapidly did the idea grow that many boards of education found themselves with a "food program" as a part of the school organization. Members of the board and teachers were not quite sure just how the program fitted into the total educational picture.

For example, it seems not to be clear whether the school cafeteria is merely a service offered to the pupil who wishes to avail himself of it or is an integral part of the school program. It still is not clear whether the cafeteria should be included as part of the learning that the school has the responsibility to provide. Unless teachers, pupils, parents, and administrators have well-defined convictions about the "lunch" program of the public school, it is difficult to fix the legal relationship of personnel to it and thus to the personnel who operate the program.

### Restriction of Pupils at Lunch Hour

There are some considerations that may help personnel in arriving at a conclusion regarding the place of the lunch program in the school program. If, for instance, the school operates the cafeteria as a service to pupils and a charge is made for this service, it can hardly be considered a part of the program of the "free" public school. However, the courts have sustained the authority of boards of education to operate a cafeteria and also to refuse to permit pupils to leave the school premises during the noon-hour period. On the other hand, the board cannot legally require pupils to buy their lunch at school. It can require the pupils to eat their "sack" lunches at a specified time in a designated spot on the school premises. Although closed noon periods have been considered by the courts as one of the reasonable regulations of the school, it does not necessarily follow that the lunch period is a part of the instructional program of the school.

### Ethical Aspects

When school principals meet, one of the topics of discussion sure to be on the agenda is that concerning the relationship between teachers and food personnel. On examination, it is disclosed that the problem between teachers and cafeteria workers usually concerns acceptance and status.

### Teachers' Attitudes Toward Workers and Service

The personality of some teachers and of some food service workers, or the type of service performed may be responsible for part of the friction created. The tendency for school systems to hire persons for jobs in the food service program who are specially trained has sometimes created problems in staff relations concerning quality of service and status.

Trouble is bound to develop when a teacher feels, looks, or acts as though he felt challenged by the workers behind the counters, stoves, and sinks. A tone of voice or action of authority is likely to be misunderstood by a person who is not a teacher. Words thoughtlessly spoken will sometimes "set things off." If a teacher makes a comment about the "over-starchy food" and poor service, perhaps within earshot of students, the cafeteria workers have a legitimate gripe. Talking about "poor fare" with a colleague may be understandable. It is, nonetheless, "out of place," at least on school premises.

Along with the pupils, the teacher looks forward to the noonday break. Difficulties mount if and when a food service employee shows partiality to some individuals. Each teacher should receive the same treatment in terms of speed of service and size of portions if harmony is to be maintained. Special privilege lays the basis for dissatisfaction. When a teacher actually requires special attention of some kind, he has the responsibility to provide for it himself. It is selfish to expect a limited kitchen staff to cater to the needs of one individual when there are literally dozens of other hungry persons waiting.

When a teacher talks directly to boys and girls about the quality of the food, he becomes a party to their "gripes" and thereby performs a disservice. He can do little good but much harm. Rather, it is the task of a teacher to speak positively about the whole program of the school to pupils. He can better engage the attention of pupils within the classroom and outside of it by speaking of the ways in which all phases of the school can be improved.

Rather than speaking in a disparaging manner about the food or poor service, an employee can take the lead to help improve the functioning of the cafeteria. He should remember that school cafeteria meals are planned, prepared, and served for the children. The objective of the cafeteria is to serve well-balanced meals for children, not to prepare attractive salads and other low-calorie foods for the employees.

## Responsibility for Supervising Children

Another area of controversy between employees and lunchroom workers is that of supervision of children while in the lunchroom.

It would seem that a teacher has at least nominal responsibility because the noon period is no longer a "going home" time as it formerly was. Because eating is a part of the regular school day, a teacher should not push off to cafeteria employees the task of supervising the children. Such personnel possess neither the training nor the authority for the task. Free time for a teacher should not be purchased at this price.

Improved personnel practices and relations are generally needed in the service area because it continues to be a bothersome one. Grievances will develop. The personnel in the service area are characterized by a big turnover rate. Individual-type inservice training of the employee can be handled by the manager of the lunchroom or other person in charge. Training can be augmented by written instructions. It must not be undertaken by a teacher who believes, rightly or wrongly, that he has been slighted or mistreated.

The task all school personnel are engaged in is extremely important. Teachers and food workers are members of the same school team. Each has a role to perform. Each needs to know and accept the rules and abide by them. There can be no place for him who must obtain his measure of security by warning others to "keep their place." A careful organization of the entire food service management under the supervision of a fully competent person is the fundamental approach to the problems of better school food for pupils (and for teachers) and of improved relations between employee and service worker.


## OFFICE EMPLOYEE-PERSONNEL RELATIONSHIPS


### Legal Aspects


Clerical services are clearly distinguishable from those which the professional staff performs. To avoid trouble, it is important to delineate clearly the duties of teachers and the secretary.

## Scope of Clerical Workers' Authority

The principal delegates certain responsibilities—and corresponding authority—to the school secretary since he has but two hands and 24 hours in the day. Teachers recognize this necessity. The tasks of the clerical staff must be kept within their scope of assignment and qualifications. The danger exists that, even with all due precautions, the secretary may assume the teacher's role. The secretary in the school office who arrogates authority to herself is acting outside of her province and can raise fundamental policy issues. Unfortunately, one need not look long nor hard to find the secretary who seems to "take on" responsibilities. It is not uncommon for one to dismiss pupils arbitrarily or to get them from study halls or classes for questioning. When such occurs, the teacher has every right to object most strenuously.

In order to provide clerical personnel, a school system must consider many factors other than the likelihood of authority's being overstepped. Besides a reasonable salary schedule, the clerical personnel are desirous of the social and welfare benefits that accrue to all employed personnel.

## Ethical Aspects

### How the Principal Sees the School Office

The aid a clerical staff extends to teachers depends, in large measure, upon the philosophy held by the principal regarding the relationship between teacher and secretary. In other words, the quality and quantity of help that a teacher will receive is related directly to the outlook held by the principal regarding the basic purpose of the school office. If he conceives the office to be a place where teachers and he can be of help to children and their parents by providing services, then teachers can expect to find the school secretary an ally. On the other hand, if the principal feels the office to be the private domain of the administrator, a teacher will have to "beg" for any assistance and be fearful of doing so. The principal who looks at the office as his "private suite" will usurp the time and energies of the office workers. They will have little or no time for teachers because their time is being consumed by tasks outlined by the principal.

## Function of the Secretary

Teacher and secretary ordinarily come into close daily contact. A teacher is usually dependent upon her for such things as school supplies, book orders, textbooks, and various school records. The school office usually is the place where records of pupil attendance and cumulative folders are kept. A teacher is dependent upon the secretary for the operation of school bells, the handling of lunch and milk moneys, and the accounting of Red Cross funds.

The secretary should assist teachers by performing clerical duties that she is trained to do better than either teacher or principal. Sometimes the load of clerical detail can fall heavily upon the teacher or principal. Perhaps the burden of clerical work has been permitted to develop without any examination of the function it serves, or the principal and staff do not employ the services of the clerical staff wisely.

Ordinarily, an important duty of the school secretary is to take dictation and transcribe it into mailable letters. She ought to be able to cut stencils, duplicate instructional materials, handle mail, and relay communications between teachers and the principal.

In large systems many types of clerical services are rendered. They include the secretary with assignments to a specific person; secretary with a general assignment; general stenographic help; receptionists; typists and transcribers; file clerks; general office clerks; record, receiving, and paying clerks; inventory clerks; business machine operators; and telephone operators.

By looking at the work of the secretary-clerk and thinking about the many jobs connected with the assignment, a teacher can get a better picture of the magnitude of the job. The assignment includes receptionist, telephoning, stenographic tasks, record keeping, making reports, marking standardized tests, helping children, helping teachers, helping patrons, receiving and storing supplies, keeping inventories, payroll reports, and first aid services.

It should be understood who is to do such things as cutting stencils, typing teachers' letters to parents, filing pupil records, compiling age-grade reports, checking registers, correcting standardized tests, and the like. When there is such an understanding, animosities and low morale are not likely to result because of "front office" trouble.

The secretary should be helped to see that she is there, whatever the division of duties, to help serve teachers in their efforts to conduct a quality school program. There are schools without secretaries and principals. There can be no school without pupils and teachers. If the school is one where all share in the services of the office workers, teachers must be considerate of the work load of the office. The principal has the responsibility to see that office services are extended to every teacher on a planned basis. Favoritism and jealousy are reduced to the degree that plans are formulated. If a teacher plans ahead to fit his request with the office schedule, each teacher will receive the help available to perform duties effectively.

The timing of requests by a teacher is most important. Complicated jobs should be submitted well in advance. If a teacher does not do so and descends upon a busy clerk one hour before class and wants forty copies of a five-page test, the teacher cannot expect to "win a friend and influence a secretary." With reports to be completed, many routine matters to be attended to, telephone calls, visitors, pupils, and interruptions of all kinds, the secretary deserves not to have additional pressure placed on her by an inconsiderate "Johnny-come-lately" teacher. If a teacher does submit work late and then complains that it is not finished, he exhibits poor judgment and demonstrates shabby manners.

A teacher usually recognizes that the task of secretary for a school faculty is important, interesting, and responsible. A large part of the secretary's time, it is noted, is spent in dealing with people —the principal, teachers, other employees, and the general public. A teacher is conscious that a competent secretary can be one of the key members of the staff in the public relations program of the school. A secretary with a curt tone over the phone or an abrupt manner to a visitor damages the school program. A large portion of the school's public has its one and only contact with the school over the telephone. The voice of the secretary is the first "school voice" that is heard. The manner and mood of that voice are most important.

The ability of a secretary to deal graciously with all persons, whatever their habits and language, and to act in the best interests of the school staff is essential.[3] Perhaps there is no other phase of the work of the school secretary that requires the display of finer personal qualities than does the receiving of callers to the school. The secretary must be able to meet visitors easily, to obtain information from them without disturbing and provoking them, to decide quickly whether they should see the principal or whether they should have an appointment later, perhaps much later. The method used by the secretary in handling callers has a direct bearing upon their attitude toward the whole school organization. A capable person develops much goodwill for the school, including the principal and all members of the staff.

The school secretary-clerk must like to be with people and be able to receive requests and to request work from others in a tactful manner. She must often act as a buffer to the administrator to shield him from outside contacts that would consume time he needs for executive duties. She must relieve him of time-consuming clerical and minor executive details. She must schedule many kinds of activities and supply him with needed information at the time requested.

A teacher, along with the pupils and public, depends on a school secretary. Her personality, integrity, and ability to work well with other adults, in addition to her office skills, are factors of high value. A teacher should understand that the key clerical person is the secretary to the principal. From the standpoint of both efficiency of operation and public relations, this person should be chosen with great care. The job is a demanding one. It should be so classified as to attract and then hold outstanding personnel.

### Teacher's Concept of the Clerical Staff

A teacher should keep in mind that many clerical employees seek their jobs because they like the atmosphere found in the school. They like the aspect of service as compared to the strictly business

[3] The ethical requirements of secretaries and the social requirements of school business are discussed in such books as Emily Post's *Etiquette* and Collins' *Etiquette in Business*. The "C.P.S." (Certified Professional Secretary) goes after a secretary's name upon successful completion of a twelve-hour examination. It covers a variety of topics including understanding and skill in human relations and personal adjustment.

office. Good relations can be maintained in the school when a teacher exercises judgment in choosing what to discuss with the office staff. Confidences should not be broken. A teacher should try to discourage office personnel from gossiping about private and personal school matters. When the "listening ear" vanishes, energies will be directed along more constructive lines.

A professional teacher will remain friendly and courteous toward office workers. He will not "probe" to determine their attitude and get free information regarding school news or the principal's problems. A teacher knows that information about the management of the school can be secured by seeking it from those responsible for the conduct of the school.

As suggested earlier, an overly conscientious worker occasionally will attempt to "take over" some of the duties of a teacher or the principal. Patience and understanding by a teacher will eventually help such an employee to see that decisions about "unexcused absences," errands to be run during school hours, and behavior problems are the direct concerns of the teacher and principal. If the officious worker is permitted to continue without any counsel, she may well create a situation difficult to remedy, where the prerogatives of the professional staff and of the office workers are sadly confused.

## HEALTH PERSONNEL RELATIONSHIPS

### Legal Aspects

Services such as those of the medical department have been added to the general program of the school in many school districts. Courts have been clear in stating that the board of education possesses the authority to employ school nurses, physicians, and dentists for "first aid and inspectional" purposes. The law is clear regarding the fact that a board of education may not employ such personnel to operate a clinic for administering treatment.

**Authority of Medical Personnel**

Neither a physician, a dentist, nor even a school nurse employed by the school board is authorized to treat a pupil beyond
giving essential first aid and acting in a consultative manner to
parents and teachers regarding the health problems of pupils.

An important item to bear in mind is that the personnel of the
medical department, as a rule, do not hold certificates to teach. They
do not in any way bear the relationship of teacher-to-pupil in the
school where they happen to work.

A teacher, however, has the duty to make regular health inspec-
tions. Pupils with unusual symptoms should be checked by the
school nurse or physician. A teacher must remember that he is not
to provide medication for the child who complains of aches and
pains. The child, in every instance, should be sent to the nurse or
one who acts in her capacity.

A physician and school nurse have certain duties of law enforcement. They must enforce quarantine legislation. They must enforce vaccination regulations. A teacher should understand this
phase of the health work of physician and nurse. He should realize
how vital the maintenance of health standards is to the entire school
program.

A teacher should know that the nurse has an educational responsibility as well as the legal one of helping to enforce regulations
pertaining to health and safety. Every school family presents re-
curring challenges. In certain cases, the nurse will suggest in an
indirect manner changes that relate to personal or work habits.
Again, she may make outright and direct comments. In no case,
however, can this action on her part be interpreted as usurping
authority from the classroom teacher.

## Ethical Aspects

Much of the success or failure of a program of health education
or rehabilitation in a school system depends upon the attitudes and
feelings that a so-called regular classroom teacher holds toward
the program. A teacher who works in a school building where some
provisions are made for the teaching and treatment of exceptional

children needs to work closely with the personnel of the special services. The classroom teacher needs to be able to recognize symptoms of disorder and to detect when a pupil requires immediate attention from a health specialist.

A teacher needs to appreciate that any program including provisions for "special education" offers opportunities for pupils who cannot profit from regular school. He will learn that in providing needed services the load of all teachers is made heavier. There are extra inconveniences plus added responsibilities.

## Cooperation Between Teacher and Health Personnel

The teacher's increased burden comes from working with an expanded staff including health personnel. A teacher can show by his actions and feelings that he respects the abilities of the nurse and therapist. Or, he can cast reflection upon their ability, directly or in front of other teachers and pupils. To build up the prestige of the nurses rather than to belittle it is the greater job.

It is essential, for the effective operation of the school, that the nurse not send children home without first contacting the teacher involved and the school office. The reason is not that "line and staff" relationships are important in and of themselves or that "going through channels" brings its own rewards. Besides the need for records to be kept in case of accidents, respect for persons is shown when all involved are given notice.

In speaking with a parent, a teacher should remember that the suggestions of health personnel regarding the child should come to the parent from the nurse, not from him. On the other hand, the nurse should be careful not to enter a classroom without first contacting the teacher. Important as examinations and routine health checks are, a nurse can respect the plans of teachers. By advance notice of the schedule, a teacher can better plan his class program. The nurse should avoid calling pupils from the classroom without the prior knowledge of the teacher.

## Teacher and Therapist

The problems of teaching in a school with provisions for special education are unique for several reasons. Perhaps the most important, from the view of personal relations, is that a classroom teacher must share the time of the child who requires special treatment with those who provide that service. A teacher must remember that the ordinary classroom creates some problems for the exceptional child. These problems are added to the special routine he must follow during the school day. Unless his teacher keeps these problems in mind, the pupil will see the teacher become increasingly irritated with the insistent and regular demands of the personnel of the treatment area. The child who must leave the classroom in the middle of the "geography lesson" to get his corrective exercise is not always viewed with the patience and understanding that his situation should merit. Threats by the teacher for inconveniences not of the pupil's making tend to harm the child and alienate the health personnel. They are bound to get to hear about the disgruntlements of the teacher. No child can or would be successful in hiding his feelings, under such circumstances.

How to organize and coordinate the many necessary activities in a school where the academic program is functioning alongside the therapy program poses unusual problems, including those of relationships between people. One of the greatest obstacles to a quality program of special education continues to be the lack of understanding of those who have some responsibility for the varied educational program of the child. Too often a classroom teacher will see little more than the value of the child's leaving the third grade with a knowledge of the "table of 5's." He cannot or will not see that the therapist must hold equally strongly to the important schedule of treatments authorized by the orthopedic surgeon.

A clash between teacher and nurse or therapist over the amount of time that should be spent by the child in the classroom and in treatment rooms is not a rarity. It is essential for the welfare of all children that some understanding exist between teacher and therapist about the child's schedule. To bicker about which phase of the child's program is the more important—the academic or treatment—is to divide loyalties and ultimately hurt the youngster. A good classroom program and treatment routine cannot be managed when energies are consumed in defending the values of either phase of the program.

A first approach is to help the classroom teacher to be fully informed about the objectives and methods of the special education program. Since special classes and special treatments are extras in the school that is organized to help the special child, the over-all program must be especially flexible. Such coordination can be achieved by careful study. Given data on the load of the health area in terms of pupils requiring treatment and facilities available, both teacher and therapist can devise schedules that make optimum use of the facilities and yet do not disrupt the program of the classroom unnecessarily. Sometimes several pupils can be taken care of at one time from one room. More frequently, however, needs are so unlike that each pupil must be attended to individually. This means that a therapist can minister to one child at a time, requiring a series of separate periods during the school day. A classroom teacher must become resigned to the fact that several children may be away from the room immediately after the opening bell right up to dismissal time.

### QUESTIONS FOR STUDY

1. Why are the relationships between teacher and nonteacher so very important for a good school program?
2. In what ways have the "nonteachers" on the school staff been classified? Why?
3. Should all personnel classified as "professional workers" be assigned some teaching duties?
4. Make a list of all "noncertified" personnel in your school. What is the job of each?
5. Who are the "auxiliary professional workers"?
6. What is meant by "dual regulation"?
7. What are the purposes of "job classification"?
8. What one particular limitation does the "nonteacher" bring with him when he joins a local school staff?
9. What are some common obstacles to the effective coordination of the program of the school?
10. Does a "breach of ethics" depend upon the conduct of the actor alone or whether the recipient has "equal status" with the teacher?
11. What does the term "teaching" include so far as school duties are concerned?
12. Does the responsibility of the custodian extend beyond keeping the floors clean and the furnace operating?
13. What kinds of "chores" are often imposed on the custodian by the classroom teacher?

14. Does the teacher have responsibilities that go beyond "instruction"?
15. Is the cafeteria a regular part of the school program or a service that is maintained for "convenience's sake"?
16. Whose job is it to supervise pupils while eating?
17. Who on the school staff has the task of seeing that the school clerk "works for all the teachers"?
18. What is the duty of the school nurse?

### SUGGESTED READINGS

Chandler, B. J., and Paul V. Petty, *Personnel Management in School Administration* (Yonkers, N.Y.: World Book Company, 1955), chap. 17, "Non-Professional Positions."

Dougherty, James H., Frank H. Gorman, and Claude A. Phillips, *Elementary School Organization and Management* (New York: The Macmillan Company, 1950), chap. XVI, "The Teacher's Relationships."

Moore, Harold E., and Newell B. Walters, *Personnel Administration in Education* (New York: Harper and Brothers, Publishers, 1955), chap. 6, "The Work and Responsibility of the Nonteaching Personnel," and chap. 7, "Coordination of the Personnel."

Pittinger, Benjamin F., *Local Public School Administration* (New York: McGraw-Hill Book Company, Inc., 1951), chap. 3, "Traditional Organization of Local School District Personnel," and chap. 18, "Administrating Student Health and Behavior."

Reavis, William C., Paul R. Pierce, Edward H. Stulken, and Bertrand L. Smith, *Administering the Elementary School* (Englewood Cliffs, N.J.: Prentice-Hall, Inc., 1953), chap. 10, "The School Office as a Service Center."

# Parent-Personnel Relationships

# 8

## PROBLEM SITUATIONS

What would you do in each of the following situations? Analyze each in terms of the questions raised at the beginning of Chapter 3 (page 56).

### CASE A

Following an outbreak of destruction of property by a juvenile gang in —————— School after which three of the gang were sent to "reform school," a seventh grade teacher received a telephone call from a mother. She reported that a "junior gang" was organized in the teacher's room. She understood the initiation fee was twelve stolen caps. The mother gave the boys' names and stated that each would have an identification card in his wallet. The teacher called the mother back the next day but was told that she knew no more to tell her.

### CASE B

Miss X was a substitute teacher who had had several "run-ins" with the father of a nine-year-old boy, a convalescent polio victim. Miss X supplied for an elderly, much-beloved teacher.

On this occasion, Miss X is alleged to have used "corporal punishment" regarding the boy. The father was angered when his wife reported the incident. He took the view that no one but himself had better use any punishment on "his Billy." The child knew of the parent's attitude and was considered to be "a real problem child."

The father came to school in a defiant mood. He went directly to the teacher's classroom. He interrupted class to scold the teacher and to threaten her. He would tell her, if she would care to listen, about the kinds of suitable punishment to be used.

The principal discovered that the boy was in no way injured as a result of the punishment.

CASE C

Ned is a fifth grader who runs and plays despite a limp. He has a stepfather, and his mother is excitable and noticeably nervous. Ned is considered "irresponsible" at school since he does not do his homework, loses his materials, and "wastes time."

His last report card showed that Ned "lacks effort." His mother became angry and the stepfather whipped the boy "quite severely." For about a week, Ned seemed to do better. Soon he slipped back despite encouragement from his teacher.

When time came for the next report card, Ned had made some improvement. Despite this, the card indicated "poor work." The teacher did not want Ned to get another beating. She took the card to the principal's office.

CASE D

One morning, before the beginning of the school day, Mr. R, principal of ——————— Junior High School, was confronted at his office door with an upset mother and her son, a pupil in the school.

Without giving her name, she insisted upon showing the principal several dark spots on her son's back. She said they were the result of an "unmerciful beating" by the print teacher. She insisted that the principal call in the teacher. She would be satisfied with an "apology" and let it go. If not, she would go "straight to the superintendent."

There seems to be a high and positive correlation between effective relationships involving teacher and parent and the quality of the relationship between teacher and pupil. In fact, satisfying relations between teacher and parent seem to have their origins in adequate pupil-teacher understandings.

However, when rapport is lacking between teacher and parent, it is often due to ignorance on the part of both teacher and parent concerning the work, the responsibilities, and the viewpoints of the other. For example, if a parent learns via the "grapevine" of certain changes in teaching method in his son's class, he may consider them to be mistakes. By some parental standards, strange methods that produce results different from expectations are signs of weakness, oversight, or plain ignorance on the part of the school. The parent sees only that his child does not know his ABC's in the first grade although he does know words and can read phrases. He may not understand that the pupil today is helped to read without first memorizing each letter of the alphabet with its appropriate markings.

## The Parent's Attitude Toward School and Teachers

Changes in method that came with greater understanding of how pupils learn and the introduction of varied activities into the school curriculum have not been explained adequately to many parents. How can the net result be less than skepticism or outright opposition to "modern education"? Course names in the high school like "driver education" and "consumer economics" sound pretty much like fads and frills when the parent is not in a position to evaluate their purposes. Until "sold," the parent wants his child to "learn his lessons" and not "keep house" and "farm" at the school, or learn to park cars during school hours or study newspapers for "best buys."

To add to the misunderstanding, parents may persist in repeating the trite phrase, "If you can't do anything else, you can at least teach." There may be school personnel within earshot of such a remark. A parent may add that "the school trains kids poorly these days for citizenship and accepting responsibility." He may allude to the recklessness of "youth," or mutter about how little the school is accomplishing these days. The assumption, implied of course, is that these ills are mainly the school's fault.

A parent may be sitting at a bridge table, with a teacher as one of the foursome. A businessman may pride himself in being one who "knows how to meet a payroll." He is one who *does,* not one who teaches. His wife may chime in with the fact that school folks have it easy, for they work only a few hours a day and only half the days a year.

Some current articles hit the nail on the head when they point up that, after all, the school's job is merely to echo the beliefs and values of the mass mediocrity. Yes, teachers are followers and not leaders. So seems to be the consensus.

Perhaps it is not too farfetched to say that in some communities there does exist a parent-school relationship in which the domination of the parent strangles the effectiveness of the relationship. The reverse could also be true, the domination of the school strangling the spirit and endeavor of the parent toward cooperation with its personnel.

### Teachers' Overtures to Parents

A parent may speak of the "unfriendliness" of teachers toward him. He may say that they are too critical of parents and that he as a parent feels uncomfortable at school. The parent may even exclaim that teachers often appear to be snobbish and superior in manner.

Do a majority of school personnel tend to ignore parents? It is not uncommon to read in educational journals that the truly professional teacher discusses plans with parents, strives eagerly to get to know them, and on occasion meets them socially. For what reasons, then, does this seemingly sound advice remain within the pages of magazines without being acted upon?

Some would say that some school people tend to be "too standoffish." Teachers must accept, then, a portion of the responsibility for misunderstandings that exist between themselves and the home. It is their fault that the parent persists in evaluating modern methods in terms of bygone standards.

When the news and information about the school at the parent-teacher meetings are well planned, the parent has the chance to see for himself the needs of today's children, if he wishes to. He will have the opportunity to get first hand the raw materials so as to understand the needs and the accomplishments of the school to date. The association of teacher and parent can do much to promote understanding between the parent and teacher.

## LEGAL ASPECTS

The possibility of legal involvement of school personnel with parents is slight. Relations usually are but indirect. It is, of course, teacher and pupil who are in almost daily proximity. It is of major concern to the parent when difficulties between teacher and pupil appear "insurmountable" and solutions are hunted.

The legal relationship of classroom teacher and parent resembles most clearly that of a partnership. It can be so defined because both have a vested interest in the business of educating the child and both stand to profit by "the product" turned out by the joint effort.

The parent on his part profits personally and as a better member of society. The teacher profits both as a member of society and as an individual who has carried out a function of the state. The partnership is bound closely by common interest and mutual concern in the educational development of the pupil.

## The Teacher's Authority and Control

One opinion often erroneously held by teacher and parent is that the parent "permits" the teacher to do this or that when the child is under the jurisdiction of the school. Frequently, a teacher will ask a parent if he may require a certain task of the pupil. Again, the parent may stalk to the schoolhouse to "forbid" the teacher to do a certain thing in reference to his child.

When such behaviors occur, the teacher needs to keep in his mind the fact that he, as a teacher, gets his authority from the state by way of the certificate to teach. He does not get authority to teach and discipline from the parent. This is so only when the teacher happens to be a tutor, employed privately by the parents. The parent is mistaken if he thinks that the public school teacher is his private manservant or tutor just because he has paid his school taxes. A teacher is in no wise paid personally by the parent. If a parent believes so, he should be considerately informed of the facts.

The relationship between teacher and parent has its basis in the legal theory of public education. The courts have been quite clear in establishing the fact that schools are not for the sole purpose of conferring individual benefits upon children. To the contrary, in fact, the state has a considerable stake in the education of every child for the "good order and peace of society."

The education of youth has been declared by the courts as a matter of vital importance to the maintenance of the democratic state and to the public wealth. The state may do a great deal, however, in the matter of limiting the control over the education of the child. A parent may choose not to send his child to the public school if he so elects, and still obey state laws. The state may not prohibit the parent from enrolling his children in private schools.

However, the law provides teachers with considerable authority over the control and education of the child, once the parent sends his child to the public school. Again, the authority of the teacher is not delegated by the parent. It is granted to the teacher by the state as an essential part of his teaching responsibility. The legal term for this relationship of the teacher and the pupil is *in loco parentis*. The teacher, in other words, stands "in place of the parent" when the child is under his supervision and care.

Quite frequently questions arise as to the legal authority of a teacher when his requirements or rules run counter to those of the parent. For example, a teacher may request the child to stay after the dismissal of school. The teacher may ask for a period of time that would be called reasonable. The parent may request that the child be sent home immediately upon the closing of school. There can be no true conflict here, for the authority of the parent is temporarily superseded by that of the teacher when the child is under school supervision.

It is a well-established principle of law that during school hours the educational program of the pupil is in the hands of those employed by the board of education. The authority to make reasonable rules is granted to teachers. To repeat, a teacher legally has the position held by the parent in his relationship to the child insofar as his authority and control go.

### Detention and the Police Power

Despite fairly clear-cut legal principles here, complaints have been filed against teachers on the ground of false imprisonment of a child. The courts have held that such restraint of the pupil by the teacher is not false imprisonment. If for a "reasonable" time and for a "reasonable" purpose, such detainment is considered to be for the best interests of the child or for the general welfare of the school. The right of the teacher to the child's time supersedes that of the parent in this particular regard.

It must be emphasized, though, that a teacher must use no physical force to restrain the child from leaving the school building. Under no condition does the classroom teacher possess the "police power" of physical restraint over the child's body. He must use no other method than command to restrain the personal freedom of the child. If the teacher "locks the child in a room or a closet," he moves beyond his legal authority. Such action would not be upheld by the courts. Physical coercion is not a legal means of control.

The question sometimes arises regarding a teacher's legal authority over the child during his coming to and going from school. Here again the authority of the school may run counter to the wishes of the parent. The child's conduct on the way to or from school must not be such as to be detrimental to the "peace, harmony, and goodwill" of the other pupils. It must not impair the effectiveness of the school itself. If so, the school's authority takes precedence over that of the parent. In other words, the child can be held accountable to the teacher and school.

Where a parent openly resists a teacher, a different problem is created. A parent may not instruct his child to disobey a teacher or to create a disturbance regarding an issue. If he does, the parent may be brought into court to answer charges of "disturbing the peace" or of "contributing to the delinquency of a minor." It makes no difference that the minor may be the parent's child. The principle of law here is clear—the school's control over the pupil, even after he leaves the school premises, has been sustained by the courts. The act or offense committed by the pupil, though, must have a direct bearing on the best interests of the school.

Most of the legal problems that arise between teacher and parent have their inception in one of two areas: (1) discipline of the child, or (2) subjects taught in the school. From the standpoint of legal problems or court issues, the most important ones have occurred in the area of pupil discipline. This subject will be treated fully in the following chapter on "Teacher-Pupil Relationships." However, some attention now will be given to the legal relationship of teacher and parent regarding the matter of discipline. For, as the old adage goes, "no teacher can do what a parent has failed to do."

## Discipline and Corporal Punishment

It is a basic principle that unless denied that right by statute, a teacher has the authority to make pupils obey by means of inflicting corporal punishment. Along with the principal, a teacher stands *in loco parentis* to the pupil. Other school employees or officials do not. But a teacher may make and enforce rules that he believes to be necessary in order to control pupils and maintain the efficiency of the school.

Even though teachers stand *in loco parentis*, their right to punish corporally is more limited than that of the parent. A teacher can do some of the things to correct the child that the parent can do, including the use of physical punishment. The courts are agreed, though, that a teacher's method must be reasonable and that there must be no injury to the person of the child. If a teacher oversteps his authority in the control of the pupil, the parent may represent the child in a cause of action in court. The child's right that has been violated may be prosecuted by the parent.

If charges are preferred by the parent against a teacher, the teacher may get in the middle of a legal tangle. Then the child upon whom punishment was inflicted becomes the third party in the case. If the parent incurs medical or hospital expenses owing to the injury of the child through wanton and malicious punishment by a teacher, the teacher, if found guilty, may be required to reimburse the parent for such expenses. The rule here is that a pupil and his parent may obtain damages from a teacher who administers corporal punishment deemed to be excessive, administered with malice, or administered to enforce an unreasonable rule. In assault and battery cases, which are criminal offenses, the parent may also make his complaint on behalf of the child.

Quite different is a case where a teacher severely punishes a child for misspelling a word. The court held here that a teacher did not have sufficient cause. It ruled that if such acts were not restrained by the court, there was danger that an outraged parent might attempt to take redress into his own hands. Sometimes parents do.

As a general rule, a teacher may not expel a pupil. In other words, a teacher may not take unto himself the authority to forbid permanently the attendance of a pupil from school. The parent must understand, however, that a teacher possesses the authority to suspend a pupil, subject to the action of administrative personnel, if the pupil commits any offense that impairs the orderly conduct of the school.

In general, the legal right of the pupil and his parent to seek redress in money damages for injuries incurred in connection with any school-connected event depends upon the liability of the school district and the liability of the teacher with respect to his degree of negligence. You will recall that the term "negligence" as usually interpreted by the courts is any conduct, including acts of commission or omission, that falls below the standard of care required for the protection of others against unreasonable risk of harm.

In case of injury of a pupil, a teacher may have to answer a parent's charge if it can be proved "beyond reasonable doubt" that the injury was due to the negligence of the teacher. He will not be held liable in action for damages when he punishes a child moderately and injuries result that could not have been foreseen by a reasonably prudent person.

As a disciplinary device, corporal punishment appears to be on the way out. Fewer cases involving this question are being brought before the courts.[1] When a teacher does administer corporal punishment and is charged criminally therewith, certain fundamental propositions of law must be borne in mind by the school and parent. Six principles of law were set up in a court decision and may be considered as a "complete expression of the law as it relates to corporal punishment."[2] These fundamental principles are:

1. The teacher stands *in loco parentis,* acts in a quasi-judicial capacity, and is not liable for an error in judgment in the matter of punishment.

2. The teacher's responsibility attaches home to home (i.e., while the pupil is on the way to and from school).

3. There is a presumption of correctness of the teacher's actions.

4. There is a presumption that the teacher acts in good faith.

5. Mere excessive or severe punishment on the part of a teacher does not constitute a crime unless it is of such a nature as to produce or threaten lasting or permanent injury, or unless the state has shown that it was administered with either express malice (i.e., spite, hatred, or revenge), or implied malice (i.e., wrongful act wantonly done without just cause or excuse), and beyond a reasonable doubt.

6. The defendant teacher is entitled to all the benefits and safeguards of the well-known presumption-of-innocence doctrine.[3]

[1] Lee O. Garber, *Yearbook of School Law 1955* (Philadelphia: University of Pennsylvania Press, 1955), p. 71.
[2] State v. Lutz, 113 N.E.2d 757 (Ohio) (1953).
[3] Garber, *Yearbook of School Law 1955,* p. 72.

## Parent's Authority to Choose Course of Instruction

The second area in which many legal problems arise between the school and parent is that of school instruction. Friction between teacher and parent develops when the parent believes that teachers encourage everything in the classroom except "real learning." In the absence of express statutory authority, there is some conflict among the courts as to whether a school board through the teacher may require a pupil to pursue a particular subject against the wishes of his parent.[4]

Within certain limits, a public school pupil has the right to learn the subjects his parent chooses for him. The courts say that a parent may make a reasonable selection of studies for his child to pursue from such studies as are taught in the school. Here a teacher is obliged to follow the parent's wishes when such demands are made through the administrative offices.

Although the parent may choose, within limits, the subjects his child is to pursue, the parent cannot determine to any degree the textbooks that the child should use. A parent cannot request that a teacher use a certain "method" of instruction. A parent cannot insist that a particular method be used before allowing his child to enroll in the subject. A pupil may not refuse to take a course because his father objects to the way the written papers are scored.

When the parent of a backward child opposes his assignment to an ungraded school because of a teacher or other objection, the courts uphold such board action. If a parent objects to the class or teacher, he must either accept the assignment offered in the public schools, place his child in a private school, or furnish the child equivalent home instruction. The principle is well established that a pupil must attend the school to which he is assigned so long as the board of education acts reasonably and does not abuse its discretion.

## Sectarian Instruction

One of the most controversial curriculum questions has to do with sectarian education in the public schools. The parent has a legal

[4] Fred E. Brooks, "The Legal Status of the Pupil in the American Public Schools, A Study of Common Law Principles" (Unpublished Ph.D. dissertation, University of Chicago, 1948), p. 72.

right to inquire into this basic question: When is religious or sectarian education being taught in, or fostered by, a public school teacher?

The problem of what is religious or sectarian instruction is a substantial one. Unwittingly, a teacher violates federal and state constitutional prohibitions against sectarian influences in the public schools if one sect is praised over another or regularity of church attendance is inquired about. This is especially so in certain sections of the country where reading of the Bible "without comment" is encouraged as part of the opening exercises of the class or home-room.

A teacher goes beyond the law when Bible reading is the means to actual services within the school. A parent has the right to inquire whether state law is not being forgotten. The Unitarian Church has enjoyed increases in enrollments in its Sunday schools in part because of parents' objections to the indoctrination of their children by well-meaning public school teachers.

The federal Constitution provides for complete separation of church and state. A number of state constitutions prohibit sectarian instruction and influence within public schools. If the law is so explicit, why, then, is the question one of great complexity? There are several reasons. Pressures from religious groups would have school personnel believe instruction in moral and spiritual values is a duty, and that support of one church plan is as good as another. A child in nonpublic schools has received state and federal aid because of the much-misunderstood "child benefit theory" from which some have concluded that "some study of religion is all right." A third reason for some of the confusion is misunderstanding over the so-called "released-time" plans.

Whatever the details, the released-time plans call for the pupil to attend whichever church his parent chooses for him to attend some-time during the school week. The plans cause all manner of friction between some parents and some classroom teachers. In the state of Illinois a parent objected to the bringing of teachers of religion into the public school buildings. His objection was responsible for the United States Supreme Court decision in the *McCullom* case. Despite contrary state court rulings, the high court supported the complaint of the parent.

Members of some religious groups object to their children's

saluting the flag during school exercises. Parents have protested that a teacher has no legal right to force the pupil to participate in exercises contrary to his religious convictions.

Under statutes or constitutions that provide that no tax funds can be used for religious schools or for the teaching of religion in the schools, the parent has the right to make objection when he feels the law is being violated. Specifically, the parent can make objection to the expenditure of tax money by any board for the purpose of maintaining a school where the teacher is a member of a religious order under the supervison of the clergy.

A statute requiring the pupil to be sent to a public school or approved private school, thus "outlawing" home instruction as a substitute for school attendance, was held constitutional in New England in 1929. A New York statute permits home instruction in lieu of school attendance. Where the law requires that a child attend a school until he has attained a certain age, the child will be required to attend school until that age is reached regardless of scholastic achievement or the wishes of parent or teacher.

## Enforcement of Health Rules

Sometimes difficulties arise because of the demand by the school that health rules be enforced. The compulsory vaccination requirement has been objected to by parents on the grounds of religious convictions. If a parent refuses to permit his child to be vaccinated, the educational authorities may exclude him from school. A teacher cannot be prevailed upon by the parent to accept the child.

The board of education has the responsibility to see that the compulsory attendance laws are enforced. A teacher can help get an unvaccinated child adjudged a "neglected child" to be committed to a children's home. When a board of health, either state or local, passes a rule affecting the health of the pupil, the courts hold that such a board has the authority to exclude or otherwise govern the action of the pupil. If a teacher acts accordingly through the school office to aid in the enforcement of health regulations, the parent should see clearly the legal duty of employee.

In some states present laws prevent a teacher from administering any kind of aid to the child, even in extreme emergency, without first contacting the parent. The basis for the restrictions are the religious convictions of the parent. To circumvent the law, some parents have given instructions in writing to the school to give the necessary aid in cases of need and when they cannot be reached. For all practical purposes, then, the parent has left a "standing order" to do what a teacher believes is wise without first having to reach the parent.

## ETHICAL ASPECTS

Between school personnel and parents, the ethical aspects of relationships loom as far more significant than the purely legal concerns. The reason is that parents and school personnel come up constantly against problems where attitudes and "deep convictions" play a part vital in solutions, or in roadblocks to possible solutions. Through home visits and conferences parents and school employees get the chance to talk about many topics such as marking and reporting practices of the school.

### Parent's Respect for the Teacher

Attitudes regarding the respect or lack of respect in which a teacher is held by a parent either help or hinder the school in its assigned task of influencing the pupil for good. There seems to be some evidence, alleged substantial by some, indicating that the public has little respect for the "learning" for which the school is one symbol. Some children and more parents stated, in a recent survey, that "they had no respect for their teachers' knowledge." Less than one in four adults polled said they admired teachers.

A parent may look down on a teacher for several reasons. A teacher may be ashamed of his occupation and be apologetic about being "in the classroom." A parent may read that a teacher must belong to a low estate since about one in three elementary teachers in 1958 had less than four years of college. A parent may also know that barely half the teachers are members of any "strong and unified professional association."

There are problems of a different sort that tend to widen the gap between teacher and parent. A parent may feel indifferent toward teachers and teaching. In his disinterest he may fail to support teachers when necessary. Or, the parent may act tolerantly amused when the name of a teacher is mentioned at the table. The child gets these convectional attitudinal currents, make no mistake about it!

### Judging the Teacher by the Pupil

A parent may be ready to accept "tall tales" of the child regarding the incompetency or laziness of school personnel. The parent may be taken in by the child's tactics when he wants his parent's attention diverted from a weak report card or the unflattering remarks about the child contained in a letter. A parent may be too ready to denounce teacher, principal, and school for not being able to "get their stuff across." A parent may thus spend his energies without investigating possible reasons for his child's behavior.

A teacher, on the other hand, may be beset with problems that stem from having to work with a boy or girl who comes from a home where an overprotective parent will not permit the child to grow up. All attempts by the teacher to broach the issue are met with resistance and by the parent's telling the child that no teacher "is going to make you unhappy by having you do all that nonsense." The parent does not stop to realize what such a remark, even made casually, can do to the child's concept of school and learning. A teacher who feels that a child is being harmed by the home environment may refer to "problem parents" in his reports. Unless both teacher and parent are "mighty understanding people," chances are that the teacher may give the impression, on contacts with the parents, of "tolerating" less able folk. Or the teacher may, quite unintentionally, snub the child's parents by making them feel that they are the sole cause of their child's poor school adjustment. The time could be ripe for retaliation. Only ways and means need be found to accomplish the mischief.

Whether school personnel like it or not, pupils are in fact "daily reporters" to parents about teachers and the school itself. The parent tends to judge all "education and teachers" in terms of what Johnny says on his own or what "Mamma can drag out of him" at odd moments. If the school day has gone well for Johnny and he feels that things are "all right with his world," the report to the parent, verbal or silent, will be a favorable one.

## How the Teacher Helps the Parent Understand ∨

A teacher who takes a clearly positive attitude toward the parent, sees his problems, and expects him to be interested and intelligent about school problems has gone "a fer piece" in the direction of setting up conditions favorable for cooperation. The teacher can assist the parent to see school problems in a variety of ways. He can see to it that news and general information releases are well planned and written so that a busy adult will get much in little reading time. A teacher can encourage parent-teacher groups to promote understanding rather than build walls between teacher and parent. A teacher can encourage the parents to plan sparkling programs, devoid of tedious minutes and parliamentary maneuverings. Here a teacher must be careful. He should assist parent groups and not attempt to "seize the helm" to promote any special interests he or the administration may happen to favor at the moment. He is not a "parent educator." A teacher must attend willingly these meetings where parents are present. If a teacher considers them a duty, a burden, and a chore, so will parents. A teacher must reach the parents who do not come to meetings at school. He should encourage classroom visits so that parents' confidence regarding school will be raised.

There are many opportunities for learning more about pupils and the community without burdening either school personnel or parents. The yearly "open house" or "teacher appreciation day" is not the best vehicle for such learning. Much better are group discussions (buzz sessions) concerning aspects of school-home relations, "workshop" sessions by means of which parent, pupil, and teacher can study problems related to their school in their community. "Fathers' night" and activities to encourage participation by alumni in school enterprises offer possibilities for improving teacher-parent relationships. Citizens who are not parents should be included in school-initiated activities. A teacher should recognize that families with no children in school are supporters of the school, or at least potential supporters or adversaries. A teacher should not ignore his responsibility to the adult who happens to have no child enrolled in school. He can help prepare school communications of many kinds to help interpret the school program for the parent and the childless or older couple.

A teacher can encourage parents to assist in school social events. Their aid and counsel tips the scales in understanding toward the school and the teacher's point of view. A teacher should make it a point to extend invitations to parents to participate in class and out-of-class activities. Their interests and hobbies are of sound educational worth. Of course, a teacher must plan carefully and well. Otherwise, he may inadvertently be giving opportunities to some adult to "take over" so that the teacher feels driven from his classroom and the principal feels apologetic for being in his office.

Diversity of opinion, if controlled, affords an opportunity for school personnel to "pull together" and indicate to parents the need for organizing and administering the school in closer accord with the aims of education in a democracy. Difference provides the opportunity for teacher and principal to help parents see that no one course or subject or activity is equally good for all children. Upon this basis—believing that the individual pupil is the reason for school organization—school personnel need to work. They should avoid setting themselves apart from parents by indicating that the school is the authority and knows what to do. A teacher and principal must help community members see that, logically, the school should provide large areas of time in which the school staff can plan and organize the school activities for the good of all who want to and must attend the public school.

There is no "chain of command" as far as the public and the professional educator are concerned. When basic objectives of the public and professional group are mutually opposed, those of the public must prevail. Parents must not be thought of as interfering with the prerogatives of the school. The decisions as to how best to achieve goals are, however, the responsibility of the school staff.

The willingness of a teacher—his readiness to talk about school doings and to explain what and why they are—go a long way in giving the parent the feeling of trust and of confidence in teachers and the school system. If a teacher happens to teach in a neighborhood with a number of foreign-born parents, his responsibility to them is all the greater. The foreign-born parent lacks the understanding of modern educational theory, and he has difficulty in comprehending reports from school that include "behavior" traits. Such a parent has language problems and fails to appreciate the purposes of American public schools. To him, the job of a teacher is "to teach" so that his child will achieve. A child who has emotional problems is likely to be thought of as "bad" or "lazy" or "stubborn."

It is to the feelings behind words and deeds that a teacher should focus attention. He must practice looking beyond overt behavior to the origins of actions.[5] At the same time, he must be on his guard against making even "well-meant" comments about parents. When these are repeated, they do not always sound as one meant them to sound when first uttered.

A skilful teacher realizes that making a parent feel guilty of his shortcomings only makes matters worse for the parent, for other home members, and for the teacher too. In and through his limited contacts, a teacher cannot hope to alter deep-seated parental attitudes. He can, however, help the parent grasp the meaning of school by keeping him informed of school practices. Ultimately, the success of relationships between school personnel and parent depends upon how wisely the parent reacts to the suggestions of teachers and others regarding the child. Often the parent will fail to make the most effective use of suggestions when left to himself. A teacher should play an active role in raising questions in parents' minds about school matters and home influences.

## Bases for Teacher-Parent Cooperation

Bases for teacher-parent cooperation have long been established. It has been common for a teacher to secure the help of the parent in promoting programs of better dental health, bodily cleanliness, and safety. It has been fairly common, in some schools at least, for the effective teacher to obtain curriculum materials from the parent. He has recognized the parent as an important human resource with talents to enrich and enliven the school program. He has called upon a father who served in the Armed Forces, one who headed a local industry, one who operated a filling station, one who planned buildings, and one who played musical instruments. The craftsmen, working with wood, stone, leather, metal, and glass, the

[5] Grace Langdon and Irving W. Stout, *Teacher-Parent Interviews* (Englewood Cliffs, N.J.: Prentice-Hall, Inc., 1954), p. 295. Chap. 13 is devoted to "Some Do's and Don'ts."

painter, and the amateur musician have helped to broaden the horizons of the pupil, teacher, and parent. Along with the tactful clerk and supervisor, a teacher can do much to help make the parent a partner in the work of the school. Through these many contacts the understanding teacher can better learn the views of the parent and thus help bridge the gap that too often separates school and home.

Cooperation sometimes gets a setback because of the thoughtless words or actions of teacher and parent. A teacher may feel, for example, that it is a nuisance for Johnny to drop out of school for several weeks so that he can accompany his parents on a vacation trip or a visit to "Grandma's house." A parent may vaguely understand the need for regular attendance because "it has something to do with the amount of state money the schools get." He may, therefore, bring the child by the school, report to the teacher, just for the record, and then want the child to accompany him on a shopping tour. A teacher who is employed as a teacher should not require the parent to pay him for "special help" if the pupil is regularly enrolled in the school system and the "coaching" is done during the regular school year. The teacher and parent should take all such "irregularities" as matters of course, using them as a basis for achieving better understanding. Absence can be used as a means for planning with the parent. A teacher can help suggest to the parent experiences to keep in mind which can then be shared by classmates.

## Records and Reporting

A teacher possesses one of the most valued of assets, the confidence of the parent and pupil, when he tells the parent truthfully how the child is progressing in school. Both parent and child appreciate, in the long run, a teacher who can be depended upon to report honestly what needs to be reported.

A report from a teacher to the parent should mean a summary or an analysis of the progress of the pupil in a form that the parent can understand and use. Unless the card or the letter indicates clearly to the parent in what ways the pupil can improve, a teacher has not met minimum professional standards.

## Reports Must Be Soundly Based

Reports that "meet professional standards" may cause ruptures in the relations between school and parent. The parent may consider the report a "sharp-edged instrument." However, a teacher can do much to build confidence in the parent by adhering to several desirable practices. First of all, a teacher should keep honest and accurate records of the pupil's learning in order to inform the parent. The records should be based on observable evidence, not upon the sex or conduct of the pupil. When a teacher places a rating of a pupil upon a record that goes to the home without having sufficient basis for it, the teacher is professionally dishonest. He is just as unjustified as though he had changed a pupil's grade to one "more in line" with those other teachers had previously recorded for the pupil.

A teacher deserves to be blamed by a critical parent for such practices. The parent must be confused and distrustful when he learns of such unethical action. When the teacher is pressed to defend the rating, meager data and personal whim are not enough. That teacher is successful only in performing a disservice to himself, to the pupil, to the parent, and to his colleagues.

## Should Children Be Compared?

A parent may want a teacher to report to him the exact scores earned by his child on achievement or other kinds of tests. The parent may want a teacher to tell him exactly what the nature of the test is and what the score means. The parent may even want a teacher to tell him of the exact comparison of his child with others in the group. If the parent lacks understanding about the wide range of differences in and between children, he is likely to be annoyed or elated, depending upon which way the advantage lies as far as his child is concerned. All a teacher asks is that the parent will use the report of his child to help the youngster grow up according to his own individual pattern.

There is a parent who causes concern for other parents and for the teacher by his excessive interest in the marks the youngsters get. His primary interest seems to be comparing his child's report with those of the neighbors' children. The effective teacher, through patience and understanding, has built up confidence within the child to accept his weaknesses along with his strengths as points to "work on." He has impressed the child with the confidential nature of his report—that it is a message for his parents about what he and the teacher already know. Along comes the inquisitive, station-wagon-owning parent on his daily round to pick up five or six of the neighborhood "gang." The parent-driver may seize the reports of all six youngsters before they have "boarded the wagon." He admonishes, so that all can hear, the lad who "went down in spelling" and praises Ned for "all those A's." The parent hopes that the boy will receive a dollar for every A earned. The parent forgot, if ever he knew, that he has undone much of what a good teacher had carefully and painstakingly constructed. Worse, the parent has violated basic principles of courtesy and respect, whether he was conscious of it or not. Few examples of adult thoughtlessness can match such conduct!

## The Parent's Responsibility: Be Constructive

/ On the other hand, a parent may appear to be indifferent to communications from a teacher. As indicated before, this may result from misunderstanding rather than just plain "cussedness." The net result for the child may be almost the same, however. The parent may blame a teacher for his child's failure to progress even though he does not say so. He may not understand the card but may use the poor marks as a whip over the youngster. He fails to see that the report could be a means for examining the work of the child and for building up confidence in the child regarding school and learning. The parent should remember that the child is likely to have only that one teacher for the entire school year. Stressing the child's strong points, even when there seems to be only one, is apt to bring its rewards in terms of increased security and improved relations between the teacher and the home.

When reports sent home are not all that parents may desire, a teacher should point out that scolding, spanking, or depriving a child of a privilege because of a poor report, are at best incitements to achievement that the child probably cannot achieve. At their worst, they may be medically harmful. Such procedures do not add up to good judgment on the part of a parent who feels compelled to employ them.

## Home Visits

Counseling of the parent by a teacher is recognized as one of the obligations of school personnel. The occasion involves many opportunities for demonstrating an adherence to strict ethical standards. Meeting the parent at home presents a teacher the chance to win or alienate a friend. Home visits can open the door to just "getting acquainted" or to thinking through emotional problems of the child.

### Need for Care in Conversation

Whether relations between teacher and parent are improved or worsened depends upon the way in which a teacher conducts the visit. He must be careful regarding problems talked about. Surely, his call may be strictly social. More generally, though, a teacher thinks a home visit is necessary to consider a pupil's problem. In the course of the conversation things may come up that a teacher feels a bit uneasy about discussing, and yet he does not quite know how best to sidetrack them. A parent may ask for information that a teacher feels would be unethical to reveal. A teacher may be "put on the spot" by not knowing how to withhold the information without offending the parent.

A teacher must guard against being led into commenting about other children and other parents. He could easily say things that would be unfair and disloyal to colleagues and unprofessional as far as the other parents were concerned. Discussions should center on the school problems of the child in whose home the teacher is visiting. The problems of other teachers, pupils, or parents should not be the business of a home visit.

### Teacher's Respect for the Parent

A teacher needs to be careful that he does not make the parent feel that he is being checked upon to see whether a teacher's suggestions have been followed. A teacher should avoid the "snupervising stare" of the overzealous social worker who would pry to "make note of irregularities." There is little to be gained by talking down to the parent. A wise teacher does not underestimate the parent's perceptions. He avoids pedagogical language and other ways of making the parent feel inferior.

A teacher should take care not to look upon the parent as a potential enemy to himself and the school who is bent upon fault-finding and broadside criticism. If he creates the impression that the parent is a nuisance by taking up his energies and time, a teacher does little for the child and weakens the home-school ties. He is a discredit to the whole teaching profession.

A teacher must be aware of the existence of unwholesome conditions and of real poverty in the home if they exist. However, he is quite powerless to prevent or to correct these conditions on his own. The establishment of constructive and positive relationships is by its very nature a painfully slow process. A teacher cannot successfully cut corners by pushing himself, by forcing issues, or by intruding into wholly private family matters.

It is true that poor family conditions handicap the backward child and cause a teacher real distress. Where the temptation is strong to help by doing just enough to "get one geranium to grow," a teacher must proceed cautiously. To barge into the home to "preach the gospel of salvation" can bring a laugh or two for someone. But any resulting "remedies" will do little for the emotional ills of parent or child.

### Keeping the Interview Balanced

A teacher must be well informed about the growth and development of children, must be sensitive to some of the problems facing parents who want to learn, and must have training in counseling and interview techniques. If not, his probings can do much harm and very little good. A teacher requires a knowledge of the basic principles of interviewing as a guide for planning and carrying out a successful home visitation.

A home visit that is carefully planned and tactfully promoted can develop desirable bases for rapport. A teacher must be on his best behavior too. He should show that he accepts the parent and his ideas. He must listen most attentively. He must respect the parent who is reserved. A teacher should pose alternative actions to the parent when the situation warrants. He must be watchful not to blame or to condemn. A teacher must be ready to make adjustments to help the child under discussion. He must be ready to explain the "what and the why" of school activities. He must show a genuine interest in what the parent has to say, even if he does not think, at the time, that the comments are pertinent. A teacher should speak openly and with an honest admiration for the child. He must be understanding of home conditions but not act sentimentally. He must take seriously what the parent says and means. He must show that he respects the confidences of the parent. Above all, a teacher should be honest and truthful in his remarks and in the impressions he creates, explicitly or impliedly.

A teacher can do much to keep from being asked back into the home of a pupil a second time. He can labor the point of untidiness or lack of play or study space. He can chide the parent about such shortcomings. He can ask personal questions or reply to questions in a manner that gives the parent the impression of being considered stupid. A teacher can belittle the occupation of the father or mother. He can fail to see ahead, precipitate an argument, get authoritative. He can act shocked by what a brother or sister happens to relate.

But home visits are not to be discouraged. Make visits to homes of exceptional children when time does not permit visits to all homes. Both problem children and talented youngsters can profit from home contacts if they are planned carefully and teacher and parent take the child into their confidence.

It is expected by the parent that a teacher will be honest in his dealings with him concerning questions asked about school. The parent will have a feeling of satisfaction to know that he will get a straightforward answer when he asks the teacher a direct question. It gives the parent a "comfortable" feeling to know that his child's teacher is willing to tell him what goes on and to explain why things are as they are.

The parent respects a teacher who has respect and consideration for him, who does not make him feel inferior and inadequate. A teacher does not compare one child with others to his detriment. He makes school challenging and interesting without demanding "too much" from the parent or child. In attempting to help parents see

that he is a human being, with a gender, a teacher should not overact
so as to break down barriers by playing the role of a "regular Joe."
A teacher is not "just a regular guy." To his pupil and to the parent,
he is and should be someone very special.

## Parent-Teacher Conferences

The conference period provides teacher and parent another opportunity to become informed about one another's job. The conference is crucial because of its direct and very personal nature.
It deals with confidential information. The attitudes regarding
school are formed as teacher and parent, and on occasion the child,
sit down together. The development of sound procedures for conferences provides one of the best foundations for effective school-
home relations.

### Focus on the Child

The conference can serve the purpose of bringing a teacher and
parent together to plan the important phases of the child's daily
living at school and at home. The conference serves its purpose
when the teacher and parent talk together, genuinely thinking
about suggestions for the good of the child.[6] The parent can learn
that home is school, that play is school, and that community living
is school.

Sometimes the parent comes into the conference to complain that
"other children pick on" his child. The parent may demand that
something be done. Brushing off such a parent will be of no help.
When a parent offers excuses for his child's behavior, there is nothing to be gained by argument or annoyed comment from a teacher.
In fact, there may be much lost. Argument only sets the teacher
and parent at cross purposes. It is better for the teacher to accept
comments and move on to a new point. A teacher cannot make
the parent over. It is his task, in the conference period, to find ways
to work with the parent for the good of the child.

A professional teacher does not use the conference as a means

[6] Langdon and Stout, *Teacher-Parent Interviews*, p. 335.

of comparing the child under discussion unfavorably with other children. He does not belittle the concern of the parent over his problem. If worry of a parent meets amusement from a teacher, the facts that would change the amusement to seriousness are likely never to come into words for a teacher to know. On the other hand, a teacher may suspect that some of what the parent says is not true. However, he must avoid any quick and glib diagnosing. It is easy to jump to conclusions but far wiser, of course, not to do so.

A teacher should understand that a startled or surprised or shocked or disapproving reaction to what is said only serves to shut off abruptly what is being said. A teacher should not only show no appearance of being shocked but should not *be* shocked by anything that is said.

A teacher who picks up the "conversation ball" and never relinquishes it has little opportunity to learn the many things that the parent has on his mind about the child. The parent who begins a sentence is in the best position to complete it. It is more courteous to let him do so. The skilful teacher-counselor can learn to be a sympathetic listener. He must learn how to highlight the parent's own sound insights and suggestions. He must learn to encourage the parent to make certain specific changes in his behavior toward the child that may, in turn, influence the way the child behaves at school and at home. By listening, a teacher can establish a close working relationship if he takes care to employ restraint, caution, and judgment in his overtures to the parent. The parent, above all, will appreciate the teacher who listens, who takes what he has to say seriously enough to give it respectful attention.

## Confidential Information

In a conference things can sometimes get on what is termed the "gossipy side." Information may be exchanged that one has no need of knowing about another. The parent may reveal information about other families or about affairs in the community. The parent may raise family matters that he would not wished "noised abroad." A teacher must hold in strictest confidence all that is told him in the conference, or anywhere else for that matter. Even the things that touch only on the pleasant side are the trust of the teacher and parent. They are not grist for the midmorning conversation mill.

When trouble about a child is spoken of, it is a temptation for a teacher to speculate with friends about the reasons. A wise teacher, needless to say, will keep his suspicions confidential. He will talk the matter over freely only with someone who can be of help in suggesting what is best to do.

For a teacher, gossipy information is simply "loose talk." Information may be passed on that may be true in whole or part or may be pure speculation. No teacher worthy of the name tells things to anyone merely for the sake of a laugh or to show that he is "in the know." He needs to be discerning enough to realize when the parent is telling things confidentially, when he is talking in the hope of eliciting some "free" information from the teacher, or when he is just talking to make pleasant conversation.

Consideration suggests that a teacher respect the parent enough to avoid any idle repetition of what is revealed in a conference between teacher and parent. The parent should never have any reason to doubt that whatever he says will be held in trust, never to be gossiped about, never even to be recounted as merely "a good story." A teacher must place himself mentally in the parent's shoes. He will then realize better how the parent may feel if he hears the retelling of confidences. This will give the teacher a real test of whether the item is the kind that a considerate person would retell. If a teacher would take the time to peer below the surface to see possible implications and consequences of his words and deeds, the chances of his saying careless words and of doing harmful acts would be minimized.

Matters can come up that a teacher feels a bit uneasy about discussing and yet does not quite know how to avoid. Maybe adverse comments are made about a colleague, the principal, the superintendent, or another parent. Though the teacher would rather not listen, he is afraid to shut off the talk lest the talker be offended. A parent may inquire about a subject that a teacher feels is not proper conversation, yet he may not know how best to withhold the unethical information without offending the inquirer. He must learn. He must not only be careful of all comment he makes but gain ability to move away tactfully from provocative topics. A teacher has an obligation to avoid saying anything that a parent might ever construe as being disloyal to the school system and the teaching profession.

Repeating what has been told on a professional basis to one concerned with the welfare of a child is vastly different from repeating information in a gossipy fashion. Knowledge gained in this way may be a means of great help to the child. Casual conversations may bring to light important details. Problems cannot be ignored or neglected. A teacher and parent should not necessarily avoid differences. Talking about them can prove enlightening and constructive.

## Truthfulness and the Constructive Approach

When the parent is critical and angry and upset, however, a teacher needs to use all the sympathy and understanding he can muster. The parent should come away from the conference in a different frame of mind—without hurt feelings or wounded pride and without having taken whatever was said personally. The irritation that comes from hurt pride or injured dignity can be minimized if the teacher keeps his thoughts centered on helping the child. Even though the parent may continue to be troublesome, a teacher can learn to pay less attention to personal feelings as such.

Words spoken about the desirable behaviors of the child will sound a responsive chord in the parent. A teacher need not worry that his expressions will be considered as flattery or the currying of favor. Words that come from genuine admiration are seldom misinterpreted. The parent may wish a definite opinion on a matter. The integrity of the teacher in withholding it and honestly telling why is likely to be understood.

Sometimes the honest answer to a parent's question is, "I don't know." The parent will respect such a reply when frankly given. The parent should not hear remarks from the teacher that are camouflaged, sugar-coated, or that in any way misrepresent the facts. Honest and truthful words imply an integrity that gives the parent reason for his trust and confidence in a teacher.

A teacher can speak the most profound ideas in everyday language if he really understands the thought back of the words. Sometimes being simple, direct, and truthful means the same as "having to face the music." On occasion unpleasant things have to be said. But unpleasant matters can be stated directly rather than obliquely.

To sum up, a teacher who is mindful always of his role as a leader will think about the relationships between himself and the parent in order that they may work well together. He will think less about bits of free advice to be given the parent.

The parent needs a teacher's help in playing down some aspects of competition and in looking for evidence of improvement in the child's record. The parent needs help in viewing his child objectively. The parent who is "all tied up" with his child needs the counsel of a sympathetic teacher and the help of a qualified analyst. He must be helped to see that his unrealized ambitions are not necessarily suitable goals for his child.

A teacher does well to look upon the problems of the parent as the parent's to carry and to solve. A teacher can be helpful. He can protect the confidences of the parent and show his understanding of the parent's needs. He can be patient and slowly learn how the parent feels about him, his child, and education in general.

There are many thoughtful and considerate things that a teacher can do in terms of his relations with the parent. These little things are to be done because the parent is a person to be respected and liked and treated with consideration. A teacher should not act civilly just for the sake of making his work go more smoothly.

There are no "open-sesames" when it comes to establishing good relations between all school personnel and parents. A few final words of caution, however, may be in order.

1. Be on special guard when speaking to parents. "Casual" remarks may turn up to hurt you, the child, and the school.

2. Hold frank conferences with parents based on factual data. Explanations should be based on feelings of empathy and sincerity, not pity.

3. Explain the "poor attitudes" of a pupil to a parent only in situations where privacy is certain.

4. Make comparisons of a child's performance to his past record, not with any other child.

5. In speaking with a disturbed parent, stress first the child's strengths as you honestly recognize them. The "bad" points will be broached by the parent in due time.

Such suggestions as those above are almost commonplace and may even smack of just "common sense." This may be so but perhaps it does no harm and a little good to remind ourselves of them. They are the things that come easy when school persons feel friendly toward parents and when they care how parents feel toward the school and the colossus we term "education."

## QUESTIONS FOR STUDY

1. What do you consider to be some reasons for lack of rapport between teacher and parent?
2. Point out specific kinds of misunderstanding that do occur.
3. Does the parent grant "permission" to the teacher to make certain demands on the pupil?
4. Upon what legal theory does the relationship between the teacher and the pupil rest?
5. What is included in the concept *"in loco parentis"*?
6. What are some of the "complaints" against the teacher alleged by parents?
7. Does the teacher possess "police power" with respect to the pupil?
8. With respect to what two areas do most of the legal problems arise involving the teacher and parent?
9. What are some limitations imposed upon the teacher regarding his treatment of children?
10. What are the six principles set out in a court decision that may be considered as a "complete expression of the law as it relates to corporal punishment"?
11. Can a parent choose the subjects he wants his child to study?
12. What is included in the phrase "sectarian instruction"?
13. Are health permits a legal requirement for admission to the public schools?
14. Give examples of remarks made at school or at home that reflect seriously on the integrity of each.
15. What is a "well-meant" comment?
16. Cite examples of "unprofessional conduct" of a teacher.
17. What are common dangers faced in a home visitation?
18. What is "loose talk"?

## SUGGESTED READINGS

Brooks, Fred E., "The Legal Status of the Pupil in the American Public Schools, A Study of Common Law Principles" (Unpublished Ph.D. dissertation, University of Chicago, 1948).

Hagman, Harlan L., *Administration of Elementary Schools* (New York: McGraw-Hill Book Company, Inc., 1956), chap. 9, "The Home and School."

Hymes, James L., Jr., *Effective Home-School Relations* (Englewood Cliffs, N.J.: Prentice-Hall, Inc., 1953), chap. 3, "Parents and Schools," and chap. 6, "Face-to-Face Relationships."

Langdon, Grace, and Irving W. Stout, *Teacher-Parent Interviews* (Englewood Cliffs, N.J.: Prentice-Hall, Inc., 1954), chap. 5, "The Teacher's Feelings," and chap. 13, "Some Do's and Don'ts."

# Pupil-Personnel Relationships

———————— 9

## PROBLEM SITUATIONS

What would you do in each of the following situations? Analyze each in terms of the questions raised at the beginning of Chapter 3 (page 56).

CASE A

Mr. *H* teaches arithmetic in the eighth grade at the Centerville School. On this particular morning, he assigned problems to be solved at the chalkboard. Dan failed to complete his work in the time allotted. Dan became very upset, making several comments to and about Mr. *H*. The teacher tried to prevail upon Dan to "get hold" of himself but apparently to no avail.

Dan was asked to leave the classroom. After some objecting, he did. He met his English teacher in the hallway. The teacher listened to Dan's story and then helped him arrange to go home. After the close of the period, Mr. *H* discovered that Dan was not in school.

CASE B

It was election time for home-coming queen at Johnson City High School. The student council had the job of setting up voting booths and of supervising the voting procedures. The president of the council saw several students "stuff" one of the ballot boxes. He took no immediate action.

Tom saw the same act and expressed his feelings strongly about "dishonesty" so that other students including some of the candidates heard him. The council president offered Tom some ballots for "his candidate." He refused to take them and went to report the two incidents to the sponsor of the council. It was during the noon hour that the sponsor asked the council president to come to the teachers' lounge.

CASE C

On the third day after the principal had taken action on the problem involving Roger *H*, the boy's homeroom teacher requested a "minute or so to talk over the matter." The trouble was that Roger had been failing

253

to report to class on time. Roger had come seven minutes late on that day and had no excuse.

It was part of school policy that a pupil must report for fifteen minutes detention for each five minutes of unexcused tardiness. Roger reported to the detention room one afternoon twenty-five minutes late with no "valid excuse." An extra hour was added to his detention time. Roger then retorted that "no specific time" had been designated by anyone for reporting after school. Finally, Roger stated that "one of us is lying and it ain't me!"

The teacher in charge told Roger, "Sit down and shut your mouth!"

Roger declared, "Nobody's going to yell at me. I'm leaving as of right now." He banged the front door closed.

The teacher stalked after him. "You had better get right back in this seat or you'll be walking permanently."

The lad continued walking away shouting back, "We'll just see about that."

When the child enters school, it is the beginning of his "immersion" in an environment where a teacher (or several teachers) exerts a very marked influence upon him. It is difficult to say at exactly what spot or time the relationships between pupil and school are first formed. A beginning is that point at which the school makes its first direct impression upon the members of the home—when the child is accompanied to school for the first time. Thereafter, teachers have almost daily contact with the pupil in the classroom, hallways, at lunch, and during play.

In some instances a teacher may come into contact with a child even before he gets to the school building. A teacher may assist with taking the school census. During home visits a teacher is able to meet preschool as well as school-age children. He can speak with the parents. Here first impressions are formed by teacher and by home members alike. At school, a teacher makes indirect contacts with the home by means of birth records, health and child-care clinics, and scheduled home visits to inquire about attendance problems.

It is generally agreed that the primary relationship of school personnel involves the children with whom they associate. Of course, this basic relationship involves many relationships, including those legal and ethical. As one text states, "the teacher-pupil relationship is the alpha and omega of education." [1]

[1] Harold E. Moore and Newell B. Walters, *Personnel Administration in Education* (New York: Harper and Brothers, Publishers, 1955), p. 88.

Understanding of what this relationship entails must come from other sources than statutes and codes of ethics. For these reveal little about what is or should be involved in pupil-school personnel relationships. Actually, a guide as to what the relationships should be ought to grow out of the ideas about people and things in which teachers and other school workers feel some stake. A teacher can help to determine what should be included in and excluded from the circle labeled "pupil-personnel relationships." He can do this partly through a study of the purposes of schools—whether his job is to spend his time and effort with potential "sputnik" creators solely or with those who will be content to remain the "bird-watchers." The legal and ethical proscriptions per se help only a little.

The purpose of the present chapter is, nevertheless, to point out some of the legal problems involved in the pupil-personnel relationship concept and some of the ethical problems (herein treated as psychological and social).

## LEGAL ASPECTS

### Pupil Control

The maintenance of control in the classroom is, of course, a concern to others besides school personnel and pupils. Parents, supervisors, and administrators are directly interested. But, the very first legal authority of a teacher is the maintenance, by whatever means is appropriate for him, of control of the pupils in the room. Teachers know this. The pupil ought to know it.

So, a teacher is entitled to know, and must understand, the expectations of the administrative staff regarding what is and what is not appropriate in maintaining "control." A teacher cannot be left with vague guides in a teacher's handbook. He must have specific notions about what is expected in terms of pupil management. A teacher must be certain about corporal punishment limitations, the detention system, procedures for sending pupils to the office, and responsibilities for pupil conduct beyond the classroom.

## Corporal Punishment

In the great majority of states, the legal right of a teacher to employ corporal punishment (any kind inflicted on the body of the pupil) is clear. However, this right has limitations and must be exercised with caution. The topic deserves attention here because the use of corporal punishment is yet fairly widespread, despite misgivings of psychologists, some educators, and some parents.

/ The courts are in accord in holding that a teacher who acts in good faith may inflict "reasonable" corporal punishment upon a pupil for offenses committed by the pupil that fall *within* the jurisdiction of the school. Rules made by a teacher, to be valid in court, must be limited strictly to supporting the purposes of effective instruction and maintaining conditions that permit teaching. Court cases bear out the contention that a teacher has "the right of correction" when such limitations are observed.

Punishment must be "reasonable in nature" and administered without malice. Where a teacher's punishment has been deemed to be excessive, the courts have held the teacher liable in damages. A rule of conduct made by a teacher is not considered by the courts to be reasonable or unreasonable per se (inherently or standing alone). Whether the rule formulated by a teacher to help govern the conduct of pupils is reasonable depends upon the circumstances in each case. The age of a child is relevant, as are his sex, physical health, surrounding room and playground conditions, and so on. The courts will set aside a rule made by a teacher only when, under the particular set of facts established, it appears to the court that the rule of the teacher was clearly not reasonable or was arbitrarily enforced or was promulgated out of malice toward the pupils.

A teacher has the authority to determine the gravity of the offense and what is suitable punishment to help deter a pupil from future similar acts. A teacher may not, however, interfere brutally with a pupil's body so as to affect his life, limb, or physical health. One case in this connection involved a third grade boy who opened windows against the order of a teacher. The pupil was pursued by the teacher and the principal together. Later, the principal sat upon the boy's chest. In the suit that followed, counsel for the plaintiff showed injury to the boy. The court awarded damages which had to be sustained by the defendant principal.

In law a teacher holds the position toward the pupil that the parent holds toward the child outside of the jurisdiction of the school. In this context, a teacher is said to stand *in loco parentis* (charged, in part, with the parent's rights, responsibilities, and duties), insofar as his authority and control extend over the pupil. But—and this limitation is an important one—a teacher does not have the general right to punish a pupil for all offenses as does the parent. The right of a teacher to administer corporal punishment is restricted to the limits of his acts as teacher.

Further, it is generally agreed that a teacher (along with the principal and superintendent) may make and enforce against a pupil those rules which are believed to be necessary in order to control and maintain the efficiency of the school when the board of education has failed to formulate rules covering the matter.[2] Where the rule enforcement entails some measure of corporal punishment, a teacher is bound by law to keep these three questions in mind to avoid legal trouble:

1. Have I acted from defensible motives in employing the punishment?

2. Am I sure that the rule for the infraction of which the pupil is being punished is a reasonable rule related to the business of the school?

3. Is the punishment to be inflicted such that it will be deemed moderate in degree?

In an emergency a teacher may not wish to use corporal punishment, even though permitted so to do. He may prefer to exclude the pupil from the classroom until administrative authorities have had the opportunity to review the facts and pass judgment upon

[2] The legal right of the teacher to punish the pupil for objectionable conduct does not depend upon the time nor the place of such objectionable conduct. Rather, such punishment depends upon whether the pupil's act has a direct and immediate tendency to harm the school and bring it into disrepute in the eyes of the general public.

States differ in their laws regarding the limits of the authority regarding the use of corporal punishment. The law of Maryland states in effect that the teacher can "pour it on." In Pennsylvania the law cautions the teacher to "take it easy," with no brutality to be used, no blows directed on the head or ears of the pupil. There corporal punishment must be administered only by the principal, not the teacher. See Robert R. Hamilton and E. Edmund Reutter, Jr., *Legal Aspects of School Board Operation* (New York: Bureau of Publications, Teachers College, Columbia University, 1958), chap. 2, "Authority of School Boards in Relation to Pupil Personnel."

the merits of the case. A teacher who does act on this theory and expels a pupil for violating an unreasonable rule will not generally be held liable in damages for such action in the absence of a showing of anger and malice.

## Teacher Liability

Pupil control in and outside of the classroom is related to the matter of the possibility of teacher liability in the event of injury to the child. In most situations where a teacher attempts by use of force to control the actions of the pupil, there is the possibility of legal responsibility in the event of injury to a pupil arising out of the teacher's action.

To repeat, the courts are in agreement that the teacher stands *in loco parentis* with respect to the pupil during the time the child is under the jurisdiction of the school. By the act of sending the child to school, as the state demands of the parent if the child meets minimum prescribed standards, both parent and teacher share in authority to "control" the pupil. Remember that the offense must militate against effective control by the school. This notion comes from the English common law and has a rich tradition behind it.

Liability of a teacher, in the event of injury, is real despite *"in loco parentis"* protection. Answers to the following questions are needed by a teacher when such an accident occurs: What constitutes "negligence" in a court of law? How are actions by a teacher with regard to negligent conduct interpreted by the courts? How can a pupil "prove" in court that negligence was present? What procedures may be followed by the teacher when he is the defendant in a suit? A teacher needs competent legal counsel when faced with a suit. The chances are, though, that he will make more intelligent use of legal services if he is familiar with "field trip" problems, with at least one definition of "negligence," with what the concept of "immunity from tort" means, and with what protection is afforded for a teacher by insurance.

## School Trips

"Beyond the classroom" is a concept of curriculum that is firmly established in many school systems. The "field trip" and yearly trek to Washington, D.C., by upper grade pupils is commonplace. It is not unusual for a teacher, who has made plans for such excursions, to cancel the trip because a parent has stated that he would "sue somebody" in case of injury to his child while off the school campus. At teachers' meetings and over bridge tables there seems to be increased discussion about "what to do" if a child gets hurt during school hours but away from the school building.[3]

When accompanying pupils on trips, a teacher must be concerned with his measure of responsibility. What are some suggestions which, if followed, may reduce the likelihood of legal trouble for a teacher? Adequate supervision should be one of the "musts." Even though teacher and pupil are not "in school" literally, a teacher must exercise reasonable caution. He must use an "average" amount of foresight with respect to his actions and the actions of pupils that he can anticipate. A teacher must act in a "reasonably prudent manner." It is easier to "be prudent" if a teacher makes visits with small groups. He should take special precautions if the trip will take pupils to private property such as an industrial plant. A teacher should remember that while on private property, he and the pupils are called "licensees." They are on the premises purely for their own purposes and advantage. If asked to come, the guests are "invitees" toward whom the company owes a duty of reasonable care. In addition, a teacher should make the parent aware of the trip beforehand by requesting the return of a written consent slip signed by the parent. This document is no "legal out" for the school, should a parent bring suit because he presumes that his child was injured owing to the carelessness of a teacher. The signed slip indicates only that a teacher has planned adequately and acted "in good faith." It means nothing more, since a parent cannot sign away the rights of his child to sue for damages in the event of injury.

A teacher must make reasonable rules governing pupil conduct

[3] Lee O. Garber, *The Yearbook of School Law 1956* (Philadelphia: University of Pennsylvania Press, 1956), p. 109.

while away from the classroom. He has the authority to enforce these regulations as he would were he and the pupil within the classroom proper. On the trip a teacher assumes responsibilities comparable to those of a parent. While on a school excursion, a teacher possesses legal authority to enforce rules as though both teacher and pupil were on school property. The jurisdiction of the school extends to the acts of pupils committed away from the campus itself.

### What Is Negligence?

A teacher needs some understanding of what "negligence" means as far as his relationships with pupils are concerned. Strictly speaking—in the legal sense, that is—acts of a teacher become negligent by this standard: the ability of a prudent teacher, in the exercise of ordinary care, to foresee that harmful results will follow the commission of the act. In short, a teacher is bound by the law to exercise that care which a person of ordinary prudence would exercise under comparable circumstances. If injuries result to a pupil as the direct result of the failure of a teacher to exercise "ordinary care" (this concept is of course a relative one and depends upon the particular set of circumstances in each case), a teacher may become personally liable for the injury sustained. Where danger is not inherent in a situation and injury to the pupil is not foreseeable, a teacher is not liable when such injury does occur.[4]

Teacher, pupil, and negligence may come together as a result of recess activities, noon-hour operations, pre- and after-school functions, as well as from trips. A teacher may chaperon a school party and not be careful to be sure everyone knows what school areas are "off limits." A teacher may realize that a pupil has remained in the building after hours because of bus trouble but go off the premises without thinking of this responsibility. An accident may occur to an automobile in which a teacher and pupil are riding with injury befalling the pupil. A teacher may allow a pupil to

---

[4] *Black's Law Dictionary* (1951 ed.) states that there are degrees of care, and failure to exercise the proper degree of care is "negligence." There are no degrees of negligence. Classifications indicate only that under special circumstances great care and caution are required rather than ordinary care, or that slight care is sufficient.

ride his bicycle across a crowded school ground with the result that a child is hurt. A teacher may request that a pupil help him to move a piano or other piece of school equipment. An injury, perhaps quite serious, could befall a pupil while thus engaged.

Sometimes the most ordinary act on a teacher's part can lead to legal trouble. A pupil may ask a teacher for "something for his sick stomach" or a "pill for a headache." A teacher is legally permitted to administer "first aid" to a distressed pupil but should avoid even the suspicion of overstepping his authority in this area. A teacher must not administer medical "treatment" to a pupil. There are emergencies, of course, where any adult must call upon his own good judgment as to what is best to do. The guide again is: act as would any prudent person under similar circumstances.

A child may be injured at school while he is playing. Here, at least ordinarily, a teacher and negligence do not come together to create the possibility of legal trouble. The school district is not an insurer of the safety of the pupil. Under the common law, the chances of a parent's collecting damages from a teacher in the event a child is injured were practically nil. To make a teacher liable, when a statute has not been violated, it would be necessary to prove negligence on the teacher's part, were he in control at the time of the injury.

However, a teacher has always been, and now continues to be, personally liable for his own negligent acts. A teacher and pupil may be driving an official school automobile going on a school errand when an accident occurs, hurting the pupil. Even though the teacher was acting for the school district, he is not relieved from any legal consequences that may ensue from the injury if his action was negligent. A driver of the teacher's car is liable for any negligence and so are the passengers if a "joint enterprise" is held to exist. This condition is said to obtain where all of the travelers in the automobile have a common purpose in the trip, share expenses, and have control over the route traveled.[5] Under these conditions, all the occupants of the vehicle are liable for the negligence of any other person, should the basis for a suit develop. In almost half of the states there are "guest statutes" which pro-

[5] See *Words and Phrases* (St. Paul, Minn.: West Publishing Company, 1956 Pocket Part), pp. 36-41, for much information about the "Joint Enterprise" doctrine.

tect a teacher-driver from suits by persons who are carried gratuitously. If the driver is grossly negligent, however, he is liable. A person is not a guest within the meaning of such laws if he pays either a fixed sum or his share of the car expense. A teacher would have to "dig into his own purse" for ordinary negligent acts. Liability may be incurred by any driver towards his passengers where no such guest statutes are in existence.

The whole issue of the degree of liability of a teacher for injury to a pupil is complicated, as can be judged from the foregoing discussion. The doctrine of negligence is involved and requires a trained legal expert. However, a teacher and principal should familiarize themselves with the body of law, including court decisions, that affect their relationship with pupils.[6]

To do less is foolhardy, for there has been a growing disposition in recent years for juries to return verdicts in personal injury cases with substantial amounts awarded to the plaintiff. From studying recent cases, a teacher can learn reasonably to anticipate danger. For, unless he does anticipate—and take precautions—he is liable for whatever consequences may ensue from injury to a pupil. A teacher has the duty to use the same degree of care that an ordinary prudent parent would exercise under like circumstances and conditions with reference to discipline and "training." Where there is a known hazard, a teacher has the legal duty to so inform the pupil before injury. A teacher must take steps to safeguard the pupil from hurt. If the pupil is exposed to a situation that is clearly hazardous, a teacher must take all reasonable precautions to protect the safety of the child. The courts have held that teachers are personally and individually liable under some circumstances for injuries suffered by pupils because of lack of proper supervision.

## The Limits of School "Immunity"

The word "immunity" appears often in connection with personal injury suits. What does it mean? In what connection is it used? Literally, it means "freedom from duty and responsibility" for whatever person or agency the concept is intended to protect. Here, the idea refers to the common law tradition that a school district

[6] See *American Jurisprudence* and *Corpus Juris Secundum,* under the topic "Schools and School Districts," for guides to such reading.

(in most of the states) is "immune," not liable, in action for torts (legal wrongs). Unless statute has altered the common law rule, a claim for damages against the school district is usually denied when entered by pupils who have sustained personal injuries while under the jurisdiction of the school.

The rule that "the state (king) can do no wrong" has meant that the school district too is immune since it is an arm of government. The negligence of a teacher as an employee, however, is not reduced or canceled out simply because the employer (the school district) enjoys immunity. A teacher is personally liable for acts of negligence while performing his teaching duties.

In some states liability for pupil injury is explicitly imposed upon the school district by statute. The common law doctrine of immunity is thus abrogated. Almost all modifications of the doctrine are partial acceptances by units of government (city, county, or state) of liability for damages when accidents occur in connection with authorized school activities. In states where such alterations have been made, the school district is now liable for torts of employees. A school district thus affected can be sued for the tortious act of a teacher.

There continue to be suggestions from informed sources that the long-standing doctrine of immunity should be abrogated in all of the states. If this suggestion were acted upon by the state legislatures involved, other problems might loom almost immediately. One is the possible effect that such a change in basic doctrine might have on the relationship between teacher and pupil. Would a teacher be made to feel more vulnerable to legal entanglements and thus circumscribe the activities of the pupil rather than extend them? Would "trips" be out? How much of a teacher's time would be taken up by appearances in court? Would a new kind of friction arise between teacher and pupil? Would a teacher suffer from "some kind of stigma" as one result of the change?

In the past the "immunity" rule has lent "moral support" if not actual "legal protection" to teachers in their relationships with pupils. A teacher has felt shielded from possible court action because the school district could not be "called into court" to answer for a tort. Teachers may be reminded that the "old law" is gone and that they had better not get involved so that a judgment can be won against them.

Thus far, the "field trip" problem has been elaborated in helping to develop the concept of negligence. One definition of negligence has been cited. The concept of "immunity" has been unraveled to some extent. The last problem to be treated in connection with liability of teachers in the event of injury to pupils is the matter of "insurance protection."

### Insurance Protection

A school district need not take out insurance to cover the negligent acts of a teacher or any other employee or agent, because the school district (with few exceptions, as noted above) is not liable for negligence in the performance of "governmental" functions.[7] A teacher should keep in mind that insurance protection purchased by a district is no protection for him if the policy extends only to the district itself.[8] If liability for negligence exists, a teacher ought to inquire whether his employer has availed itself of the right to buy insurance to protect teachers from a suit for accidents in school or on "trips."

Some states have authorized the purchase by the school district of insurance that covers a variety of contingencies. For instance, in some states teachers enjoy insurance protection against accidents to their persons and against being held liable in the event of injury to others, including the pupils with whom they work.

Teachers are becoming more conscious of the value of insurance. They are being urged by public and private groups to accept the notion that the "pupil has the right to be protected." The argument runs like this: The pupil must be in school by law and has a right to be protected if injured. For himself, a teacher needs protection since he is required to assume responsibilities because of the nature of his work. If a teacher has caused a loss while acting within the

[7] Here the teacher's attention is called to a difference between acts of a school district that are governmental in nature and those which are deemed to be "proprietary." The former are those connected directly with providing educational opportunities; the latter are nongovernmental or are related to business undertakings for profit.

[8] Lee O. Garber (ed.), *Law and the School Business Manager* (Danville, Ill.: Interstate Printers and Publishers, Inc., 1957), p. 243.

range of his assigned responsibilities, he should have the protection insurance affords.

When it is necessary for a teacher to use his automobile for school purposes, insurance is at least one kind of security he knows he has. The legal consequences in case an accident occurs under the above conditions should make a teacher "stop, look, and listen." Without some protection, a teacher is placed in a vulnerable position when he uses his own automobile for a school function. A teacher should investigate the nature and extent of his own insurance coverage, including protection of his person, other persons, and the vehicle itself.

If, for example, a teacher's automobile has so-called "extended coverage" on it, the policy would protect a teacher and any other person using the vehicle with the teacher's permission. A teacher's insurance may be suspended or voided in toto if he accepts payment for making the trip with pupils. He should make sure there is no provision in his policy that precludes his "carrying passengers for hire."

A teacher should carry adequate insurance to offset his liability in the event of accident to a pupil. A personal liability policy is one means of safeguarding life earnings and protecting against the disaster of a large verdict. The pupil should be covered by accident insurance. A teacher could work more effectively since he would be free from the strain that sometimes accompanies uncertainty.

## The Curriculum

Prescription of subjects to be taught in school by teachers is common practice in all forty-nine states. The legislatures and state boards of education have generally prescribed more subjects to be taken by the elementary pupil than by the high school pupil. Because of the regulations, teachers have been required to teach pupils facts and understandings in such areas as agriculture, physical education, the "evil" effects of alcohol and of narcotics, the federal and state constitutions, the conservation of natural resources, and the meaning of "Americanism."

### Pressure Groups and Public Opinion

A teacher is required to spend time in certain areas and provide instruction to the pupil depending upon how the legislators have left the "school law" after the adjournment of the current session. All manner of pressure groups impinge upon the legislators, as is well known. Their barrage of propaganda and "personal attention" results in many kinds of things including new legislation covering what must be taught pupils in the public schools. Legislative requirements regarding the curriculum correspond, at least in part, with successive waves of popular opinion with regard to the importance of the issues that happen to be in the limelight at any one time.

Recently, some groups have been disturbed about what is alleged to be the poor showing by pupils about the meaning of "Americanism." Scores on certain tests covering selected items in the area of American history were said to indicate that "our boys and girls know little about the heritage of their fathers!" In the State of New York the Feinburg law was directed at teachers and others who attempted to "subvert" the basic allegiance of pupils to the United States and "to the Republic for which it stands." The alleged purpose of the law was to protect the pupil from contamination by teachers who were deemed to hold alien ideologies. A teacher so identified was to be kept from obtaining employment within the state. Apparently New York legislators had been convinced by someone that communists had infiltrated the teaching profession and were thus able to use the forum of the classroom as a means of indoctrinating the pupil of "tender years" who was susceptible to such subversion.

Even more recently, there has been much stir about the "poor showing" that pupils make in the area of science. Teachers have heard either that they omit science in the classroom or that they do a poor job of building within the pupil the attitudes of work that make science education successful. Surely there will be legislation in some, if not most, of the states requiring that teachers provide instruction in "basic principles of science" and in "how the future will be shaped" by science.

### Religious Teaching in the School

Besides having to be concerned about "Americanism" and science, teachers must comply with the law with respect to introducing religious teaching in the school. Laws in many states limit a teacher regarding what materials may be used for classroom instruction and on bulletin boards and in display cases. According to supervisors, some teachers have "gone far," especially in southern school systems in mixing "ordinary learning" with religious teachings, despite existing legal cautions.

Some observers have pointed out that a teacher, where the law so permits, is only to read or have read without comment a passage from the Bible (with some version stipulated). The charge is that teachers have imposed on the pupil the memorization of Biblical passages, the singing of "sectarian" songs, and acceptance of particular religious biases. These unidentified "observers" have stated that a teacher should be prevented from using his "captive audience" to promulgate denominational doctrine and from making pupils feel uncomfortable when they report that they attend this or that church or do not attend at all. A recent case seems to indicate that in certain systems at least the "swing away" from sectarian teaching in the schools is quite far. On order from a board of education, it will be unlawful for the schools within the system to show drawings or pictures of the Nativity or other scenes with a purely Christian orientation.

Teacher and pupil and the law come together with regard to the problem of declaring allegiances to persons and symbols. The courts have generally sustained members of certain sects who have, on personal grounds, objected to giving the "Pledge of Allegiance" to the flag of the United States. For at least one enterprising teacher, the requirement to salute the flag and the pupil's objection posed no problem at all.[9] Apparently a pupil said, "Mr. Teacher, I can't salute the flag because my religion won't let me." What did the teacher do? He saw to it that Robert was the one to hold the flag while his classmates did the saluting during the required opening ceremonies.

[9] See Robert R. Hamilton, *Bi-Weekly School Law Letter* (November 22, 1951), Vol. I, No. 20.

## Other Regulations

### Activities for Personal Gain

Certain prohibitions that a teacher must respect are related to curriculum but not actually part of the content as such. One is that a teacher employed by a public board of education (one in the United States whose operations are dependent upon collection of taxes) is not to teach or coach for money when the pupil so aided is then enrolled in the school system. Admittedly, the point raised here is not alone a legal one. The question of "good judgment" and therefore "ethics" is involved. This question is even more in evidence when a teacher struggles with the problem of whether such service should be performed after school hours rather than during regular hours.

A matter only slightly different in import is raised where a teacher, employed by a board of education, makes use of school property, during or after school hours, to augment his monthly salary check. A case in point is that of a piano teacher who provides "private lessons" to pupils using board musical instruments. He may pocket the money thus earned while being paid by the board for instructing pupils on school time. Whether such a practice is actually illegal or merely "sharp" is perhaps dependent upon the way in which local regulations (if any) are interpreted.

A teacher, however, who at one time was employed by a board of education and is now "retired" for any reason has no authorization for coming into a public school classroom to use equipment when the proceeds are to add to the income of the teacher. It provides an opportunity for someone to cry "poor taste" and actually is an example of a teacher's using school facilities for instruction that results directly in his own monetary gain. Tax funds allotted for schools should be spent only in the prescribed manner.

### Compulsory School Attendance

A more basic rule or regulation is that pertaining to school attendance. In the United States the compulsory attendance of the child at a public or a "comparable" school is now recognized as the responsibility of the parent. Under the English common law— that law "comprising the body of those principles and rules of action, relating to the government and security of persons and property, which derive their authority solely from usages and customs of antiquity"—a father had almost unlimited control over the education of his child. This principle has been modified, of course, so that "we are at a point where no one questions the obligation of the state to make education available to all its citizens." [10] The parent realizes and voluntarily discharges his duty to send the child to school where a teacher can exert his influence.

A teacher has a "captive audience" since the pupil, with few exceptions, must attend school, whether willingly or without too much opposition. On a teacher's side is a body of school laws requiring the child who is within a certain chronological age bracket to attend school. Both teacher and pupil are aware that some pressures operate to make attendance at school five days a week for nine or ten months of the year a familiar pattern for school-age youngsters. State statutes require that the pupil be served by a teacher—or several teachers—during the course of about 180 days every year. The form of government cherished by most Americans has demanded this. That the arrangement is not a voluntary one is important for both teacher and pupil to remember.

However, the laws requiring the attendance of the pupil at a school are not self-enforceable. The state cannot depend solely upon the willingness of the parent to send his child, the complaints of neighbors when violation occurs, or the action of the local police. Legal responsibility to enable the child to be taught by a teacher must be placed in regularly constituted officers. Child labor control is of concern to the school because of regularity of attendance of the pupil. The state is responsible for such laws. The issuance of work permits is usually handled locally and entails the filling out of forms in the principal's or the superintendent's office.

[10] Charles K. Woltz, "Compulsory Attendance at School," as part of "School Pupils and the Law," in *Law and Contemporary Problems,* Vol. XX, No. 3 (Winter, 1955).

## The "Right" to Be Taught

Neither the pupil nor the parent holds any constitutional right to schooling. It may be limited by reasonable requirements. For instance, the pupil has no legal right to insist that he be admitted to a particular class or grade or group. The pupil's, teacher's, or parent's wishes have nothing to do with the problem. This is a prerogative of the school if and when the basis for the choice or the classification is a reasonable one. The school must retain the power to classify, to grade, and to reject the pupil on the basis of board discretion, using the "best-interests" rule as the sole criterion. The organization of a school, including the choice or assignment of teachers, cannot be made to depend upon personal preference.

Because of the *Oliver Brown* decision by the United States Supreme Court, statutes of some states requiring that a teacher of one race may not legally instruct a pupil of a different race are under attack. The Court said nothing about the skin color of pupils or teachers, it is true. However, the unanimous Court stated that separation of pupils from others of similar age and qualifications solely because of race "generates a feeling of inferiority." Subsequent orders of the Court would seem to suggest that the ultimate rule may be that all services provided at public expense must be available on a nonsegregated basis.[11]

## Liability of Parents

Sometimes a teacher makes a rule that damage to school property must be paid for by the pupil. He communicates with the parent and states that restitution must be made. There is a distinction here which it is important for teachers to bear in mind. If a pupil cuts up auditorium seats or robs the classroom, the parents of the pupil *are* legally liable for such damages. Parents are civilly liable for the acts of their children. For the criminal acts of their children parents bear no legal responsibility.

To elaborate the point, the bill-of-attainder provision in our Constitution forbids the enactment of any law punishing anyone for the misdeeds of a relative. This includes sons, daughters, fa-

[11] Edward S. Corwin, *The Constitution and What It Means Today* (Princeton, N.J.: Princeton University Press, 1954), p. 266.

thers, and other relatives. Because the old practice of punishing one for the misdeeds of his family was so grossly abused back in early Anglo-Saxon times, the framers of the Constitution specifically sought to prevent such assessment of blame.

## Secret Societies

A teacher should be acquainted with local regulations regarding secret societies. A teacher must not affiliate himself with groups of students outside of school when those students are banded together in organizations not recognized by the board of education. Court cases show that secret groups may be outlawed. A teacher may not legally belong to or sponsor organizations that exist outside of school regulations.

## Withholding the Diploma

If a pupil has notes during an examination period, and such possession is against school rules, the pupil can fail the subject or course. If, however, his diploma is withheld as punishment by the school authorities when the pupil has sufficient academic credit to be graduated, the court may order his diploma awarded. The pupil who refuses to wear a certain garb at commencement has been kept from receiving his diploma by the superintendent. It is essential for the teacher in charge of such activities ever to keep in mind that academic and disciplinary problems are distinct and separate in their handling and should not be confused.

# ETHICAL ASPECTS

The relationships between pupil and school personnel that are best described as being "ethical" in their nature are more elusive and therefore more difficult to describe than are legal boundaries. A teacher can and occasionally does show favoritism toward one or several pupils. Perhaps a teacher even may grade papers in a fashion that gives the charge of "unfairness" some validity. A new teacher may confuse respect and fondness and seek to obtain the latter first by encouraging the pupil to use a teacher's first name in his associations outside of the classroom. In these situations violations of ethics are quite clear, for there are no *legal* obstacles to stand in the teacher's way.

However, a teacher influences the pupil in more subtle ways. By means of attitudes expressed or merely "implied," a teacher can encourage effort or disparage attempts of the pupil. A teacher can, if he wishes, be unprofessional or even unscrupulous toward the pupil by acting indifferently or by undermining the pupil in the eyes of his peers and his teachers by encouraging "whispers" at appropriate opportunities. A teacher may have failed to organize and temper the forward-pushing urges and strivings that help build a strong superego.

To help bring into focus the complicated problem of the ethical aspects of pupil-personnel relations, this subject is divided here into two subdivisions, "Psychological Factors" and "Social Factors."

## Psychological Factors

The influence upon the pupil of the personality of a teacher is considerable—whether good, bad, or indifferent. In contrast to the fairly constant personality structure of teachers, that of the pupil is impressionable and susceptible to a teacher's glances and gestures, posture, work habits, and his wisdom.

### The Teacher's Professional Role and Insights

Two teachers within the same school may possess similar knowledge of "geography content" as measured by achievement test scores. They may have similar mental and social maturity ratings as judged by standardized tests. Each may have marked success in working with adult groups of various kinds. Yet each may have a radically different effect upon the pupil in and outside of the classroom.[12] It is recognized here, in the development of this idea, that some of the factors that are psychological and account for the difference in effect upon children are related not so much to ethical precepts as to job competency—professional insights and role-

[12] One conclusion reported by Bernice Baxter in *Pupil-Teacher Relationships* (New York: The Macmillan Company, 1946).

concepts. The difference does stem, in part, from unwillingness of one teacher as opposed to another to practice or live up to those ideas pertaining to teaching which a teacher knows are professionally right and befitting.

For example, teacher *A* may be talking with a visitor in the front of a classroom where eight- and nine-year-old youngsters are assembling items for the class store. During the teacher's conversation with the visitor, Sally may leave her work and come near the teacher to ask him to "fix the flap" on the milk bottle. As the child gets near the two adults, the teacher may say, breaking away from the visitor, "Sally, you can see I'm too busy to bother with you now. Go back to your seat!" Teacher *B*, in a similar situation, may say, "Look, Mr. Visitor, see the big quart bottle that Sally has made for our store. And class, hasn't Sally made an attractive front for it?" By this time the teacher has quietly tucked the flap in where it fits. How different! How vital is the support given to Sally and the recognition of her efforts, if she is an especially reticent child. How wholesome the effect on the other class members and the impression left with the visitor. Strange, is it not, that both teachers could have earned the top grade at State University the previous summer in a workshop on "Child Development"? Perhaps teacher *A* is not exactly "unethical" in a strict sense. But teacher *A* may as well have slapped Sally as far as the hurt that was bestowed. He knew differently. He must have. Rudeness to a child should never be excused away.

Or, a boy may be telling a small group in the classroom about a nest he found as a teacher smiles and nods approval to one who "needs to share the limelight" whenever it is possible. Another youngster in another room may be seen scowling as he haltingly hands a paper to a teacher who, with body tense and erect, holds out his arm grudgingly. This teacher may have similar paper scores, but unlike his colleague he does not see any reason why a teacher must treat unequals unequally. He sees little need to learn the names of the pupils since they are in the grade book and on the class roll anyway. He conducts class discussions but plans them around the contributions of three pupils "who can at least be depended upon." He provides opportunities in class for pupils to examine only the ideas he has previously selected as worthy. By the close of the first school term he has not bothered to "spot" the

few or many pupils who need special help. He has not taken time
to probe for likely causes of reticence.

### Effect of the Teacher's Personality

One investigator desired to explore the "receptivity-producing
effect" of teachers upon children. In the study on teacher-pupil
relationships, she came to the conclusion that certain definable relationships between teacher and pupil do exist within the classroom. These relationships apparently are not fleeting but do occur
with sufficient regularity to be used in describing the teacher.[13]
The finding stated in part that

> . . . the good teachers were free from restricting inhibitions and
> restraints common to the poor teachers. They sought ways to im-
> prove their teaching and were open-minded and desirous of sugges-
> tion. The poor teachers defended their shortcomings whether called
> upon or not to do so. They called attention to that which they
> thought would lead to commendation.[14]

In addition, a teacher who defended his shortcomings to others
and who sought out data to bolster his sagging ego seemed to fail
to get from the pupil the responses that the teacher wanted. However, the teacher did get from the pupil the responses that coin-
cided with his own behavior. A teacher who defended his own
shortcomings was easily disturbed and distracted. His efforts were
rewarded with inattention from the pupil. The whole class tended
to become disorganized and unruly with the self-concerned and
self-interested teacher.

Does the pupil "get molded" into the pattern of behavior of a
teacher, whether integrative or disintegrative? Some psychologists
stress the influence of a teacher upon the thoughts, feelings, and
the very actions of the pupil with whom he makes almost daily
contact. Many teacher rating scales include some items that in
effect "describe" the personality pattern of teachers. There seems
to be some agreement that teacher personality patterns are reflected
in the pupils. The lazy, the indifferent, the arrogant, or the "un-

---

[13] Daily records of the observed behavior of six teachers and their pupils made
possible a fairly complete description of each teacher's personality in terms of
her influence upon pupils' reactions.

[14] Baxter, *Pupil-Teacher Relationships*, p. 30. Used with permission of The
Macmillan Company.

principled" teacher has no less influence upon the thoughts and actions of pupils.

## Putting the Child's Needs First

Books in professional education are full of statements that boil down to "teaching the child and not subject matter." For teacher and pupil, this admonition is more than rhetoric and sound pedagogy. Implicit in the phrase is basic philosophy. In other words, a teacher should consider the Freds and Dorothys first and the textbook content of arithmetic or of Latin second—as the means to ends.

What does this mean as far as the ethical relationships between teacher and pupil are concerned? A teacher will, above all, avoid resorting to threats and similar devices when faced with uncomfortable decisions. He will avoid intimidating the child. There will be an absence of nagging and apathy. Rather than a "spirit-killing" attitude, indifference, disdain for the exceptional child, a teacher will understand that children have emotional as well as physical and mental needs that require fulfillment.

A teacher does not choose to be in conflict with children, of course. He wants and really hopes to avoid parent and general community complaints. However, in his anxiety to rid himself of classroom troubles—or at least keep them at a minimum—a teacher may fall into the error of attacking symptoms. In such procedures, causes are not explored. When frustration is encountered, a teacher may neglect or boss the children, whichever suits his particular whim at the moment.

A teacher should avoid threats or reprimands if he wants to reduce classroom disorder. Threats and high-pitched voices beget more threats and increased pitch. Disorder becomes its own breeding ground. Failure in school, of whatever nature, should be considered as the partial responsibility of a teacher. When it concerns an individual child, the teacher is directly involved. He makes the daily direct contacts. In a large measure, he controls the school situations that induce success or failure.

A discriminating teacher knows that sometimes an underdeveloped Jerry plus "crummy" clothing make for a situation where the boy may become the butt of school jokes. Size notwithstanding,

Jerry can become a fighter and learn to enforce respect with his two fists. From the school bully to the adult menace is not an unfamiliar road. Jerry can be well on his way before a court of law finally intervenes.

A teacher who in his teaching employs the principles of child development and governs his actions by the concepts of sound teaching-learning theory will take Jerry in stride. He willingly accepts the notion that extreme deviate behavior, even lawlessness, is more a matter of circumstances than inclination or "inborn cussedness."

Teachers know that stealing is one of the most common of juvenile offenses. In such instances a thoughtful teacher wonders to what extent Jerry's stealing is "for show," out of bravado. To what degree is the boy breaking the rules of society to gain some much-needed respect from his peer group?

A teacher offers no sermons on sin. He acts on the assumption that misdeeds are an unconscious revenge upon the social group whose code is not tenable for him. A teacher acts on the belief that the first signs of resentment against the world may build up into fixed patterns unless ways are found to get at sources of the real trouble.

A wise teacher provides opportunities wherein the pupil learns of his inadequacies but without sacrificing his confidence and feeling of status with his peers. He finds ways of solving problems and of sharing both the work and results of work with the pupils. Such a teacher is not partial. He shows consideration for every variant child. He trusts children, is eager to learn with and from them, and demonstrates his interest in their problems. He guides children by quiet, humorous, and sometimes inaudible suggestion. Enthusiasm and spontaneity are his distinguishing marks.

In short, a perceptive teacher treats all pupils with respect and interest in them as people. He is friendly and courteous. There is no "Take your seat, George, can't you see I'm talking!" A teacher helps the pupils to take an interest in the plans of the class. The pupils stand out, not the "gold stars" on the bulletin boards where the A papers of the "chosen few" are displayed. The individual pupil is worthy because of his best efforts. A teacher has little need to call attention to rules that have been violated. The room is guided by a person who is relaxed and non-striving.

For the child, the thrill of grasping an idea has its own reward. A teacher is fully aware of this truth. He knows the value in avoiding the demand for hurried results before the pupil has had time to think things out for himself. Because of a sensitivity for the rights of the pupil, a teacher is not impelled to dominate. He does not rob the youngster of the just fruits of his own efforts by prematurely shoving an answer at him.

A teacher, nevertheless, appreciates the importance of discipline and takes seriously his responsibility of helping the pupil understand what self-control and good judgment mean for him and for others. He strives to understand the pupil's deeply rooted need for recognition. He plans events so that each pupil has some successful experience. Thereby the child can feel his own worth and sense his developing powers. He gets encouragement at school. A teacher helps to enhance the child's sense of well-being. The "golden rule" is practiced.

## Social Factors

The social development of the child takes place outside of the school and under the influence of the home long before the pupil and teacher face each other. However, poor home treatment of the child (owing to a variety of emotional, economic, and physical factors in the environment) may be reflected in poor school adjustment. A child rated by a teacher as having good social adjustment and work habits in school may well be the child who is "well adjusted" in his home. When a teacher "spots" a problem pupil and refers the youngster to a psychological clinic, the skilled clinician will "go to work" on the parents.

For a teacher to be of help and assistance, the child must be in school. He must "be around" to participate in the "socializing" activities planned. Pupil absence is high in some classes and in some teachers' rooms. It is not unusual for a pupil, when questioned, to raise every excuse "in the book" to explain away inattendance or irregularity in attendance. He may state that he tries to evade the monotony of a dull daily program, an inflexible routine, or the antics of a "queer teacher."

## The Teacher's Fairness and Friendliness

Any conclusions based upon the judgments of a pupil regarding school must be analyzed carefully. The criticisms made by pupils of their teachers and their schools have been catalogued by various persons at various times. These compilations are available for examination. Despite limitations, the items are "food for thought." When pushed for a reply under proper circumstances, a pupil may state that a teacher has been unfair and partial. The pupil may add that a teacher has been unsympathetic about helping pupils in out-of-class activities. The pupil may believe a teacher to be one who sets standards for all which "must be maintained at all costs." Perhaps a teacher believes that impartial treatment of pupils means equal treatment. If so, he has not learned the kind of behavior that is required of a teacher who recognizes the principle of individual differences within and among pupils.

There is the teacher who encourages relationships with pupils that are not consistent with his professional obligations. A teacher who lets himself be invited to the home of one pupil for a dinner and refuses another invitation from a second pupil is "asking for trouble." Another example is that of a teacher accepting favors from a boy or girl who is his current pupil but refusing favors from other youngsters. "Bad manners" and "poor taste" best describe a teacher who permits a pupil to perform "personal services" for him. Familiarity and respect in a school social situation are miles apart. Relations between teacher and pupil are apt to deteriorate from the "purely professional plane" when a teacher fails to make clear by his own conduct those marks which separate friendliness and license.

A professional teacher is careful to avoid such errors. He guards his actions and words when on visits to homes of pupils. He watches the places of entertainment he visits so that his presence or absence will not be construed as approval or disapproval "by teachers" of the particular brand of relaxation. A careful teacher avoids "pumping" the pupil for information about matters that are clearly the private concern of the pupil and his family members. He guards against allowing his social contacts to degenerate into "rounds of visits" and fraternization for its sake only.

## How the Teacher's Behavior Teaches

A teacher ought to help the pupil to discriminate between those social contacts which may well lead to lasting satisfactions and those which could prove only fleeting. A teacher should be highly sensitive to the social problems that exist within the school. If he fails to be, the social activities could degenerate into cliques and special interest groups that leave the total welfare of all pupils far behind.

There is, unfortunately, a teacher who in the presence of pupils belittles other teachers and teaching. Often it is such a teacher who avoids situations where a forthright exchange of ideas about limitations and weaknesses could be profitable and not hurtful. When a pupil hears about the limitations of teaching even from only one teacher, any potential interest he might have in education as a career may well "fly right out the window." If he is normal, he will perhaps run as fast as he can in the opposite direction.

There is also the forensic or athletic coach or musical director who considers it "fair game" to find out the weaknesses of opposing individuals or teams no matter how this is done. The pupil onlookers get the impression that it is right and proper to "get access to" confidential reports from district or regional officials by devious means. Or, the pupil participants may get the impression from their teacher coaches that the participant on the team or squad is entitled to spend school-earned funds freely for personal items or to keep part of the school equipment as his own property for "having served Old Bemish School so ably."

Last, by way of illustration, there may be a teacher who serves as the coach of debate. On occasion he may display, in front of the school debate team members, the most blatant bad manners and rudeness. In his anxiety to win, he jockies for the most favorable committee of judges for "his team" or for the "best position" on the tournament program. He demonstrates not only bad manners but an immaturity and impatience that sets a poor example. Worse, he undermines the very values he is paid to help encourage. His behavior shouts out loud a philosophy that discourages the teacher who is thoughtful and who holds convictions regarding what is fair play that are different from those displayed by the "winner-at-all-costs" person.

## Working Principles for the Teacher

It is easy to "show up" a teacher who fails to practice those precepts taken as minimum in building solid and wholesome relations between himself and pupils. To emphasize the positive and de-emphasize the negative, there follows a numbered list of suggestions which, if accepted and put into daily practice, should tend to foster desirable relationships between teacher and pupil.

1. Build up a sufficient number of privileges in the classroom or in the club so that certain of the privileges can be denied for a reasonable length of time when a pupil uses poor judgment.
2. Use a private conference for a rule-transgressor, thus avoiding a scolding in public.
3. Have freedom to do the sensible thing regarding a pupil, unfettered by the administration with special restrictions, promises, rewards, or punishments coming from a third person.
4. Make sure that a pupil who is eliminated from the class goes to a certain spot with something to occupy his time. (Otherwise the pupil has the opportunity to cause further trouble for himself and the school.)
5. Deal with difficult problems in different and unexpected ways each time. A child is unique, an individual, all his own!
6. Believe that the primary responsibility for the behavior of a child (whether in school or out) rests with his parents or guardian.
7. Extend to the parent the privilege of consultation. Do not avoid such opportunities because of feelings of apprehension.
8. Suspend judgment and avoid immediate punishment. Perhaps the parent will take the task off your shoulders.
9. Give thought to handling serious disciplinary problems.
10. Help a child see a good reason to stay after school for special help.
11. Arouse feelings of self-respect rather than of humiliation in the pupil.
12. Act on the assumption that certainty and not severity of remedial action is what counts with children.
13. Believe that "freedom" and "order" are two terms that take on meaning from the type of activities carried on.
14. Avoid familiarity!
15. Know that private informal talks with a child about a problem of behavior will usually be successful.
16. Keep the school principal informed when arranging for parent conferences.
17. Show by your attitude that you will work with all types of children.

18. Give of your time and energy willingly.
19. Live by the dictum that all children deserve respect and courtesy.
20. "Make-up" assignments should vary considerably in each case.
21. Have facts and other kinds of data to back up grades earned by pupils.
22. Be free when a pupil comes for a scheduled conference.
23. Make all statements about a pupil in a brief and constructive manner.

To summarize, one can excuse almost everything that a teacher may do except his being rude and hurtful to a child, thus "selling himself and the child short." A thoughtful and careful teacher realizes that physical ailments of the pupil may frequently result in learning problems and that such discomforts may be related to a boy's belligerent attitude toward a teacher, school, and the world in general. A teacher can be sensitive to the fact that the school plays a major role in helping the pupil to conserve energies or to cause them to be dissipated in meaningless and random activities. A truly professionally-minded teacher spends his efforts helping to reduce tensions in and between children. He attempts to make preliminary diagnoses of pupil difficulties in order to see if and what kind of help is required. He makes use of the conference and demonstrates his fund of patience in working with the pupil and parent who have problems that need solving.

The tensions created by the tempo of modern living affect boys and girls as well as their teachers and parents. Nerves become taut. A wise teacher regards the pranks and more serious misbehavior of children as deviations from good citizenship rather than as personal insults. He considers them as offenses against the group, not against himself. A teacher appreciates the meaning and importance of discipline and takes seriously the responsibility he has for aiding the pupil to understand what self-control and judgment mean for himself and for others.

There have been numerous attempts to define the "professional teacher." As early as 1929, the National Education Association adopted a code of ethics with a preamble and three articles. From that date to the present there have been other declarations. All have had elements that are substantially the same. A teacher is admonished in the "statements of general conduct" to be truthful in his relationships with pupils. He should limit his promises but fulfill those he makes. He should avoid mass discipline. He should inquire about the pupils who are ill or who have illness in their homes.

A pupil's successful orientation to the social life of the school is influenced by the conduct of a teacher, by his insight and ability to promote in the pupil a feeling of well-being. If a pupil's classroom relationships are such as to assure him of acceptance of himself by others, it is safe to assume that he is well on the way toward behavior patterns that should prove satisfying to both himself and the group.

A good teacher helps the pupil establish such desirable relationships. He helps him grow in understanding concerning the necessary balance between freedom and responsibility, between rights and duties. The teacher provides opportunities for the pupil to work under conditions that foster respect for the rights and the privileges of others. He helps the pupil see the need for tolerance of viewpoints different from his own and for sharing the responsibility for decisions affecting the welfare of the members of the group.

An informed teacher recognizes that children have emotional needs that require particular attention. He knows also that under the pressures of daily living these needs often become intensified and more complex, more difficult to understand. He realizes the ineffectiveness of many of the methods in common use for attempting to overcome some of the "undesirable" emotional reactions in children. A teacher appreciates the heavy demands made upon the physical and emotional reserves of children because of the tempo of modern living and constantly changing conditions.

### QUESTIONS FOR STUDY

1. What single factor affects relationships between the teacher and pupil to a greater extent than any other?
2. What is the first legal responsibility of the classroom teacher?
3. What standard is commonly used to measure the degree of corporal punishment that can be inflicted by the teacher on a pupil?
4. Are local school rules and regulations valid if and when the board has remained silent on the matters?
5. What determines the "reasonableness" of a school rule?
6. Is the teacher protected from suit for negligence because he is an employee of the state?

7. What precautions should be taken by the teacher in preparation for a field trip?
8. What is a "workable" definition of sectarian teaching?
9. What part does the teacher play in enforcement of compulsory school attendance regulations?
10. Is the parent legally responsible for the civil acts of his children? What is your reason?
11. Are all inconsiderate words or acts of a teacher examples of unethical behaviors?
12. In the last analysis, are breaches of good faith by the teacher causes or merely symptoms of unprofessional conduct?

## SUGGESTED READINGS

Bush, Robert N., *The Teacher-Pupil Relationship* (Englewood Cliffs, N.J.: Prentice-Hall, Inc., 1954), chap. 8, "Matching Teachers and Pupils."

Edwards, Newton, *The Courts and the Public Schools* (Chicago: University of Chicago Press, 1955), chap. XXI, "Rules and Regulations of Boards of Education," and chap. XXII, "Discipline and Punishment of Pupils."

Garber, Lee O., *Handbook of School Law* (New London, Conn.: Arthur C. Crofts Publications, 1954), chap. VIII, "Pupils."

————, *The Yearbook of School Law 1956* (Philadelphia: University of Pennsylvania Press, 1956), chap. VIII, "Pupils and Pupil Services." See chap. VIII on "Pupils" in the 1954 and 1955 Yearbooks.

Hamilton, Robert R., and Paul R. Mort, *The Law and Public Education* (Chicago: The Foundation Press, 1941), chap. XI, "Rights and Responsibilities of Pupils and Parents."

————, and E. Edmund Reutter, Jr., *Legal Aspects of School Board Operation* (New York: Bureau of Publications, Teachers College, Columbia University, 1958).

Remmlein, Madaline Kinter, *The Law of Local Public School Administration* (New York: McGraw-Hill Book Company, Inc., 1954), chap. 7, "Pupil Regulation."

Sumption, M. R., "The Control of Pupil Conduct by the School," as part of "School Pupils and the Law," *Law and Contemporary Problems* (Winter, 1955), Vol. XX, pp. 80-90.

Wahlquist, John T., *et al.*, *The Administration of Public Education* (New York: The Ronald Press Company, 1952), chap. 6, "The Administration of Pupil Personnel." There is an excellent bibliography at the close of the chapter.

Yeager, William A., *Administration and the Pupil* (New York: Harper and Brothers, Publishers, 1949), chap. 16, "School Control."

# Bibliography

Adams, Harold P., and Frank G. Dickey, *Basic Principles of Supervision.* New York: American Book Company, 1953.

American Association of School Administrators, *Staff Relations.* Thirtieth Yearbook, 1955. Washington, D.C.: N.E.A., 1955.

American Association of University Professors, *Bulletin* (Winter, 1954-55).

Avent, Joseph E., *The Excellent Teacher.* Knoxville, Tenn.: Joseph E. Avent, 1931.

Ayer, Fred C., *Fundamentals of Instructional Supervision.* New York: Harper and Brothers, Publishers, 1954.

Bartky, John A., *Supervision As Human Relations.* New York: D.C. Heath and Co., 1953.

Baxter, Bernice, *Pupil-Teacher Relationships.* New York: The Macmillan Company, 1946.

Bills, Robert E., *About People and Teaching.* Lexington: University of Kentucky Bulletin.

Black, Henry Campbell, *Black's Law Dictionary,* 4th ed. St. Paul, Minn.: West Publishing Company, 1951.

Brooks, Fred E., "The Legal Status of the Public in the American Public Schools, A Study of Common Law Principles," Unpublished doctoral dissertation, University of Chicago, 1948.

Buros, Oscar K., *The Fourth Mental Measurement Yearbook.* Highland Park, N.J.: The Gryphon Press, 1953.

Burton, William H., and Leo J. Brueckner, *Supervision; a Social Process,* 3rd ed. New York: Appleton-Century-Crofts, Inc., 1955.

Bush, Robert N., *The Teacher-Pupil Relationship.* Englewood Cliffs, N.J.: Prentice-Hall, Inc., 1954.

Carney, Marie L., *Etiquette in Business.* New York: McGraw-Hill Book Co., Inc., 1948.

Chamberlain, Leo M., and Leslie W. Kindred, *The Teacher and School Organization.* Englewood Cliffs, N.J.: Prentice-Hall, Inc., 1949. (See also Revised Edition, 1958.)

Chandler, B. J., and Paul V. Petty, *Personnel Management in School Administration.* Yonkers, N.Y.: World Book Company, 1955.

Chase, Francis S., "Professional Leadership and Teacher Morale," a Midwest Administration Center Study in *The Administrator's Notebook*, Vol. I, No. 8 (1953).

Cook, Lloyd, and Elaine Cook, *School Problems in Human Relations*. New York: McGraw-Hill Book Company, Inc., 1957.

Corwin, Edward S., *The Constitution and What It Means Today*. Princeton, N.J.: Princeton University Press, 1954.

Cubberley, Elwood P., *Public Education in the United States*. Boston: Houghton Mifflin Company, 1919.

Denneson, Charles P., *Faculty Rights and Obligations*. New York: Bureau of Publications, Teachers College, Columbia University, 1955.

Deuel, Leo, *The Teacher's Treasure Chest*. Englewood Cliffs, N.J.: Prentice-Hall, Inc., 1956.

Dougherty, James H., Frank H. Gorman, and Claude A. Phillips, *Elementary School Organization and Management*. New York: The Macmillan Company, 1950.

Edwards, Newton, *The Courts and the Public Schools*. Chicago: The University of Chicago Press, 1955.

Elsbree, Willard S., *The American Teacher*. New York: American Book Company, 1939.

———, and Harold J. McNally, *Elementary School Administration and Supervision*. Englewood Cliffs, N.J.: Prentice-Hall, Inc., 1954.

———, and E. Edmund Reutter, Jr., *Staff Personnel in the Public Schools*. Englewood Cliffs, N.J.: Prentice-Hall, Inc., 1954.

Faulkner, William, "On Privacy," *Harper's Magazine*, CCXII (July, 1955).

Fisk, McKee, and James C. Snapp, *Applied Business Law*. Cincinnati: South-Western Publishing Company, 1955.

Garber, Lee O., *Handbook of School Law*. New London, Conn.: Arthur C. Crofts Publications, 1954.

———, *Yearbook of School Law 1955*. Philadelphia: University of Pennsylvania, 1955.

———, *Yearbook of School Law 1956*. Philadelphia: University of Pennsylvania, 1956.

Greider, Calvin, and William E. Rosenstengel, *Public School Administration*. New York: The Ronald Press Company, 1954.

Griffiths, Daniel E., *Human Relations in School Administration*. New York: Appleton-Century-Crofts, Inc., 1956.

Hagman, Harlan L., *Administration of Elementary Schools*. New York: McGraw-Hill Book Company, Inc., 1956.

Hall, Robert K., and others, *The Yearbook of Education, 1953*. New York: World Book Co., 1954.

Hamilton, Robert R., *The Bi-Weekly School Law Letter*. March 15, 1951; July 8, 1953. Laramie, Wyo.

————, *Legal Rights and Liabilities of Teachers.* Laramie, Wyo.: School Law Publications, 1956.

————, *The National School Law Reporter.* New London, Conn.: Arthur C. Crofts Publications (August 4, 1955).

————, and Paul R. Mort, *The Law and Public Education.* Chicago: The Foundation Press, 1941.

————, and E. Edmund Reutter, Jr., *Legal Aspects of School Board Operation.* New York: Bureau of Publications, Teachers College, Columbia University, 1958.

Hepburn, William M., *Cases on the Law of Torts.* St. Paul: The West Publishing Company, 1954.

Hymes, James L., Jr., *Effective Home-School Relations.* Englewood Cliffs, N.J.: Prentice-Hall, Inc., 1953.

Jessup, John H., "Violators of Ethical Standards," *Phi Delta Kappa,* XXIX (November, 1947).

Jewett, Robert E., "Why the Able Public-School Teacher Is Dissatisfied," *Educational Research Bulletin* XXXVI, No. 7, Ohio State University, 1957.

Kennedy, Millard F., *Schoolmaster of Yesterday.* New York: McGraw-Hill Book Company, Inc., 1940.

Langdon, Grace, and Irving W. Stout, *Teacher-Parent Interviews.* Englewood Cliffs, N.J.: Prentice-Hall, Inc., 1954.

Lieberman, Myron, *Education as a Profession.* Englewood Cliffs, N.J.: Prentice-Hall, Inc., 1956.

Linn, Henry H., and others, *The School Custodian's Housekeeping Handbook.* New York: Bureau of Publications, Teachers College, Columbia University, 1948.

Mayer, Lewis, *The American Legal System.* New York: Harper and Brothers, Publishers, 1955.

Moehlman, Arthur B., *School Administration.* Boston: Houghton Mifflin Company, 1951.

Moore, Harold E., and Newell B. Walters, *Personnel Administration in Education.* New York: Harper and Brothers, Publishers, 1955.

National Education Association, Research Division, "Professional Salaries for America's Teachers," *Education Digest* XX (September, 1954).

Norton, A. O., *The First Normal School in America;* the Journals of Cyrus Pierce and Mary Swift. Cambridge: Harvard University Press, 1926.

Overstreet, Harry, and Bonaro Overstreet, *The Mind Alive.* New York: W. W. Norton & Company, Inc., 1954.

Pittinger, Benjamin F., *Local Public School Administration.* New York: McGraw-Hill Book Company, Inc., 1951.

Reavis, William C., Paul R. Pierce, Edward H. Stulken, and Bertrand L. Smith, *Administering the Elementary School.* Englewood Cliffs, N.J.: Prentice-Hall, Inc., 1953.

Reeder, Ward G., *The Fundamentals of Public School Administration,* 3rd ed. New York: The Macmillan Company, 1951.

Reeves, Charles Everand, *School Boards.* Englewood Cliffs, N.J.: Prentice-Hall, Inc., 1954.

Reisner, Edward H., *The Evolution of the Common School.* New York: The Macmillan Company, 1930.

Remmlein, Madaline Kinter, *The Law of Local Public School Administration.* New York: McGraw-Hill Book Company, Inc., 1954.

Rorer, John A., *Principles of Democratic Supervision.* New York: Bureau of Publications, Teachers College, Columbia University, 1942.

Ross, Donald H., "Employment Practices and Working Conditions in the Elementary and Secondary Schools," chap. IV, "Teacher Personnel," in *Review of Educational Research* XXV (June, 1955).

Snygg, D., and A. W. Combs, *Individual Behavior.* New York: Harper and Brothers, Publishers, 1949.

Sumption, M. R., "The Control of Pupil Conduct by the School," as part of "School Pupils and the Law," *Law and Contemporary Problems* XX (Winter, 1955).

Tead, Ordway, *The Art of Administration.* New York: McGraw-Hill Book Company, Inc., 1951.

Wahlquist, John T., and others, *The Administration of Public Education.* New York: The Ronald Press Company, 1952.

Werwick, Robert, "Modern-Style Mind Reader," *Life* XXXIX (September 12, 1955).

Wiles, Kimball, *Supervision for Better Schools.* Englewood Cliffs, N.J.: Prentice-Hall, Inc., 1955.

Willing, M. H., *Schools and Our Democratic Society.* New York: Harper and Brothers, Publishers, 1951.

Woltz, Charles K., "Compulsory Attendance at School," part of "School Pupils and the Law," in *Law and Contemporary Problems* XX (Winter, 1955).

Yeager, William A., *Administration and the Teacher.* New York: Harper and Brothers, Publishers, 1954.

# Index